Praise for *Mining Group Gold*

"I have been a student of *Mining Group Gold* for more than twenty years, since first being exposed to it during my career at Xerox. Subsequently, in two senior leadership roles at MBM Corporation and at CARQUEST, I have personally used Tom's processes to run my own meetings and have taught it to others and the feedback was always the same. *Mining Group Gold* increases productivity and the quality of work performed, as well as the satisfaction of participants. While I have acquired a significant number of business books over the years, only a handful remain close by to reference. *Mining Group Gold* is one of the few."

> —Edward V. Whirty, President, Coral Ridge Consulting

"*Mining Group Gold* works! Using MGG concepts in my coaching work with corporate executive clients and entrepreneurial business owners has been a key factor in their ability to align their teams, accomplish desired outcomes, and deliver millions of dollars in improved bottom-line performance."

> —Rod Buchen, CEO, The Buchen Group

MINING GROUP GOLD®

MINING GROUP GOLD®

HOW TO CASH IN ON THE COLLABORATIVE BRAINPOWER OF A TEAM FOR INNOVATION AND RESULTS

THIRD EDITION

THOMAS A. KAYSER

New York   Chicago   San Francisco   Lisbon
London   Madrid   Mexico City   Milan   New Delhi
San Juan   Seoul   Singapore   Sydney   Toronto

The *McGraw·Hill* Companies

2 3 4 5 6 7 8 9 0   DOC/DOC   1 9 8 7 6 5 4 3 2 1 0

ISBN: 978-0-07-174062-3
MHID: 0-07-174062-7

This publication is designed to provide accurate and authoritative information in regard to the subject matter covered. It is sold with the understanding that the publisher is not engaged in rendering legal, accounting, or other professional service. If legal advice or other expert assistance is required, the services of a competent professional person should be sought.
—*From a Declaration of Principles Jointly Adopted by a Committee of the American Bar Association and a Committee of Publishers and Associations*

McGraw-Hill books are available at special quantity discounts to use as premiums and sales promotions, or for use in corporate training programs. To contact a representative, please visit the Contact Us pages at www.mhprofessional.com.

This book is printed on acid-free paper.

CONTENTS

FOREWORD

"If you want to go fast, go alone. If you want to go far,
go together."
—*Warren Buffett, Chairman, Berkshire Hathaway*

I read this quote long after meeting Tom Kayser, yet the words in many ways typify how I remember him when we worked together at Xerox Corporation. I first met Tom over 25 years ago. I was just out of graduate school and joined Xerox as an analyst in Human Resources. Tom was leading a small team of Organization Effectiveness specialists. Working with Tom gave me a front row seat to effective organization change in progress. At the time, Xerox was embarking on a journey we called Leadership Through Quality. There were many aspects to this performance and culture changing initiative. None were more impactful and pervasive than driving better decision-making through disciplined processes and teamwork.

Today, process discipline and collaboration are well studied, practiced, and written about. But back in the early 1980s, these ideas were considered innovative and relatively untested across large enterprises. Champions of innovation are often big personalities and the sheer force of their conviction can produce the momentum needed for adoption of new ideas. That was not Tom. Tom's approach was understated yet always confident that if managers utilized just a few simple collaboration tools with their teams, then they could extract, that is, mine gold within the group.

And who wouldn't want to get the very best out of their team--individually and collectively? Work is challenging, issues are complex, and answers are not obvious. Imagine having a very difficult problem to solve (that should be easy to do!) and you have been identified as the leader of a newly formed task force. There are opposing views, emotions are running high, there are power struggles and, yet, the required knowledge and experience to solve the issue reside among the very same people. How do you maximize all that human capital?

Over the years I have participated in numerous exercises that demonstrate time and again the collective power of the group. One exercise consisted of administering a set of questions to individual participants, who were then placed in teams. The teams then competed with one another to "win" by submitting the most correct responses that represented the collective agreement of the group. In debriefing the exercise the team discovered that, while their group answered many of the questions correctly, all of the right answers were actually known by at least one of the individuals on their team. All the knowledge they needed to win was right there, and yet the group was not effective at drawing out the contributions of each team member. And that was the "Aha!" moment—the realization that having individuals with all the knowledge, skills, and capabilities necessary for our business, school, or not-for-profit agency is not enough unless we can unleash both individual and collective capabilities.

Mining Group Gold started out simply as a set of tools that Tom developed to facilitate groups of people who were trying to solve problems. The tools started to work almost immediately and they turned into a small primer for Xerox managers to learn how to be effective meeting facilitators themselves. By the late 80's, the methods became pervasive throughout Xerox. The book, *Mining Group Gold*, was first published in 1990 and is still found on the bookshelves of Xerox senior leaders, managers, and human resources professionals.

In 2010, over 25 years after Tom first introduced his approach, his basic meeting tools are embedded in our Xerox culture: meeting leaders spend time preparing, meetings have agendas, agenda items have defined desired outcomes and time allotment, meetings are facilitated by the leader and participants, and assessments are conducted at the end of every meeting to determine the effectiveness of the time spent and behaviors exhibited. And we make changes based on those meeting assessments.

So how do we maximize human capital? As a practitioner for over two decades, I would suggest that you invest in learning the tools described in this book. Tom Kayser relies on proven approaches to what works in any organizational setting at any level. It provides a step-by-step process on how to develop team facilitation skills strategically to enable break-through thinking and outcomes. If you are tired of reading about theory and want to unleash collaborative power in your organization and become a more effective leader of team outcomes, then start here. This is a journey you will want to take!

Barbara L. Koontz
Vice-President
Human Resources & Learning
Xerox North America
January 2010

PREFACE

"Take the complexity out of this complex subject, boil it down to its essence, make it readable and applicable, and you'll be doing all managers a tremendous service." That was the advice I got many years ago from a highly regarded senior vice president at Xerox when I first thought about writing a book on a subject loosely titled "The Manager as Facilitator." That was then, leading to what is now! This book is now the third edition of my original work, first published in 1990. Even so, as I made the many revisions to create this version, the senior vice president's mantra still rang through my head.

Making things simple for managers to comprehend does not mean making them so watered down as to be useless. Albert Einstein's maxim stated that "everything should be made as simple as possible, but no simpler." Leonardo Da Vinci's "Simplicity is the ultimate sophistication" and Antoine de Saint Exupéry's "It seems that perfection is reached not when there is nothing left to add, but when there is nothing left to take away," drive home the point more elegantly than I ever could.

A story has been told that Kelly Johnson, the lead engineer at the Lockheed Skunk Works—creators of the Lockheed U-2 and SR-71 Blackbird spy planes, among others—gave his team of design engineers a handful of tools, with the challenge that the jet aircraft they were designing must be repairable by any mechanic using only those tools, under combat conditions in the field.

This third edition of *Mining Group Gold* is analogous to the handful of tools Kelly Johnson gave to his design engineers. Learning how to use these few tools well—to have terrific execution of the fundamental principles under the "combat conditions" of a meeting—will increase your ability to plan and lead productive group sessions to an extent you did not think possible. Although I am familiar with much of the research on facilitation, collaboration, teams, and teamwork, this book is neither a compilation nor a summary of that material. It is more—much more.

Mining Group Gold is an integrated approach for thinking strategically about the facilitation of teams to maximize their collective wisdom in the pursuit of innovative ideas and results. It is a book about facilitation—the manager as a facilitator with the help of all others present as secondary facilitators. Specifically, *Mining Group Gold* is a set of fundamental—but potent—tools, processes, techniques, and templates that any person, at any organizational level, can readily apply to increase his or her ability to plan and facilitate work sessions that help build a collaborative organizational culture.

The procedures covered in this book truly are combat-tested and have withstood the challenge of decades of time. The initial framework was developed in 1984 and has undergone many additions, refinements, and developments since then. Tens of thousands of people in multinational corporations, small businesses, school districts, government agencies, non-profit organizations, and colleges and universities have read the previous editions this work and learned how to become "miners of group gold." I have spent my career as an organization effectiveness professional and facilitator personally using, teaching, and honing what you will be reading about here.

One thing I have discovered in my personal journey is that managing efficient and effective collaborative sessions requires a set of skills that you must deliberately set out to acquire. I'm convinced that the necessary skills are the relatively simple ones presented in this book. However, without your desire to master these skills, all the ideas presented here will be useless. You are completely in charge of what *Mining Group Gold* will ultimately mean to you and your organization. There is nothing overly complicated here. You do not have to be a group dynamics expert, a marriage counselor, a skilled arbitrator, or a seasoned facilitator to make these tools and processes work for you.

As the title suggests, by reading and practicing the ideas presented here, you will learn how to extract and process the gold nuggets of wisdom brought to the conference table by the participants—*the gold mine*—so that everyone can cash in on the collaborative brainpower of the team producing innovation and results.

I will not get you bogged down in a lot of ivory tower theories, formulas, esoteric psychological or sociological experiments, or meta–data analysis. Instead, I will give you some concise, easy to understand information that will put you on the leading edge of common sense—"just a handful of tools so you can repair your jet aircraft under combat conditions."

What You Will Learn from Reading This Book

This is a "how to" book! *Its core purpose is to show you how to plan and facilitate collaborative group sessions.* It is *not* a book on how to become a master of meeting politics, how to crush your opponent, how to dominate a session and get your own way, or how to win at the expense of others.

Chapter 4, "A Map of the Gold Mine," gives you a pictorial representation of the full *Mining Group Gold* process and outlines the set of 18 principles that underlie its operation. Throughout the book you will learn how to execute the model and its principles by means of a number of fundamental actions.

You will become acquainted with a set of task-and-maintenance interpersonal behaviors to be shared by all attendees in pursuit of a successful collaborative session. You'll learn five steps for successfully planning the structure of a session; you'll learn a number of considerations for planning the processes you will use to move your meeting through the three critical phases of "Start-Up", Move-Out", and "Wrap-Up." These three phases do not occur by chance; they require process planning, and you'll learn the necessary guidelines for developing excellent process plans for each phase. Also, you'll gain knowledge about how to initiate a collaborative climate, how to maintain it, how to constructively deal with feelings, how to manage group conflict, how to handle disruptive behavior, how to reduce confusion, and more.

When you have finished this book, you will have learned how to be more accomplished in the art of facilitative leadership whereby you lead people from the center of the circle rather than dictating to them from the top of your personal pyramid. You will have acquired the important facilitation strategies and skills necessary to carry your team to new heights in the pursuit of innovative thinking and results by mining everyone's gold nuggets of wisdom.

Some Thoughts to Keep in Mind

While the spotlight of this edition remains focused on a manager facilitating his or her work group, these techniques are applicable to any group session in a host of environmental settings. Any person responsible for leading any type of group session will find this material relevant and valuable.

To obtain the greatest benefit from this edition, read it straight through to learn from each chapter's content as well as from the flow of the whole book. During your initial reading, highlight key points that are of particular interest, then go back to those points for a more detailed review and study. Write a final set of key learning points to yourself on the fill-in worksheets at the end of each chapter.

The tools, processes, and techniques presented here are not ironclad rules and regulations to which you must inflexibly adhere. Rather, they are ideas for guiding you and helping you expand your knowledge and skills in the practice of excellent team facilitation and leadership.

Because these are guidelines, you are encouraged initially to practice the techniques and processes as described. However, after gaining experience and confidence in their use, you are encouraged to supplement and refine this solid core of knowledge and skills in order to further develop your leadership style and abilities in building collaborative teams.

The key to success in acquiring and/or improving your team facilitation skills is the old refrain: practice, practice, practice. There are no shortcuts. You can read books on swimming, talk to experts about swimming, watch videos on swimming, go to swim meets and watch swimmers perform in person, but if you are going to become a swimmer yourself, you have to jump in the water sometime and start doing it. It's the same thing with becoming a facilitative leader. You must do it.

A Few Tips for Skill Development in Your Work Environment

Skill development can be an organized endeavor using *Mining Group Gold* as your central resource. The skill acquisition process involves a series of successive approximations as shown by this little diagram:

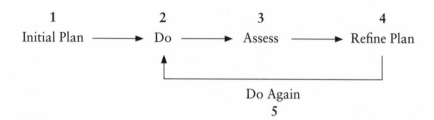

Step one is planning the structure and process of your initial group session; step two is facilitating the initial session; step three—with the help of everyone present—is assessing where the session went well and where it did not go well; step four is taking this assessment to heart, making a new plan for your next session that preserves the positive aspects of the previous effort while reducing its negative aspects; and step five, is doing it over again. With each new cycle, you and your teammates will be learning and improving your ability have diversity of thought and critical thinking while still pulling together and collaborating to achieve agreed-to desired outcomes.

You soon will discover that the art of team leadership is personally rewarding. It is a powerful lever in building the collaborative culture so necessary to accomplishing the tough, complex tasks that lie ahead for organizations regardless whether they operate in the public or private sector. Equally important, facilitation done well not only will heighten job satisfaction for you, but for your teammates as well, by unleashing greater synergy and accomplishment in an environment of trust, collaboration, and commitment.

Above all else, do not regard an unsuccessful facilitation effort as a failure; instead consider it as another opportunity to try again—more intelligently!

ACKNOWLEDGMENTS

The actual writing of a book is a lonely, solo endeavor. Acquiring the unique insights and experiences around a particular core of knowledge so you have something relevant to say in book form, and then getting a book published, marketed, and sold is a collaborative effort of the first degree. Since my initial step into the facilitation arena took place in 1984, and the first edition of *Mining Group Gold* was published in 1990, you can be certain there are influential fingerprints of hundreds of people all over this third edition.

First of all, I extend my thanks to all of the talented Xerox managers I had the privilege of interacting with over several decades as the initial internal facilitation manual and the first two editions of *Mining Group Gold* were created, reshaped, and improved. You praised; you questioned; you challenged; you suggested; you moved me to expand, to sharpen, and to refine my thinking about the "manager as a competent facilitator of his or her own team." But most of all you applied the tools and process being advocated back on the job. Your feedback was invaluable and you proved beyond any doubt that the ideas and concepts worked and that collaborative work sessions were within the reach of any team willing to learn and consistently practice a few fundamental principles. Without your influence and endorsements along the way, there never would have been a book; certainly no third edition.

In particular, my appreciation is given to Don Zrebiec, former V.P. of human resources, for his friendly hounding to "get off the dime" and just write the darn thing (the first edition) because the subject matter and methodology were too important not to. I am grateful to Barbara Koontz for listening and sharing when I needed it most and for being an excellent ambassador for my work. Also, many thanks to Wayland Hicks, Debbie Smith, Jim Sierk, Eric Steenburgh, Jim Stoffel, Jim Horn, Vic Muth, Joe Marino, and Gil Hatch, senior executives all, for giving these facilitation practices and me high visibility in their global divisions.

Phil Chirico, Ann Delehant, Harv Paris, Josephine Kehoe, Meg Keller-Cogan, Tom Flood, Diane Reed, Colleen Bonar, Mark Bower, and Roger Gorham all must be recognized for their advocacy and proactive efforts to infuse the principles and philosophy of *Mining Group Gold* into the school districts of Rochester, New York, and a number of surrounding towns.

Thanks to the many clients who have participated in the *Mining Group Gold* workshops taught by me or by my wife Carol using the materials from previous editions. What we've learned in those numerous interactions also has added value to this edition.

I owe much gratitude to Gary Krebs, vice president and group publisher, of the McGraw-Hill Companies, Inc., for being a highly proactive believer in this material and being passionate about publishing it. Gary truly was the straw that stirred the drink. Also, my kindest regards to Judith McCarthy, my editorial director, for her masterful job of moving the book through all the internal bureaucratic complexities that led to its publication. She was my point person and confidant throughout the entire process. Every writer should be so lucky to work with a person of Judith's caliber.

Finally to my son Chad, his wife Megan, and their miniature schnauzer, Otto, thank you for your numerous timely visits to take me away from my writing at what always seemed to be my moments of greatest frustration or writer's block. Your visits with Otto always energized me. And to my wife Carol, a special thank you for just being there, for constantly bringing me "healthy treats" to snack on, and for many content revision suggestions based on her *MGG* workshop teaching experiences.

Part *I*

ESTABLISHING THE FOUNDATION TO MINE GROUP GOLD

Chapter 1

THE DISCOVERY: A BRIEF HISTORY OF MINING GROUP GOLD

CHAPTER OBJECTIVES

- To examine the dire business situation, and the resulting cultural transformation at Xerox, that spawned Mining Group Gold.
- To prove a retrospective look at Mining Group Gold's evolution over time.

Introduction

It's unbelievable to me as I now reflect back, but it was June of 1984 when I first became involved in a seemingly short-term project at Xerox. Little did I know back then that I was taking the first steps in a career-defining assignment that would enrich and develop me beyond my wildest expectations and set me on course to write three editions of a book sharing what I discovered about maximizing the collective wisdom of teams.

The terrain of facilitation experiences that I have covered in the intervening years since then, both inside Xerox and with clients outside, has been vast and varied. Lessons have been learned, group structures and processes have been sharpened, and a philosophy of how to cash in on the collaborative brainpower of a team for innovation and results has been confirmed.

At the dawning of the 1980s, the external marketplace, the business and economic climate, and the values of American managers concerning the art of successful management were immensely different from those today. Looking back, it's easy to see how American organizations at that time—in both the public and the private sectors—had self-selected themselves into three categories.

Category 1 contained the few American companies, like Xerox, that were just beginning to awaken from their deep slumber of complacency and to realize that they had to change the fundamental way they did business in order to become world-class competitors in a new, global economy.

Category 2 contained firms in industries such as steel and autos that scurried to hide behind the fortress of government tariffs, regulations, and bailouts as their protection against the onslaught of worldwide competition.

Category 3 contained everyone else—the overwhelming majority of government and business organizations. All of these organizations felt comfortable and secure as they whistled past the graveyard. "Change our culture? Why would we do that? Our bureaucratic systems, policies, procedures, and high-handed management style have worked for us since the beginning of time. Why transform anything now? We'll do what's always worked before. We'll downsize our current operations, squeeze suppliers, pressure everyone to do more with less, broker takeovers through mergers or acquisitions, then get rid of all redundancies in IT, finance, HR, marketing, and PR, and everything will be fine."

That was the reality of the 1980s. However, looking back on the decades-long personal journey I've taken with many organizations of different shapes and sizes, and after reviewing the general literature on organizational behavior and change, I'm struck by one simple but over-whelming truth. *I'm convinced now, more than ever, that the one constant in the wrenching change to become a world-class competitor in a global economy, the single road over which "the new order of things" rides, is collaboration and its facilitation within and across interdisciplinary work teams!*

Tim Brown, CEO and president of IDEO, ranked independently as being among the most innovative companies in the world, reinforces my contention with his unique perspective.

> There is a popular saying around IDEO that "all of us are smarter than any of us," and that is the key to unlocking the creative power of any organization. We ask people not simply to offer expert advice on materials, behaviors, or software but to be active in each of the spaces of innovation: inspiration, ideation, and implementation.
>
> . . . A creative organization is constantly on the lookout for people with the capacity and—just as important—the disposition for collaboration across disciplines. In the end, this ability is what distinguishes the merely *multidisciplinary* team from a truly *interdisciplinary* one. In a multidisciplinary team each individual becomes an advocate for his or her own technical specialty and the project becomes a protracted negotiation among them, likely resulting in gray compromise. In an interdisciplinary team there is collective ownership of ideas and everyone takes responsibility for them.[1]

To understand why I am so adamant in my belief that building and maintaining collaborative interdisciplinary teams and cultures will be the lifeblood of the most admired and successful organizations in the twenty-first century, we need to begin by tracing the antecedents to a massive cultural change effort within a company that was literally fighting for its business life.

Before the Transformation Began

My first attempts at operating as an internal process consultant within the Business Products & Systems Group (BP&SG) of Xerox in 1982 were very frustrating. Initially, the culture was extremely resistant. My mere suggestion that we plan the structure and process of group sessions, initiate and maintain a collaborative climate in meetings, acknowledge and understand the feelings of others, share power, work in interdisciplinary teams, search for consensus, or build win-win solutions was enough to send many managers into a tirade that would leave my ears ringing for hours.

A few visionary managers did see the power of teamwork and collaboration and enlisted my help in turning their work groups into teams. These initial efforts—and the hands-on learning that I gained from them—while producing just tiny oases scattered randomly across the huge desert landscape of Xerox, did provide me with information, data, and experiences that would prove invaluable later on. It was tough, slow, in-the-trenches work. But after a couple of years of feeling like Sisyphus, a confluence of internal and external circumstances changed all of that. The whole Xerox Corporation was about to be thrust into a race for its life—a marathon race on a global track that even today still keeps reconfiguring itself and has no finish line.

Back in 1982–1983, Xerox was a bruised and battered company. Let David Kearns, chief executive officer of Xerox from 1982 to 1990, candidly describe the situation he faced at the beginning of his tenure at the helm.

> To many in the outside world, we still looked very much like the invincible copier giant and bedrock of the *Fortune 500* that we had always been. It was evident that we were having a few problems. But still, we were making hundreds of millions of dollars a year. We were turning out fresh products. We were employing a hundred thousand people. How bad could things be?
>
> Unfortunately, I knew. We were gravely sick. A lot of our problems boiled down to the Japanese. They were really eating us for lunch.
>
> One thing I gleaned [from over two dozen trips to Japan] was the Japanese had consciously made the decision to select our company as a "target." . . . They had good reason to do so; they were selling products for what it cost us to make them. Our market share had tumbled from more than 90 percent in the early 1970s to less than 15 percent. Every year, competitors nibbled away a few more share points. We were being decimated. Whether we liked it or not, we were in a war to the death. . . . How bad off were we? To put it bluntly, if nothing

were done to correct things, we were destined to have a fire sale and close down by 1990.

Our only hope for survival was to urgently commit ourselves to vastly improving the quality of our products and service. . . . It meant changing the very culture of Xerox from the ground up. . . . In our near-death situation, I felt we had no choice but to accomplish this.[2]

The Challenge Facing the Transformation

A well-ingrained bureaucracy to protect the status quo, plus an autocratic managerial style that had worked fine during the glory days of Xerox, ensured that the task of changing was not going to be an easy one. Few managers or senior professionals responsible for running team meetings, chairing committees, or leading task forces fully understood the basics of planning the structure and process of a truly participative group session, and even fewer cared about the fundamentals of facilitating a collaborative session in which power is shared with the whole group; the wisdom of everyone is systematically processed in an open, trusting way; and consensus is used at appropriate opportunities to make decisions.

Why should they care? They had built highly successful careers the old-fashioned way—by telling others what to do and how to do it, and in the few cases where that didn't work, by selling others on why it was in the best interests of their careers to go along with what was being advocated by the boss.

This lack of understanding and commitment to interdisciplinary collaborative processes was not unique to Xerox; far from it. It was the standard bill of fare for most of American business, industry, and government at that time. Participative management was far too often dismissed as a soft, "touchy feely," country club approach to running things. Hardball, or Theory X, was the only game in town. If you were good at it, you were viewed as a winner and your career blossomed. If you weren't good at it, or if you chose not to play that game, you were branded a loser, and your career withered.

While a top-down approach to running organizations, where the "top" dictates to the "middle" what to force upon the "bottom," certainly still exists today, it is a strategy for organizational dry rot and marketplace failure. Dominating, power-hungry egos driving a culture of intimidation, fear, and noncollaboration may ring up some short-term financial successes. But in the long run, how can any organization survive as a healthy, vibrant, innovative entity if it continually abuses and destroys the *most valuable* competitive advantage that it possesses—its gold mine—the collaborative brainpower of its people? My short answer is that it can't.

Uncovering the Need for *Mining Group Gold*[3]

It was apparent that if a significant cultural change based on total quality were to succeed, the highest levels of management would have to own it. Kearns, with the help of outside consultant David Nadler, spent the bulk of 1983 working hand in hand with the corporation's 25 senior operating executives from around the world. They hammered out a quality policy, the broad outlines of a quality strategy, and a worldwide implementation plan. All of this was given the name Leadership Through Quality. Once the broad plans were in place, several senior-level quality improvement teams were formed to flesh out the myriad details, including a comprehensive training program.

In early March of 1984, with much excitement, Leadership Through Quality was launched at corporate headquarters, with Nadler training Kearns and his executive staff in the weeklong curriculum. Upon completion of the training, the executive team had to select and complete a quality improvement project before the training could be cascaded down to the senior level of the business groups. The intent of this requirement, baked into the worldwide strategy, was to ensure that, as the training moved down an organization level by level, those in the group that was currently being trained could look up one level and know that their own managers not only "had been to school" but could put what they were taught into practice.

Six weeks later, in mid-April of 1984, I was assigned the lead in training the executive team of the Business Products and Systems Group as we became the first business group to commence the required cultural change. The nature and scope of Leadership Through Quality can be shown by the "*from*" and "*to*" goals that articulated the gap that had to be closed if Xerox was going to have a successful transformation.

- Movement *from* unstructured and individualistic problem solving and decision making *to* disciplined and predominately collaborative efforts.
- Movement *from* an ambiguous or incomplete understanding of customer requirements *to* the use of a systematic, interactive approach to fully understanding customer needs and requirements.

- Movement *from* acceptance of a certain margin of error and subsequent corrective action as the norm *to* an environment in which we collaborate within and across functions for error-free outputs that fully satisfy customer requirements the first time.

However, shortly after the BP&SG executive team was trained and we began the cascade of Leadership Through Quality down to the senior-level department managers in May 1984, we discovered a glaring problem that put the program in jeopardy before it really got underway.

As stated earlier, before the launch of its systemic Leadership Through Quality effort, Xerox was no different from most organizations in terms of its general bureaucratic policies and procedures, command-and-control meeting processes, win-lose power interactions, and closely guarded and patrolled fiefdoms. Far more enemies were deemed to exist inside other Xerox business groups and functions than outside in our competitors' organizations.

In launching Leadership Through Quality, the company provided a host of terrific, state-of-the art technical, operational, and statistical tools and processes for improving quality across all aspects of the business: a systematic six-step process for analyzing and solving problems; a powerful nine-step quality improvement process for determining, analyzing, and meeting customer requirements; a world-renowned benchmarking methodology; a unique customer satisfaction measurement system; a whole new product development process; and lots of cutting-edge, hands-on training within each of those areas. However, the implementation strategy lacked one essential ingredient: specific tools and processes for facilitating team collaboration. We quickly knew, as Tom Hanks succinctly said in the movie *Apollo 13*, "Houston, we have a problem."

Everything that Leadership Through Quality stood for, from the standpoint of transforming our business operations and culture, hinged on executives, managers, and individual contributors within and across all divisions and functions, and at all organizational levels, operating as collaborative interdisciplinary teams.

The short supply of collaborative facilitation skills among senior and upper-middle executives quickly became evident as they attempted to apply the newly acquired quality and problem-solving tools and processes with their staffs to get their initial business improvement projects successfully completed.

The vast majority of these managers took one of two approaches in running their chosen improvement projects after being trained. Most of them drove their projects hard, using the same autocratic style that they knew and loved; others got the wrong impression that being a facilitative manager meant staying removed from things and took a hands-off, laissez-faire approach. In a few isolated instances, managers tried to operate as collaborative, facilitative leaders, but they did not have a true understanding of what to do or how to do it. Regardless of the style that was being used, the improvement projects were grinding along at a snail's pace, bringing little in the way of quality improvement and retarding further deployment of the strategy to the lower levels.

Without the managers at the top few levels being helped to modify their behavior and style to become less "order givers" or "avoiders" and more "facilitator-collaborators," we knew that becoming a total quality company would be impossible. Our senior managers were the key population. Everything that they did and said set the tone for the practices and behaviors that would follow as the training moved down the hierarchy.

Enthusiasm for Leadership Through Quality was rapidly diminishing, and it was fast gaining the reputation of being just another ice cream flavor of the month. Simply requesting (or mandating) that managers be more collaborative with their direct reports, and each other, when working to solve tough business issues using these new tools and process was a waste of breath.

The Evolution of the Mining Group Gold Material

In order to help *all* managers and senior professionals within BP&SG learn some fundamental tools and processes for planning and conducting productive, team-oriented, collaborative work sessions, I was asked to write an internal handbook on this subject.

I discussed my project with more than 70 people, ranging from vice presidents to first-line managers, and their requirements were made clear. The handbook had to

- Present practical, easy-to-understand, and simple-to-apply collaborative tools and processes that would make a difference in group session productivity.
- Not be dependent on mandatory training; instead, a careful reading of the material would provide the knowledge and confidence to allow a person to get on with it.[4]
- Reinforce the tenets and philosophy of Leadership Through Quality.
- Be tightly written, user friendly, and interesting.

With these requirements met by October 1984, the handbook was distributed to 1,200 managers, project leaders, and senior professionals within BP&SG. Soon thereafter, requests for copies began to come in from organizations outside BP&SG, as well as from people within BP&SG who were not part of the first distribution.

By October of 1990, when the first edition of *Mining Group Gold* was published as a textbook, more than 14,000 copies of the handbook had been distributed across Xerox, including Europe, Latin America, Mexico, Canada, and the Pacific Basin.

The first edition of the *Mining Group Gold* textbook emerged as a significantly revised and expanded version of the core material from the original internal manual. It also included new approaches and insights based on the firsthand knowledge and experiences I had gained by being intimately involved in this "manager as facilitative leader" side of Leadership Through Quality between 1984 and 1990.

For the second edition, my enhancements and additions were drawn from many diverse experiences in the intervening years between 1990 and 1995: (1) the continued learning that I gained from conducting hundreds of Mining Group Gold seminars, team-building workshops, and third-party facilitation activities inside of Xerox; (2) my interactions with Xerox managers and senior professionals who were actively applying the tools and processes in a wide variety of situations; (3) my feedback from users of the first edition of the book; (4) the development and filming of a commercial *Mining Group Gold* video with CRM*learning* (Carlsbad, California) in 1992; (5) the tremendous insights that my wife gathered from utilizing Mining Group Gold with various consulting clients, especially from her pioneering work in MGG's application to school administration and school district leadership; and finally, (6) my review of the business literature.

For revisions and refinements in this third edition, before retiring from Xerox in 2004, I had the advantage of drawing from nine more years of Xerox experience (1995–2004) in practicing and refining the Mining Group Gold methodology in a wide variety of interdisciplinary team-building workshops, problem-solving meetings, quality improvement meetings and numerous high-priority organizational change strategy sessions for senior- and mid-level executive teams. Since 2006, driven first by my extensive work with the senior executives and mid-level managers running a 1,500-store retail operation regarded as the leading provider of total automotive care, along with interactions and feedback gathered after speeches given at professional meetings and the stimulation of teaching a leadership course at Ursuline College in Cleveland, I have continually learned and honed new insights along the way.

All revisions for this third edition have been made in the spirit of continuous improvement, while being mindful of the need to minimize the complexity of this complex subject, keep it boiled down to its essence, make it readable, and make it applicable so that anyone who reads the book will be energized to put into practice what he has learned.

WORKSHEET

Develop written responses to the two items listed below.

1. What do you feel are the main learning points from Chapter 1?

_____

_____

_____

_____

_____

2. Elaborate on why you feel these points are key for you.

_____

_____

_____

_____

_____

Notes

1. T. Brown, *Change by Design: How Design Thinking Transforms Organizations and Inspires Innovation* (New York: Harper Business, 2009), pp. 26–28.
2. D. T. Kearns and D. A. Nadler, *Prophets in the Dark: How Xerox Reinvented Itself and Beat Back the Japanese* (New York: HarperCollins, 1992), pp. xiii–xvi.
3. The reader should keep in mind that Mining Group Gold was just one piece—albeit an exceedingly critical one—of the total Leadership Through Quality strategy. The development of the strategy, the creation of the organizational infrastructure to support it, the development of numerous state-of-the art quality tools and processes, and its global implementation involved hundreds of dedicated people to make it all work. The result of everyone's passion was a successful corporatewide transformation that culminated in Xerox's winning the Malcolm Baldrige National Quality Award in 1989.
4. However, not long after the handbook was released, there was a call from managers all across BP&SG for some type of classroom training to help them better understand and practice the tools and techniques covered in the handbook. Hence, I developed an optional two-day Mining Group Gold Workshop that was available to anyone who wanted the extra classroom experience, beyond just reading the manual. I taught more than 250 of these workshops around the globe, and I also certified other experienced Xerox trainers to lead the workshop in their organizations—both national and international. Mining Group Gold then became the Xerox global standard for teaching the facilitative side of leadership.

Chapter 2

WHEN YOU NEGLECT THE GOLD MINE: HIGH COSTS, LITTLE GOLD

- To document the staggering cost of meetings in terms of time and money.
- To establish the leverage ratio as the most incisive way to understand the relationship between time and monetary meeting costs.

Introduction

Meetings, bloody meetings. For most managers, they start early on Monday and go on and on and on throughout the week. There even is an old cliché that defines a manager as a person who is either coming from, going to, or sitting in a meeting.

In the modern organization, where collaboration and interdependence are inescapable requirements for success, group sessions are a fact of life. Today, more than ever, meetings have become the forum for sharing, sorting, processing, regrouping, and distributing data and information.

In view of their role as the backbone of an organization, it is tragic that most meetings are so poorly conceived and poorly conducted. The gold mine of ideas, information, data, knowledge, and creativity that participants bring to group sessions is being misunderstood, put down, ignored, or, even worse, left buried in the minds of the participants.

The liabilities of shoddy meetings are legendary: too much talking and not enough listening; too much assuming and not enough understanding; too much attacking and not enough crediting; too much taking and not enough giving; too much storming and not enough performing; too many people and not enough room; too many topics and not enough time. The list could go on, but you get the point.

Meetings can be like vampires, sucking the life out of intelligent and creative people. And sucking the funds out of businesses. In fact, it is these negative aspects of group sessions or, as Luke Skywalker might describe them, "the dark side of the force," that gives rise to the caustic jokes about meetings. Here are some of my favorites.

- "A meeting is a gathering where people speak up, say nothing, and then all disagree."
- "A meeting is indispensable when you don't want to accomplish anything."
- "A meeting is an interaction where the unwilling, selected from the uninformed, led by the unsuitable, to discuss the unnecessary, are required to write a report on the unimportant."
- "A meeting is a place where you keep the minutes but throw away the hours."
- "The best meeting is a group of three with one person sick and one out of town."
- "A faculty meeting can be described as a bunch of screaming anarchists tied together by a common parking lot."

- "A meeting is a place where many things get reshaped, especially our waistlines from eating too many donuts.
- "Our meetings always provide a fantastic aerobic workout. We jump to conclusions, off-load decisions, dodge responsibilities, push for more breaks, carry things too far, and toss others' ideas out the window."

The thing that is most disturbing about group sessions is the lack of effort on the part of most group leaders to do anything about how meetings are planned and facilitated. We know that there are problems with a significant percentage of the group sessions that we attend or lead, but we have come to accept mediocrity as the norm. Why? Perhaps this debilitating condition has been created in many organizations by a phenomenon best defined by a Chinese proverb that says, "To the mediocre, mediocrity appears great."

In any event, inefficient, ineffective, and unproductive meetings are tolerated within educational institutions, business enterprises, government agencies, hospitals, and voluntary associations as an everyday cost of doing business, much as leasing office space and paying taxes are everyday costs. However, while organizations are continually looking to obtain the most favorable lease arrangements, pushing for the best terms and prices from every supplier, searching for loopholes to cut their taxes, and watching over their labor and benefits costs with a sharp pencil, these same organizations virtually ignore the tremendous cost of execrable meetings.

Costs of Group Sessions

Before we can turn out to be "miners of group gold," we first need to become acutely aware of an endemic situation: the incredible amounts of wasted costs associated with unproductive meetings. In other words, little gold from big expenses—not your best ROI scenario!

Figures can sometimes be misleading; we've all heard about the man who drowned while wading across a lake with an average depth of three feet. This section is not intended to mislead you or overwhelm you with numbers. It is intended to underscore the terribly high costs of bringing three or more people together inside the four walls of a conference room to share and process information.

Every time you get up from your desk to attend another meeting, your actions are sending a powerful message. They are visibly saying: "This meeting is so important to me that I am willing to set aside everything else that I could be doing to head for the conference room." And when others join you in making that same decision, the costs to you, your meeting partners, and the organization are higher than you might imagine.

Think of the *direct costs* this way. If 8 people each spend ½ hour preparing for a 2-hour meeting that wastes everyone's time, that's a total of 20 work hours lost: 4 work hours in preparation time (8 people times ½ hour each) plus 16 work hours in meeting time (8 people times 2 hours each). Those hours come "right out of the hides" of the participants. Add another hour of administrative support time that the meeting caller required for tasks like scheduling, typing, e-mailing, phoning, copying, and so on, and you are up to a total of 21 direct work hours wasted on one two-hour session.

But that's not the end of the calculations. There is another associated cost: *lost opportunity*. Collectively, the 8 meeting participants and the secretary have lost the opportunity to apply those same 21 work hours to more productive tasks. Now, if we take the 21 direct-time work hours lost in the wasted meeting plus the 21 work hours of lost opportunity, our seemingly routine 2-hour session with 8 people ends up carrying a price tag of 42 squandered work hours!

There is no such thing as a free meeting. Each time you decide to call a meeting of your own, or decide to attend someone else's, you are not making a trivial decision. The time spent in, and the costs of, meetings in the United States is truly staggering, as shown in this research report, "Meetings in America," prepared by InfoCom of Greenwich, Connecticut, on behalf of Verizon.[1]

> Meetings dominate business life in America today. According to the National Statistics Council, 37 percent of employee time is spent in meetings. Other data indicate there are 11 million business meetings each and every day.
>
> . . . According to our survey, business meetings dominate the landscape of American work today. On average, our respondents attended 12.2 meetings/month involving travel, audioconferences, or videoconferences plus an estimated 49.6 internal or local face-to-face meetings, for a total of 61.8 meetings/month!
>
> . . . Looking at the average costs for all types of meetings attended, those employed by smaller companies (firms not included in Fortune's list of the 2,000 largest companies) tend

to spend less per meeting. Fewer plane trips for employees of smaller companies contribute to the overall lower costs for all types of meetings.

Employed By	Average Cost per Meeting
Fortune 500	$527
Fortune 500-2000	$547
Other	$412

What's more, a study of 2,000 business leaders by Harrison Conference Centers and Hofstra University reveals that unproductive meeting time has a direct cost to American business of more than $37 billion a year.[2] Mosvick and Nelson state that one carefully costed-out analysis of a midsized Fortune 500 company yielded a conservative estimate that this business lost $71 million a year because of poor meeting management.[3] And research by Nelson and Economy conclude that over 50 percent of meeting time is wasted.[4]

So, if we look back at the "Meetings in America" research showing that professionals attend more than 61 meetings per month, and we couple that with the Nelson and Economy metric that 50 percent of meeting time is wasted, and if we assume that each of these meetings is just 1 hour long, then what it tells us is this: *more than 30 hours of productivity per professional employee evaporates each month.* If we assume instead that each meeting is 1.5 hours, lost productivity per employee per month increases to 45 hours, or, *one week* of productivity lost each month per employee. Can your organization actually afford that kind of waste?

Quick Meeting Cost Calculation Table

Table 2-1 can serve as a mechanism for quickly calculating a meeting's fully loaded direct costs.[5] Fully loaded direct costs include base salary, payroll taxes, fringe benefits, and GAO (general administration and overhead). However, if car travel is also a requirement, then car mileage reimbursement for local travel to sites within driving distance must be included. For out-of-town sessions, airfare, hotel rooms, meals, car rentals, airport parking, and so on will ignite participant costs beyond just fully loaded salaries. Bumping up the numbers in Table 2-1 by an additional 30 percent for those people traveling out of town is a reasonable estimate to account for those additional dollars. Still, just looking at meeting costs from the dimension of fully loaded salaries is stunning.

Annual Salary	Number of Participants in Session									
	10	9	8	7	6	5	4	3	2	1
$100,000	$834	$750	$666	$584	$500	$417	$333	$251	$167	$84
90,000	$750	$675	$600	$525	$450	$375	$300	$225	$150	$75
80,000	$666	$600	$534	$467	$401	$333	$267	$200	$134	$66
70,000	$584	$525	$467	$408	$350	$291	$234	$176	$117	$59
60,000	$500	$450	$401	$350	$300	$251	$200	$150	$101	$50
50,000	$417	$375	$333	$292	$251	$209	$167	$125	$84	$42
40,000	$333	$300	$267	$234	$200	$167	$134	$101	$66	$33
30,000	$251	$225	$200	$176	$150	$125	$100	$75	$50	$26

Table 2-1 Costs of Meetings Using Fully Loaded Salaries (Nearest Dollar/Hour)

To use Table 2-1, add up the various hourly salary figures (which include base salary plus a 50 percent "load factor") for all persons present. The total then will be the fully loaded per-hour cost of the meeting. For example, if two individuals in the $50,000 bracket and two in the $60,000 bracket meet for one hour, the fully loaded cost that the company is paying for that time is $185 ($84 + $101). When the meeting extends to two hours, the cost is $370. If a company averages 10 two-hour meetings like this each week, the real dollar cost for one year is $192,400 ($3,700 × 52 weeks).

You can easily consider salaries midway between the figures shown here—like $35,000, $45,000, $55,000, and so on—by using midpoints between the table data. For example, if you held a one-hour meeting with five people where the salary was $65,000 per person, the loaded cost for that session would be $271 (this is the midpoint between $60,000 and $70,000 for five participants).

So far, we have been dealing with direct meeting costs. Often over-looked are the indirect costs—the ripple effect that poor meetings have as their negative consequences spread beyond the meeting room to encroach on other parts of the organization. Doyle and Straus explain.

> When a meeting blows up, when nothing gets accomplished or people become frustrated and angry, the participants take their frustrations back with them to their jobs or homes. Not only do participants of the meeting waste time cooling off, but they waste other people's time griping about what happened. These are some of the hidden costs of unsuccessful meetings. Harold

Reimer, a researcher in the field, estimates that the cost of time lost after ineffective meetings amounts to $800,000 per year for every 1,000 employees. We call this the "meeting recovery syndrome."[6]

This "meeting recovery syndrome" is not something to be taken lightly. It is a stealthy, lethal bacterium that invades many of your meetings and spreads its debilitating effects across your organization without anyone even realizing the havoc it is causing. Patrick Lencioni describes the unrelenting toll it takes on your human assets.

Bad meetings exact a toll on human beings who must endure them, and this goes far beyond the mere momentary dissatisfaction. Bad meetings, and what they indicate and provoke in an organization, generate real human suffering in the form of anger, lethargy, and cynicism. And while this certainly has a profound impact on organizational life, it also impacts people's self-esteem, their families, and their outlook on life.[7]

Time and money, money and time—with respect to meetings, they intertwine. And, when all the costs are added up, it blows your mind.

The Power of the Leverage Ratio

If you have ever put 20 percent down on a $200,000 home or put $2,000 down on a $20,000 automobile, you have leveraged your money. You have invested a small amount of your own money and gained control of an asset that is worth 10, 15, or 20 times your investment. Utilizing small, up-front cash investments (equity) that yield high returns is leveraging.

This concept also applies to meeting improvement, and it must be understood in any organization that is seriously bent on salvaging some of the time and money that are being squandered on wasteful, unproductive meetings. Let's use a little vignette to illustrate the power of the leverage ratio in recouping meeting dollars currently being wasted.

Cynthia's Session

Cynthia, a manager, calls a meeting of herself and nine other people in her department. Cynthia has not read *Mining Group Gold*, nor has she had any training in the tools and processes of good meeting management. She does not take time to plan the structure and process of this session. She is too busy with other, more important tasks. Instead, Cynthia goes in, as she often does, and "wings it."

The meeting is scheduled to run from 1:00 to 4:00 p.m. The first 15 minutes are taken up arguing over "why are we here?" and "what do we want to achieve by the end of this meeting?" Another 20 minutes are spent pounding out an agenda. Facilitating the side conversations and personal attacks between Sam and Mary, who have no interest in the meeting's subject matter, requires 10 more minutes. Another 5 minutes are consumed arguing over whether or not George should be present to provide his insights on the topic. A vote reveals that a majority of the group wants George to be there. Then, because the session is interrupted searching for George, getting him to the session, and bringing him up to date, another 10 minutes are lost. Another 12 minutes are lost backtracking over data and decisions because no one is recording and posting this information as it comes up. Matt requires 18 minutes of special facilitation to keep him focused. His only interest is in how the project will be implemented, and he keeps bringing up numerous issues that are out of place for this strategic-level discussion.

The whole group eventually shares and processes the appropriate information. They reach a consensus on the issue under discussion, and the session adjourns at 4 p.m. Was this a productive session? Cynthia thinks so, and the other attendees feel the same way. They finished on time. They worked through a tough issue and reached consensus on how they wanted to proceed. Three hours to reach consensus on a sensitive issue—"hey, not bad."

Let's review this episode from a different perspective. In fact, 1 hour and 30 minutes of the 3 hours were consumed by disruptive activities that could have been prevented or reduced through proper planning of the meeting's structure and process and through better meeting leadership skills. For the purpose of this illustration, let's say that up-front planning and better in-session facilitation could have eliminated the 1.5 hours of misused time. We now can demonstrate the power of the leverage ratio.

Leverage Ratio Calculations

Let's say that Cynthia has read *Mining Group Gold* and is familiar with the tools and processes advocated here (especially the leverage ratio). Therefore, instead of being too busy to plan, Cynthia invests 1 hour of her most precious resource, her personal time, in planning the structure and process of her upcoming session. The session achieves its desired outcome in 1.5 hours instead of 3. Her planning and in-session meeting management skills have cut the meeting time by 50 percent through improved session productivity.

With 10 people at the group session (Cynthia plus 9 others), each person is given a gift of 1.5 hours of time. For the whole group, that translates into 15 work hours saved. And 15 work hours saved for a 1-hour investment is a *15:1 time investment leverage ratio!* The 10 people are released to go back to their jobs. They can perform 10 other tasks that would otherwise have had to wait while the group unproductively "burned" that same period of time. Also not to be overlooked, Cynthia's personal investment of 1 hour is returned to her 150 percent. Table 2-2 shows calculations for figuring the monetary investment leverage ratio.

No matter how you look at it, the leverage ratio is a critical meeting concept. It clearly demonstrates how small investments in advanced planning and the practice of basic meeting leadership skills are returned to the organization many times over.

These savings do not all flow neatly and cleanly to the bottom line, of course. What they do is translate into increased productivity—more and better work for the same dollars. They surface as increased time for people to learn new skills in areas that are critical to the organization. They show up as expanded work capability—people have more time to take on more tasks and wider responsibilities.

For many organizations, recovering just a fraction of the time and money that are being blown on poorly planned and facilitated group sessions could mean the difference between being able to ignite a vigorous climate of growth and prosperity and being forced to struggle for mere survival.

Whatever you do, do not follow the insanity of the manager who called his team together and proclaimed, "We are going to meet every day for two hours until we can find out why so little work is getting done around here."

Participant	Salary	Hourly Cost from Table 2-1
Cynthia	$60,000	$ 50
Average for other participants	$50,000	375
Cost per hour for the session		$425

Return: 1.5 hours saved × $425/hour = $638
Cynthia's investment: up-front planning time, 1 hour at $50
$638 returned on an investment of $50 is well over a 12:1 return on planning investment

Table 2-2 Leverage Ratio: Great Monetary Returns from Small Planning Investments

WORKSHEET

Develop written responses to the two items listed below.

1. What do you feel are the main learning points from Chapter 2?

_____

_____

_____

_____

_____

_____

2. Elaborate on why you feel these points are key for you.

_____

_____

_____

_____

_____

_____

Notes

1. "Meetings in America: A Study of Trends, Costs, and Attitudes toward Business Travel and Teleconferencing, and Their Impact on Productivity," a Verizon Conferencing White Paper prepared by InfoCom, Greenwich, Conn. See full report online at https://e-meetings.verizonbusiness.com/global/en/meetingsinamerica/uswhitepaper.php.
2. "Study Says Meetings Waste Precious Time," *Cleveland Plain Dealer*, March 31, 1989, p. 15C.
3. R. K. Mosvick and R. B. Nelson, *We've Got to Start Meeting like This* (Glenview, Ill.: Scott Foresman and Company, 1987), p. 4.
4. Robert B. Nelson and Peter Economy, *Better Business Meetings* (Burr Ridge, Ill.: Irwin Professional Pub., 1995), p. 5.
5. These calculations were made using a handy meeting calculator found online at http://www.effectivemeetings.com/diversions/meetingcost.asp. The calculator accounts only for base salaries, so all the dollar calculations shown in Table 2-1 were increased by 50 percent to accommodate the additional "load factor."
6. M. Doyle and D. Straus, *How to Make Meetings Work* (New York: Berkley Publishing Group, 1976), pp. 8–9.
7. P. Lencioni, *Death by Meeting* (San Francisco: Jossey-Bass, 2004), p. 253.

Chapter 3

THE KEY TO UNLOCKING THE GOLD MINE: THE MANAGER AS FACILITATIVE LEADER

CHAPTER OBJECTIVES

- To define the role and fundamental behaviors of a facilitative leader.
- To explain why practicing facilitative leadership is an organizational requirement for innovation and results.
- To show how facilitative actions complement and strengthen one's ability to lead.

Introduction

The message so far is that meetings cost money—a lot of money. This is a cost that must be controlled. Every meeting must pay its own way. Quit accepting abysmal meetings as the cost of doing business by using the worn-out excuse, "Well, that's just the way we do things around here; it's baked into our cultural DNA." That is wrong-headed thinking. Reduced meeting costs and improved productivity are fully within your reach if you want to change things. The approach advocated throughout this book revolves around one word: *facilitation*—the manager acting as a facilitative leader.

Facilitation is the key to unlocking the gold mine of wisdom and knowledge that is buried in the heads of your people. When it is released, this wisdom can be used to solve problems, make decisions, resolve conflicts, develop alternatives, create strategies, heal interpersonal strife, and much, much more. The vice president, manager, administrator, school principal, committee chairperson, supervisor, team leader—anyone running a meeting in order to cash in on the collaborative brainpower of a group—will be practicing the same set of skills: facilitation skills.

What happens without facilitation? The following story demonstrates the point in a light-hearted manner.

The sixth-grade safety patrol boy limped into the school principal's office with black eye and a bruised knot on his forehead. The principal asked, "Tyler, what on earth happened to you?"

Tyler replied, "I tried to help a little old lady across the busy street in front of our school."

The principal, in a voice filled with disbelief, responded, "Oh, come now, you didn't get beaten up because you tried to help an old lady across the street!"

Tyler exclaimed, "Oh yes I did. She didn't want to go!"

Force, power, authority, resistance, no commitment to the final destination, lack of mutual understanding of the situation, ill will between people, bruises—all of these elements are found in this little narrative.

These same elements, plus many others, are found in thousands and thousands of meetings across America each day where everyone is doing battle over content and no one is paying attention to facilitation—to the *group process.*

Even though the little old lady achieved her desired outcome of not going across the street, the wasteful, dysfunctional, energy-consuming process that transpired exacted a heavy toll on both parties.

Since facilitation is the key to the gold mine, let's start by defining the role of the facilitator.

What Is a Facilitator?

Very simply, a facilitator is a person who helps a group to free itself from internal obstacles or difficulties so the meeting's desired outcomes can be pursued more efficiently and effectively. Lao-Tse, one of the great Chinese philosophers who lived under the Zhou dynasty, developed a superb definition of a facilitator more than 2,400 years ago when he said, "A good leader is best when people barely know that he leads. A good leader talks little but when the work is done, the aim fulfilled, all others will say, 'We did this ourselves.'"

Building on the wisdom of Lao-Tse, over the years I have evolved the following descriptive definition to help my workshop participants envision facilitation as a dynamic, active process, as opposed to a passive, hands-off one.

In the purest sense, when wearing the "facilitator's hat," an individual acts as a neutral servant of the people. By that I mean that the person focuses on guiding without directing, bringing about action without disruption, helping people self-discover new approaches and solutions to problems, knocking down walls that have been built between people while preserving structures that are of value, and, above all, appreciating people as people. All of this must be done without leaving any fingerprints.

Effective facilitation is at the core of team-based organizations emphasizing collaborative approaches to problem solving, planning, and decision making. As more and more managers come to understand what facilitation means, internalize the philosophy, and practice the fundamental behaviors in a quality way, the payoff will be significant in terms of holding fewer and shorter meetings while increasing innovation and better results in the ones you must conduct.

A General Discussion of the Manager as Facilitative Leader

There is little doubt that managers are facing the challenge of their professional lives. Downsizing, restructuring, redistricting, mergers, acquisitions, and consolidations are responses to fierce global competition. In addition, an unrelenting need to improve customer satisfaction, product quality, and level of service are pressing managers into more demanding and more facilitative roles. They are being asked to take on more responsibilities in flatter organizational structures. As a consequence, they are being driven closer to problems where they often lack the understanding and technical expertise to handle the difficulties that arise.

Leaders everywhere are being asked to do more with less. Learning and practicing how to facilitate collaboration will be the surest way for you and others like you to provide the kind of leadership that is required to meet the challenges of people and project management. And this is true regardless of your industry or professional occupation.

Although the emphasis of this chapter is on the manager, and the corresponding facilitation requirements for creating open, collaborative climates in companies, everything said here also rings true for school and hospital administrators, agency deputies and supervisors, heads of not-for-profit organizations, and the like.

Communication and listening are undisputed building blocks for facilitating superior collaboration. This point is well articulated by "The Genius," Bill Walsh, late coach of the three-time Super Bowl champion San Francisco 49ers:

> Communication creates collaboration; big ears are better than big egos. . . . Collaboration is required more than ever these days to obtain optimal results. These results only occur when you are able to bring out the full potential of your personnel. Quality collaboration is only possible in the presence of quality communication; that is the free-flowing and robust exchange of information, ideas, and opinions. And having "big ears"— the skill of being a good listener—is the first law of good communication. . . . The second law is when you are not listening [i.e., you are speaking], ask good questions.[1]

Building facilitation capabilities throughout all levels of an organization's hierarchy is not some passing fad; it is a necessity. It is an ongoing response to the unrelenting question, "What must we do to meet the demands of our customers faster, with less cost, and with higher quality than any of our competitors?"

Organizations that take the lead in making certain that the knowledge and practice of facilitation behaviors permeate all levels of their hierarchy will be the ones that will be leading the race during the twenty-first century. Why? Because they will be "mining their group gold" and using it as an asset in the formulation of strategies, plans, decisions, and solutions to provide a level of customer satisfaction that is beyond the reach of their rivals.

Henry Mintzberg, a management thought leader and consultant to many Fortune 500 companies, strengthens the case for the manager as facilitative leader with his argument that effective managers are *engagers*, or, to put it differently, collaborators. They make certain that their subordinates, peers, and supervisors collaborate to achieve their goals.

> [T]he past century has seen a steady shift from managing as controlling to managing as engaging. We hear more and more about knowledge workers, contract work, networked and learning organizations, teams and task forces, while many subordinates have become colleagues [or associates] and many suppliers have become partners.
>
> . . . [With engaging] there is a sense of respecting, trusting, caring, and inspiring, not to mention listening. . . . Managing seems to work well when it helps to bring out the energy that naturally exists within people.[2]

John Maxwell builds on the power of facilitative leadership to maximize a team's collective wisdom with these insights on shared thinking.

> Two heads are better than one. . . . It's like harnessing two horses to pull a wagon. They are stronger pulling together than either is individually. Did you know that when they pull together, they can move more weight than the sum of what they can move individually? A synergy comes from working together. The same kind of synergy comes into play when people come together.
>
> Because shared thinking is stronger than solo thinking, it's obvious that it yields a higher return. That happens because of the compounding action of shared thinking.[3]

Finally, to avoid the impression that business and industry are the only sectors in which a significant increase in the demand for facilitation expertise is taking place, a word about school-based (or site-based) planning will show that the same requirement, possibly on an even grander scale, is occurring within our educational system.

The purpose of school-based planning is to improve the educational performance of all students via shared decision making involving school administrators, parents, teachers, and students.

Although school-based management takes many forms, the goal is to empower each school building in a district by providing it with the authority, flexibility, and resources to solve the educational problems that are peculiar to that building. The principal of each building is required to chair a regularly scheduled monthly meeting with her school's planning team, typically a group of teachers, parents, students (at the high school level), one designee appointed by the principal, and sometimes other constituencies as determined by the team.

The day-to-day operation of the school building and general administration of the school staff remain the responsibility of the principal. But the planning team can have a great deal of influence over many of the long-range issues affecting student performance. Examples of critical areas where school-based planning teams operate include tasks like analyzing student performance data, setting objectives that are consistent with student needs, planning activities to accomplish these objectives, monitoring and adjusting the plan, and reporting the plan and its progress to the community.

Principals in particular, but all other members of the school-based management team as well, must become adept at facilitation. This is mandatory if school-based planning is to succeed.

General Requirements for the Collaborative, Facilitative Leader

Rensis Likert[4] articulated the role of the leader in highly effective groups in the early 1960s, but it took until the mid-1970s for American business, educational, and governmental organizations to begin to seriously buy into them. Decades later, however, the role remains essentially unchanged, but the corresponding behaviors are now being fully embraced and practiced in the enlightened organizations of today.

Drawing on Likert's seminal research, and weaving in the references made earlier, we can unequivocally state that no matter what your formal title may be, you must routinely incorporate a minimum set of activities if you are to be recognized as a facilitative leader. And these activities, practiced a thousand times over in team meetings by you, acting as a facilitator, will be the keys that open the doors to your gold mine.

- Focusing the energies of your teammates on defining and accomplishing common desired outcomes.

- Helping your teammates use efficient communication processes that provide better information, more technical knowledge, more facts, and more experience for decision-making purposes than you working alone could marshal.
- Using team decision making at every *appropriate* opportunity to earn each member's support for the final decision, thus gaining members' commitment to executing it fully.
- Knowing that at times decisions must be made rapidly and cannot wait for team processes; therefore, you anticipate these emergencies and, with the team, establish procedures for handling them so that action can be taken rapidly with team support.
- Taking primary responsibility for establishing and maintaining a supportive atmosphere throughout the team and encouraging every member to participate.
- Strengthening the team and its processes by being careful to see that all matters involving and affecting the team are dealt with by the team, while at the same time avoiding those items or tasks that do not concern the team. (These items are handled by higher authorities, appropriate subgroups, or colleagues who give feedback on progress and results to the whole team.)
- Fostering self-discovery of alternatives and solutions by protecting team members and their ideas from attack, so that members feel secure in sharing and exploring a multitude of proposals, ideas, thoughts, and opinions.

To have the fullest impact on organizational success, the philosophy and behaviors of facilitation have to be shared values among a majority of the line managers and administrators in an organization. The facilitation role must not evolve into the exclusive domain of a few staff people on whom the line groups depend for these services.

Even if facilitation experts exist in an organization, there are likely to be very few of them—one person for every 3,000 to 5,000 employees is a common ratio. With such a small staff, the third-party facilitation help that does exist internally—or is purchased on the outside—will be concentrated on a few highest-priority sessions. In most cases, work groups, task forces, and committees must learn to facilitate themselves. It is the only way they can count on day-to-day facilitation within their unit.

For the goal of self-facilitation to be realized, every manager needs to be at the forefront, learning and modeling the basic facilitation behaviors presented in this book and encouraging others on the team to follow his lead.

Facilitation Is Always a Shared Responsibility

Although one person (a group manager, administrator, task force chairperson, or other designated individual) has the formal responsibility of being the primary facilitator for a particular session, facilitation must be shared by everyone in attendance. In other words, *all other attendees are designated as secondary facilitators*, and this must be impressed on the participants at the start of every session until it becomes internalized as "the way we do our meetings." This is a nonnegotiable I-beam upon which the whole Mining Group Gold approach rests!

Whenever a group comes together to trade information, strategize, solve problems, or make decisions, every member of the group must share the responsibility for making the session as successful as it can possibly be. By recognizing that facilitation is a group function to which all members can contribute, the primary facilitator helps to develop a culture of teamwork and group cohesion. Developing a shared responsibility for facilitation ensures that all group resources will be used productively.

No one person can possibly be sensitive to all of the task, process, and individual problems that exist at any given moment in a group session. Some members may be more skilled at using task-oriented behaviors, such as proposing, seeking information, testing comprehension, and summarizing. Others may be more prone to concentrate on group-oriented behaviors, such as encouraging, harmonizing, and performance checking. Some may be more adept at helping particular members understand how, perhaps unconsciously, they are sidetracking the group, while others may be more skillful at gate opening and drawing in quiet members or at resolving conflict. Still others may be better able to write quickly and neatly on flip charts, and so on.

The key point is that the facilitation of a session is not the sole responsibility of the primary facilitator. That person should set expectations and receive facilitation assistance (i.e., secondary facilitation) from everyone in attendance if a session's productivity is to be maximized.

The Need for Hat Switching

Initially, most people are not effective at both being the primary facilitator and, at the same time, being a full participant in the ongoing content discussion. Experience has shown that more often than not, if the primary facilitator actively participates in the content of the meeting, she gets swept up in the debate, discussion, analysis, disagreement, and other such matters, and forgets about the facilitation. It is true that some people can do both jobs quite effectively; however, they are the exception rather than the rule.

If the manager, committee chairperson, or administrator is the primary facilitator for a group and is not able to move naturally between the dual roles of group facilitator and full group participant, then these roles need to be consciously split.

The reason for mentally separating the two roles is to emphasize and preserve the integrity of the facilitation process. By thinking in terms of "having two hats" and switching them as required throughout the meeting, the primary facilitator will not forget about the facilitation role whenever he enters the discussion as a group participant.

For the primary facilitator, the chief concern must be *facilitation* (helping the group free itself from internal obstacles or difficulties so that it can pursue its desired outcomes more efficiently and effectively) and not *content* (getting enmeshed in the task-related dialogue and activities).

Obviously, when you are facilitating your own group, you will want to contribute your perspectives and ideas to the ongoing dialogue and activities. When this occurs, you need to signal that you are stepping out of the facilitator role and into the role of group participant. Your inputs should be shared with the group and processed in line with the approach being utilized. When you are done, announce that you are returning to the primary facilitator role and proceed with assisting the group process until the next occasion arises where your personal input is deemed appropriate. Here is an example:

> For the moment, I need to slip on my manager's hat and provide my ideas on the bonus plan. I do agree that it is a complex problem with ramifications cutting across many functions. Therefore we have to be careful that we don't . . .
>
> So, those are the main thoughts I wanted to inject right now, especially the concept of a 10 percent initial buy-in for all eligible participants. Now, putting my facilitator's hat back on, Chloe, you have been quiet during this discussion. I know that you are fairly new to our company, but I also know that you had some experience with bonus plans in your previous job; what do you think we ought to do to improve the link between pay and performance in our current plan?

Please remember, *being primary facilitator in no way removes you from participating in meeting content*. However, it is imperative that you distinguish your facilitator role from your active group member (content) role each time these roles change during a group session. Also, from a group member's point of view, if you are not clear as to the leader's role, stop the discussion momentarily and ask, "I'm not certain which role you are operating in at this point. Would you please clarify which hat you are wearing?"

Granted, role splitting by the facilitator is somewhat mechanical and artificial. However, this procedure does deliver a significant two-pronged payback: it ensures the integrity of the facilitation process, while at the same time offering a means for the primary facilitator to provide her personal inputs regarding the issues at hand.

You Are Always in Charge as a Facilitative Leader

From a managerial standpoint, being a miner of group gold does not diminish your assigned responsibilities, compromise your ability to make tough decisions, or weaken your ability to lead the group. Practicing the art of excellent facilitation is not being soft on your people; it is not "turning the candy store over to the kids." Practicing the art of excellent facilitation does require self-discipline and, in some situations, even requires behavioral or stylistic changes in the way in which you currently interact with the group.

Simply put, practicing the art of excellent facilitation never compromises your ability to manage the group. The underlying reason is that as the formal leader of the group, you always retain full responsibility for the group's performance and for seeing that the group meets the demands, goals, and strategies placed upon it by the larger organization. Actually, by being assigned this full responsibility, you are afforded the opportunity to decide whether you want to take advantage of the various facilitation behaviors described in the upcoming chapters in order to enhance your effectiveness in "managing *with* people."

WORKSHEET

Develop written responses to the two items listed below.

1. What do you feel are the main learning points from Chapter 3?

_____

_____

_____

_____

_____

_____

2. Elaborate on why you feel these points are key for you.

_____

_____

_____

_____

_____

_____

Notes

1. B. Walsh, with S. Jacobson and C. Walsh, *The Score Takes Care of Itself: My Philosophy of Leadership* (New York: Penguin Group, 2009), p. 112.
2. H. Mintzberg, *Managing* (San Francisco: Barrett-Koehler Publishers, Inc., 2009), pp. 14–15.
3. J. Maxwell, *How Successful People Think* (New York: Center Street, 2009), pp. 95–96.
4. R. Likert, *New Patterns of Management* (New York: McGraw-Hill, 1961), pp. 170–172.

Chapter 4

A MAP OF THE GOLD MINE: YOUR PATHWAYS TO INNOVATION AND RESULTS

CHAPTER OBJECTIVES

- To provide a conceptual illustration portraying mining group gold facilitation.
- To couple the illustration with 18 operating principles to create a full process map.

Introduction

Over time, I have gone through several attempts to create a diagram that would succinctly conceptualize what I was professing. I knew that if I could show others a pictorial representation of the mining group gold facilitation activities and their corresponding flows and linkages, it would make it easier for others to absorb the overall strategy for cashing in on the collaborative brainpower of a group. The illustration depicted in Figure 4-1, along with the corresponding principles that follow, is the latest version. This one is the most inclusive while still representing the mining group gold facilitation process in a simple, yet highly instructive manner.

Examine this conceptual framework and its associated principles, then "dog-ear" pages 41 and 43–47 so that you can easily return to them. Those pages will always be your high-level mental model for planning and facilitating any session where you will be in charge. They truly are a map of the gold mine, giving you activity sequences, routes, and reference points guiding your actions as you become a miner of group gold. If you want to be a successful miner, you first need to have a good map of the mine!

Reviewing the Map

If you check out the conceptual illustration, the first thing you will notice is that it's broken into two major segments. On the left side are the activities that must be completed prior to the start of the session. These activities are shown in the dashed box titled " I. Preplanning." Then there is the large rectangle that shows the various facilitation activities and their sequential flow, which make up the meeting itself. Notice that it is broken into three phases: "II. Start-up," "III. Move-out," and "IV. Wrap-up." These headings draw attention to the three distinct phases that excellent meetings pass through as they unfold. Finally, take note that the facilitation of mining group gold is a closed-loop system. At the close of each session, a critique is held to evaluate "what we did well" in this session and "what we could do better" in our next session to grow and develop as a collaborative team. The wrap-around arrow signifies how this critique information becomes valued input to the primary facilitator in planning the next session.

Preplanning (Chapters 5 and 6)

Excellent meetings don't just happen. Any meeting, except for the most mundane or casual, requires some forethought, some preplanning.

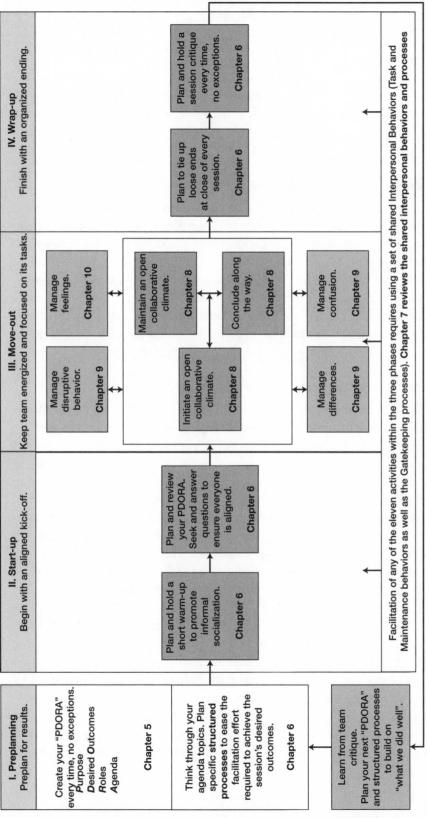

I. Preplanning
Preplan for results.

Create your "PDORA" every time, no exceptions.
Purpose
Desired Outcomes
Roles
Agenda

Chapter 5

Think through your agenda topics. Plan specific **structured** processes to ease the facilitation effort required to achieve the session's desired outcomes.

Chapter 6

Learn from team critique. Plan your next "PDORA" and structured processes to build on "what we did well".

II. Start-up
Begin with an aligned kick-off.

Plan and hold a short warm-up to promote informal socialization.

Chapter 6

Plan and review your PDORA. Seek and answer questions to ensure everyone is aligned.

Chapter 6

III. Move-out
Keep team energized and focused on its tasks.

Manage disruptive behavior.
Chapter 9

Manage feelings.
Chapter 10

Initiate an open collaborative climate.
Chapter 8

Maintain an open collaborative climate.
Chapter 8

Conclude along the way.
Chapter 8

Manage differences.
Chapter 9

Manage confusion.
Chapter 9

IV. Wrap-up
Finish with an organized ending.

Plan to tie up loose ends at close of every session.
Chapter 6

Plan and hold a session critique every time, no exceptions.
Chapter 6

Facilitation of any of the eleven activities within the three phases requires using a set of shared Interpersonal Behaviors (Task and Maintenance behaviors as well as the Gatekeeping processes). Chapter 7 reviews the shared interpersonal behaviors and processes

Figure 4-1 A Map to the Gold Mine: Your Pathways to Innovation and Results

Preplanning means doing two things: (1) developing a PDORA (the Purpose for holding your session, the Desired Outcomes to be achieved, the specific Roles to be assigned to participants, and the sequenced Agenda), and (2) determining the specific processes you will use during the session to help ensure a successful outcome. These activities are shown in the light gray dashed boxes on our map.

Task, Maintenance, and Gatekeeping Shared Behaviors (Chapter 7)

Along the bottom of the map (the wide, narrow box with three vertical ascending arrows) is the common interpersonal communication foundation for phases II, III, and IV). This foundation consists of *ten task-oriented communication behaviors* concerned with the group's effort to define and accomplish its desired outcomes; *five maintenance communication behaviors* promoting the group's efforts to survive, regulate, grow, and strengthen itself as an effective body for achieving its desired outcomes; and *two gatekeeping actions* for regulating the flow of group participation by bringing in and shutting out group members.

Start-Up; Move-Out; Wrap-Up (Chapters 6, 8, 9, and 10)

These three phases are the meeting in action. Ideally, you would like to move across the three phases along the centerline flow, following just the seven boxes shown in light gray. That is, with your preplanning completed and the time to begin your session at hand, you would like to be able to hold a short warm-up, review your PDORA (start-up); then initiate an open, collaborative climate to get things underway; maintain an open, collaborative climate as you share, discuss, and process information in the pursuit of your stated desired outcomes; draw meaningful conclusions along the way (move-out); and finally, tie up loose ends and hold a session critique to learn what went well and not so well so that both the planning and the facilitation can be improved next time (wrap-up).

Sometimes that centerline path will happen; on other occasions, you will hit bumps in the road. There are four common points of contention that arise in sessions, causing them to flounder. Sooner rather than later, you will be pulled off your centerline flow and have to manage participants' disruptive behaviors, manage differences, manage confusion, and/or manage feelings. These are indicated on the map by the broad two-headed arrows and the four darker gray boxes outside the centerline route. Facilitating these troublesome areas comes with the territory. Dysfunctional behavior cannot be allowed to sidetrack any meeting. The best approach is to deal with it quickly when it arises, reestablish the desired outcome, and keep moving forward.

18 Mining Group Gold Operating Principles

In addition to Figure 4-1, which depicts the overall interaction among the facilitation activities, there are 18 core operating principles that support the collaborative nature of the Mining Group Gold approach. Together, Figure 4-1 and these operating principles form the map of this book and define how facilitative leadership can be practiced within and across work teams. The first 4 principles originate from the material in Chapter 3. The remaining 14 are derived from the content in upcoming chapters and are keyed back to our conceptual diagram for easy reference.

A MAP OF THE GOLD MINE: THE 18 OPERATING PRINCIPLES

General Facilitation Principles (Chapter 3)
1. *Primary facilitation rests with the person who calls the people together.* If you initiate the meeting, you must assume the nonnegotiable responsibility of being the primary defense against the propagation of a wasteful session by taking on the "primary facilitator" role.
2. *Secondary facilitation is a shared task.* This principle ties back to the first. Everyone in attendance must team up with the primary facilitator in the complementary role of secondary facilitators. Without this joint effort, the potential for collaboration significantly diminishes.
3. *Primary facilitation does not preempt extensive content contributions.* The primary facilitator always has the opportunity to be an active contributor to the content of the team session. Principle 2, shared facilitation, is the key to allowing this to happen. However, since the primary facilitator is often the manager of the team or the person of influence who is running a task force or committee, verbally "switching hats" to signal a distinction between content and facilitation contributions is essential to avoid role confusion in the minds of group members.

---

4. *Facilitate collaboration authentically.* Attempting to manipulate these tools and processes into a command-and-control style won't work. Giving people a "feeling of collaboration" by first asking them for their inputs, so that you can tell them that their ideas aren't any good, and then telling them what you really intended to do all along is inauthentic facilitation. The ability to conduct a truly collaborative session always rests on your personal credibility and integrity. When your credibility is shot, you cannot facilitate collaboration. You can only accomplish things through fear, intimidation, and brute force.

Preplanning (Chapters 5 and 6)

5. *Develop a PDORA document before every team session—no exceptions.* The four tickets for admission that the primary facilitator must have in hand before entering the gold mine are the session's purpose (**P**), the session's desired outcomes (**DO**), who will play the roles (**R**) of timekeeper, minute taker, and scribe (in addition to their standard secondary facilitation role), and a sequenced agenda (**A**) with clock times. If these admission tickets are not available on any given occasion, the primary facilitator is trying to sneak into the gold mine "illegally" and should be stopped from holding the session (Chapter 5).

6. *Invite only the smallest number of people necessary to achieve the sessions desired outcomes.* If you don't do this, you will create meeting Hell. You will end up filling a conference room with people who have little or nothing to say, but who will take an eternity to say it (Chapter 5).

7. *Plan, in advance, any procedures that you will employ to help the group meet the stated desired outcomes.* A streamlined, structured process that outlines a set of organized steps to move the participants through to hit the desired outcome(s) target is as essential to facilitating a collaborative group session as the storyboard is to making a successful movie. It is through a preplanned, structured process that you ensure that an efficient collaborative session will be proactively facilitated (Chapter 6).

Shared Interpersonal Behaviors (Chapter 7)

8. *Establish the ten task-oriented behaviors, the five maintenance-oriented behaviors, and the two gatekeeping processes as standard communication behaviors for all sessions, by all attendees.* The marked improvement in collaboration, teamwork, and general effectiveness once all members understand and begin practicing these basic communication behaviors is quite astounding. Also, particular emphasis by everyone on seeking information and opinions, testing comprehension, and summarizing will immeasurably enhance shared facilitation (Chapter 7).

Start-Up (Chapter 6)

9. *Allow for informal socialization; plan more extensive, formal warm-ups when necessary.* People need a few minutes to get settled in for the meeting; allow five minutes at the beginning of your agenda to account for this. For large meetings where most people will be strangers, plan a formal warm-up that involves everyone present. Depending on the size of the group, 10 to 30 minutes may be needed to conduct this kickoff activity properly (Chapter 6).

10. *Plan to review your PDORA as part of the start-up and answer any questions before moving out.* Aligned meeting kickoffs are driven by the PDORA review and clarification. Only if a glaring problem is pointed out in the review should the PDORA be changed; otherwise, the PDORA you have created and brought to the session is the one that should be utilized (Chapter 6).

Move-Out—The Centerline Flow (Chapter 8)

11. *Initiating a collaborative climate in a team session is the primary facilitator's responsibility.* It is incumbent on the primary facilitator to initiate a collaborative climate by first setting the stage for information processing and then, while withholding his views, encouraging open expressions of thoughts among all others present. George Odiorne describes what happens when this principle is violated: "There is a law of administration which I'd suggest holds true for almost

every situation. That is, if the boss presents his solution first and then asks for opinions about it, a vote of approval will follow almost every time."[1] So if you have strong views on a topic and are not interested in collaboration, tell the people what you intend to do and get on with it; otherwise, hold back and get everyone involved first (Chapter 8).

12. *Maintaining a collaborative climate in a team session initially rests with the primary facilitator, but overall is a shared responsibility.* The people in a group session take their behavioral cues from the leader. One person cannot sustain collaboration alone. As primary facilitator, you should expect others to follow your lead and share responsibility for maintaining it. If this is not understood by all, state it explicitly (Chapter 8).

13. *Concluding along the way is always a shared responsibility of all group members.* Maximizing content value and understanding by making certain that conclusions are drawn from team discussions and noted to ensure that pertinent information is not lost is fundamental to facilitation excellence. Everyone in attendance must be alert so that this key principle is not overlooked (Chapter 8).

Move-Out—Behavior Issues (Chapters 9 and 10)

14. *Encourage the handling of disruptive behavior as a responsibility that is shared by everyone.* Each person shares with all others present the responsibility not to be disruptive in the first place. But if someone is disruptive, in the spirit of secondary facilitation, any member is free to confront the disrupter. The primary facilitator is never the sole facilitator of disruptive behavior (Chapter 9).

15. *Encourage constructive conflict; facilitate against destructive conflict.* Constructive conflict is a normal, healthy occurrence in teams. It is the key to a team's critical thinking; encourage it. Destructive conflict can destroy a group beyond repair. Facilitate against it as soon as the signs of destruction begin to appear (Chapter 9).

16. *Encourage process checks as soon as a person feels confused by some aspect of the content discussion or where the meeting is headed.* If someone is confused and does not speak up, you have lost that individual as an active participant. Keeping

team members' minds clearheaded and focused on the task at hand enhances meeting productivity. As soon as someone feels lost, that person must call a time-out and, with the help of the other group members, get her questions answered and/ or be reoriented to the group's current direction (Chapter 9).

17. *Don't duck emotions in group sessions.* Emotions typically are not something that managers, team leaders, or team members are comfortable facilitating. That is understandable. Still, this must be done in order to preserve teamwork and collaboration. While you are never asked to agree with the emotions that are being expressed, you must never deny people the feelings that they are expressing (Chapter 10).

Wrap-Up (Chapter 6)

18. *Tie up loose ends and conduct a meaningful critique at the close of every session.* Finishing with a snap is essential to superb meetings. The importance of an organized ending where decisions and action items are spelled out and where performance assessments focused on the specifics of the processes used and the quality of the interpersonal behaviors utilized cannot be overstated. Continuous meeting improvement will never happen with poor, disorganized endings to your sessions (Chapter 6).

With the conceptual diagram and its 18 integrated operating principles in place, you now have the 35,000-foot view of "how to cash in on the collaborative brainpower of a team for innovation and results." From here on, we'll reduce the altitude and explore the specific how-tos for being a facilitative leader and a miner of group gold.

Since the rest of the book's content has been organized for you by this "mapping chapter," you will be able to fit the details of each succeeding chapter into the bigger picture to aid your comprehension and learning.

Meetings: A Forum for Leadership and Achieving Innovation and Results

Before making the transition to the remaining "roll up your sleeves and get your hands dirty" chapters of *Mining Group Gold*, a few final points are in order. In spite of the drawbacks and expenses associated with bringing people together, as laid out in Chapter 2, one fact remains: group sessions are the lifeblood of organizations.

Whether we like it or not, sitting down face to face, or in some cases via teleconference or videoconference, is the right way—the *only* way—to process information and achieve goals. Meetings are an essential medium for leadership and managerial work. If you are still not convinced that demonstrating skilled facilitative leadership in group settings is critical to your personal career growth and development as well as your business success, this series of comments, first by Kieffer, then by Green and Lazarus, and finally by Maxwell, ought to persuade you to reexamine your thinking.

> Meetings are the fulcrum for all commercial and noncommercial transactions, the central nervous system of an information society, the center stage for personal performance. . . . [O]nce you perceive that meetings are perhaps the single most important "window" on business and professional life, the window through which we see and evaluate and are seen and evaluated, you will be far less casual about invitations to meet and far more demanding of the meetings you choose to call or attend.
>
> General judgments about you will inevitably be made because how you handle a meeting reveals how you might handle a future job necessarily full of meetings. There are few visible bases on which to make judgments regarding managerial and leadership skills, and the ability to manage meetings is as accurate a reflection of such skills as one can find.[2]

Green and Lazarus, documenting their findings based on the results of a survey of more than 1,000 executives from a wide range of functions, including general management, sales, finance, marketing, manufacturing, and human resources, fully substantiate the perspective laid down by Kieffer.

> Make no mistake about it, meetings are management. Or stated more accurately, meetings are a microcosm of management. Better meetings are inextricably linked to better management.
>
> One of the survey's most important findings is that, in terms of human resources and the development of management potential, business people do indeed see meetings as management. And how well [people] manage and participate

in business meetings can play a crucial role in how fast they climb the corporate ladder. The study revealed that executives who run meetings well are perceived to be better managers by both their superiors and their peers. Conversely, those who fail to run meetings effectively are often considered to be lacking in critical management skills. Statistically, 87 percent of those surveyed found that a person's ability to lead meetings affects peoples' perceptions of their management ability.

[Regarding participation in sessions,] 81 percent of the respondents said that their perception of a participant's ability is definitely affected by the quality of his or her participation in a meeting. . . . [O]ne thing seems perfectly clear: an individual's performance in meetings is a key to promotability. Those people who most effectively participate in, and manage, meetings are most likely to head the companies of the future.[3]

So, in today's competitive, turbulent, complex, interdependent economic environment, teams, teamwork, and collaboration, by necessity, are the heart and soul of world-class organizations. Teams have two assets that exceed those of any single person: they possess more knowledge, and they can think in a greater variety of ways. These potential assets may not always be exploited. Because of poor facilitation and leadership, teams may fall into so much dysfunctional conflict that they cannot operate.

However, as John Maxwell astutely points out, a collaborative culture, where the leadership values shared thinking and practices excellent facilitation, can move an organization to produce superior innovation and results and, at the same time, propel everyone's commitment and feelings of satisfaction to their zenith.

Great organizations possess people throughout the organization who produce great ideas. That is how they become great. The progress they make and the innovations they create don't come down from on high. Their creative sessions are not dominated by top-down leaders. Nor does every meeting become a kind of wrestling match to see who can dominate everyone else. People come together as teams, peers work together, and they make progress because they want the best idea to win.

. . . [G]reat thinking comes when good thoughts are shared in a collaborative environment where people contribute to them, shape them, and take them to the next level. A good team leader helps to create such an environment.[4]

The message should be quite clear by now: "Group sessions must never be blown off and simply accepted as a necessary evil." Your organization's financial and marketplace success, along with your own personal growth, development, and promotability, depends on your ability to seize every meeting opportunity as a forum for role-modeling facilitation and collaborative leadership.

In order to achieve this "best case" result, certain tools, techniques, and processes must be learned and routinely practiced by managers and nonmanagers at all levels of your organization. What these tools, techniques, and processes are, and how they can increase the value and productivity of your company's group sessions, constitutes the remainder of *Mining Group Gold*.

WORKSHEET

Develop written responses to the two items listed below.

1. What do you feel are the main learning points from Chapter 4?

   _____

   _____

   _____

   _____

2. Elaborate on why you feel these points are key for you.

   _____

   _____

   _____

   _____

Notes

1. L. D. Eigen and J. P. Siegel, *The Manager's Book of Quotations* (New York: AMACOM, 1989), p. 262.
2. G. D. Kieffer, *The Strategy of Meetings* (New York: Simon and Schuster, 1988), pp. 12–13, 20.
3. W. A. Green and H. Lazarus, "Are Today's Executives Meeting with Success?" *Journal of Management Development* 10, no. 1 (1991), pp. 22–23.
4. J. C. Maxwell, *Teamwork 101: What Every Leader Needs to Know* (Nashville: Thomas Nelson, Inc., 2008), pp. 114–115.

Part *II*

PLANNING REQUIREMENTS TO MINE GROUP GOLD

Chapter 5

PLANNING THE STRUCTURE OF A SESSION TO MINE GROUP GOLD: SIX STEPS TO SUCCESS

CHAPTER OBJECTIVES

- To present the six major considerations when planning the structure of a group session.
- To explain the specific methodology for creating a PDORA, the mandatory meeting document.
- To present two PDORA templates as models for the reader to follow.

Introduction

Because group sessions produce results that cannot be achieved in any other way, careful planning of the meeting structure is a must. An effective structure aids the facilitation process, ensures optimum participation from group members, and greatly increases the chances of cashing in on the collaborative brainpower of the group.

Nothing you will do in your role as a facilitative leader who is bent on mining group gold will be more essential to preventing meeting breakdowns than bringing a PDORA document to every meeting you call, every time, without exception. *PDORA* is an acronym for **P**urpose, **D**esired **O**utcomes, **R**oles, and **A**genda.

A clear understanding of each meeting's PDORA is the cornerstone upon which all collaborative sessions rest. By not defining your PDORA in advance, you are taking a giant step toward meeting failure. Without it, your group session will meander. You will find confusion, misunderstanding, and verbal sparring ruining your chances of conducting a collaborative meeting. Heated debates over why we are here and what we are trying to accomplish will abound. Group members' time and talents will be wasted, resulting in cynicism and strained relationships. Many participants will either withdraw or contribute at a level far beneath their true capabilities.

When a group doesn't know where it is headed, then any road will do. However, in the realities of our work, these random roads often lead us to address the wrong issues or to address the right issues incorrectly. So to create a focused, collaborative session and to maintain that approach for the duration of the meeting, you must create and utilize a PDORA document.

The value of the PDORA structure and its positive impact on the efficiency and effectiveness of a group session is demonstrated by recounting a popular TV commercial for oil filters from a few years ago.

The setting for the commercial is an auto repair garage. A mechanic is in the foreground. An automobile with its hood up and chains from an overhead pulley running into the engine compartment can be seen in the background. The mechanic yells over his shoulder, "OK, take it away, Joe." The chains tighten, and the car's engine is lifted out and swung over to a workbench.

The camera focuses on the mechanic in the foreground as he says, "You know, this guy didn't have to spend $1,500 on this expensive engine repair job. If he had spent $8 twice a year for one of these" (he holds up an oil filter as the camera zooms in), "all of this could have been avoided." As

Planning the Structure of a Session to Mine Group Gold: Six Steps to Success • 57

the camera pulls back and refocuses on the mechanic, he ardently states, "The choice is yours. You can pay me now, or you can pay me later!"

So it is with planning the structure of a group session. If you are too busy to make a small investment in planning time to create a PDORA (an $8 oil filter), you may have to suffer the consequences of wasting everyone's time and energy on an unproductive session (the $1,500 cost for a blown engine). Sooner or later, you will pay dearly for not planning the session's structure.

The "you can pay me now, or you can pay me later" illustration once more drives home the message that a little time and effort invested in up-front PDORA planning will be paid back—with interest—in time and effort saved both during and after the session just like the "leverage ratio" calculations demonstrated in Chapter 2.

Bluntly put, taking the time to plan a PDORA for any group session that you call is not a discretionary activity; it is your nonnegotiable obligation.

Planning the Structure of a Group Session

Six Vital Questions Guiding the Planning of a Meeting's Structure

1. What are the session's purpose and desired outcomes?
   This question must *always* be answered first!
   Only when the P and DO (of PDORA) have been determined can you intelligently answer the second question.

2. Is a group session necessary?
   If your answer is no, use another means to share and process the needed information.
   If your answer is yes, move on to answering questions 3 and 4.

3. Who should attend the session?

4. What is the macrocomposition of the group, and what can be concluded about its potential "chemistry"?
   These questions force you to consider whom you invite and the potential dynamics involved.

5. What are the roles for this session, and who will be assigned them?

6. What is the agenda content, and what is the sequential flow of its topics?
   These final two questions direct you to complete the R and A (of PDORA).

These six questions form a planning checklist and need to be answered in the sequence presented here. By following this format each time, you will be able to formulate the basic structure of a group session successfully. Let's look at each question in detail.

What Are the Session's Purpose (P) and Desired Outcomes (DO)?

A clear understanding of what is to be accomplished is the foundation on which the entire session rests. If the group leader cannot clarify the purpose and desired outcomes of the session before bringing the participants together, that person does not deserve the right to hold a group session. That's how fundamental the purpose and desired outcomes are. If a clear purpose statement and succinctly defined desired outcomes are not developed beforehand, you are taking a giant step toward meeting failure. Basically, the stage has been set for meeting chaos.

If it lacks a purpose and explicit desired outcomes, the session will wander. Confusion, irritation, acrimony, and impatience will abound. This undercurrent of discontent and exasperation will become a tidal wave, and many participants will either tune out completely or fail to contribute their best efforts. The mood of the meeting will not be conducive to success.

Few things kill the spirit and drain the energy of a session more quickly, or with more devastating effect, than a group of frustrated people who don't want to be in the meeting in the first place arguing over "why are we here?" and "what are we trying to accomplish?"

If there is no stated purpose and no set of desired outcomes to help a meeting refocus and get back on track when necessary, "where the session ends up is where it ends up." Whether or not the correct issues were addressed, or, if they were, whether they were addressed properly, is anybody's guess. That profound contemporary philosopher, Yogi Berra, said it best: "If you don't know where you are going, you'll wind up someplace else and not know how you got there."

Purpose. The *purpose* is a general statement that organizes your thinking as to why you believe you need to pull people together.

A *meeting's purpose* is defined as: "The reason I must pull people away from their desks and gather them together inside the four walls of a conference room for a face-to-face or a virtual meeting."

Zeroing in on a purpose is not difficult to do. By completing the phrase, "*To share and process information relative to . . .*," an incisive purpose can be written every time. Several examples of different purpose statements are presented here.

- *To share and process information relative to* reducing our spare parts inventory.
- *To share and process information relative to* our technician training schedule.
- *To share and process information relative to* the 201x departmental budget.
- *To share and process information relative to* our point-of-sale collaterals for the national June tire sale.
- *To share and process information relative to* topics of mutual interest to the entire staff. *Note:* This should be the standard purpose for any staff meeting.

A purpose statement should be brief and to the point—12 to 18 words, including the opening "boilerplate" phrase, is about right. It is a broad-brush statement that forces you to define why you believe it is necessary to take people away from their current activities and bring them together. Be careful that you don't mix desired outcomes or "how-tos" into the purpose statement. Going beyond 18 words is a sure sign that you're including too much detail in your purpose statement.

Desired Outcomes. Simply defining the session's purpose—*why* you are bringing the group together—is not enough. In addition to the purpose, you also must give forethought to the session's bottom line—*what must be accomplished* as a result of bringing this set of individuals together.

A meeting's *desired outcomes*—or, as they are sometimes referred to in the literature, its goals, objectives, or outputs—are defined as: "What do I want to have achieved when the meeting has been concluded and the people have just walked out of the conference room?"

Because of the major role that desired outcomes play in the scheme of productive meetings, four points require special emphasis.

1. You (the meeting caller) must define the desired outcomes in advance of every meeting that you initiate.
2. You must communicate the desired outcomes at the beginning of the session, in writing, as part of the PDORA so that the attendees will have something in front of them to keep them centered on "what we are trying to achieve in today's meeting."
3. In some cases, you will have desired outcomes that are not open to debate and modification. This is fine, as long as you clarify it up front. In other situations, you may decide to change a desired outcome after some attendees have made compelling arguments for altering what

you initially proposed. In those instances where changes are discussed and agreed to, the modified outcome should be noted on a flip chart and posted for all to see.

4. At any point in a session, the group may pause, reexamine a particular stated desired outcome that it is striving to achieve, and decide to stay with it or to make changes. For example, suppose that one hour into a two-hour meeting, it is obvious that the outcome as presently stated will not be achieved. It is better for the manager to put on his facilitator's hat, stop the discussion, redefine the outcome so that everyone's expectations are in harmony, and move forward together, accepting the fact that "we will not be able to accomplish what we originally set out to do; however, what we do accomplish will be the 'right stuff.' "

Let's now develop desired outcomes for each of the purpose statements shown earlier. Notice each one is written in a simple, clear-cut manner to precisely define what is to be achieved when the information processing is concluded.

- *Purpose:* To share and process information relative to reducing our spare parts inventory.
- *Desired Outcome:* The three proposals from last session analyzed and a final proposal selected.

- *Purpose:* To share and process information relative to our technician training schedule.
- *Desired Outcome:* District technician training schedule revisions developed and agreed to.

- *Purpose:* To share and process information relative to the 201x departmental budget.
- *Desired Outcome:* All budget accounts finalized and agreed to.

- *Purpose:* To share and process information relative to our point-of-sale collaterals for the national June tire sale.
- *Desired Outcome:* A common look and feel for all U.S. in-store point-of-sale brochures, signage, and banners agreed to.

Desired outcomes perform four essential functions with respect to meeting excellence.

1. They create common expectations among all participants.
2. They provide constant reference points to keep the group session on track.
3. They actually define the type of session that will be conducted.
4. They provide a benchmark against which the actual outcomes can be compared to gain a sense of the session's productivity.

In his comedy routine, Woody Allen asks, "How can you possibly be lost if you don't have a final destination?" Similarly, in workshops I pose the question: "How can you tell if your group session has gotten off course if you haven't defined your desired outcomes?" The answer to both questions is the same, "You can't!" However, when the desired outcomes are agreed upon, all group members have a target—a reference point for monitoring and controlling the direction of the session.

The misuse of targets is graphically illustrated by this tale. A traveler was passing through a small town in central Ohio. As he entered town, he saw a big billboard. On the white portion, someone had drawn a target, and right through the middle of the target was an arrow—a bull's-eye. He went down the road a bit, and there was a big, broad oak tree with a white target on it, and right through the middle was another bull's-eye. All over this town, there were bull's-eyes.

The traveler thought to himself, "Somewhere in this town there's one heckuva marksman, and I'm going to find him." By asking a lot of people, he finally did. The marksman turned out to be the son of a local farmer.

The traveler said, "Young man, you certainly have a great gift. No matter what the town folk say about farm boys, you have developed a unique skill. Tell me, how did you get to be such a champion marksman?"

The boy answered, "There's nothing to it. First you shoot, and then you draw the target!"

Thousands of meetings are held each day following the farm boy's philosophy: meet first, decide after the fact that whatever was achieved was on target, then declare the session a rousing success. This process might be described as "how to always feel great about what was accomplished, regardless of what it was."

Meetings are serious business. Don't waste people's time and the organization's money. As a miner of group gold, set your desired outcomes (targets) first and then facilitate team effort toward the achievement of those outcomes.

For every session, ask yourself: "What is this meeting intended to achieve, and how shall I judge whether it was a success or a failure?" And keep asking yourself that over and over until it is clear in your mind why having people come to your meeting is more important than having them at their desks or out in the field doing their jobs. If you do not have very clear predetermined requirements in the form of desired outcomes before you hold your meeting, there is a very high probability that it will be a waste of everyone's time as you go in and just "rely on your wits."

For clarity, keep the desired outcomes as brief as possible. Try writing the desired outcomes as simple sentences using a subject/verb format. Desired outcomes are written in the past tense so that going into the session, the team already has a feeling of accomplishment. Some examples of desired session outcomes are

- Draft of lease contract reviewed and modified.
- Program schedule for the T-4 inkjet printer revised.
- Fourth-grade math textbook selected.
- 201x training budget finalized.
- Pricing changes for all 8.5 × 11 coated papers agreed to.
- Curriculum proposal for "Principles of Economics" reviewed.
- International travel policy established.
- Foodservice vendor for Plants 1 and 2 selected.
- Departmental administrative assistant agreed to.

Is a Group Session Necessary?

Once the purpose and desired outcomes of a group session have been crystallized, the most fundamental of all questions must be asked: "Is a group session really required?"

As pointed out in the planning guidelines, this question must always be answered second, not first. A manager cannot know if a meeting is necessary until its purpose and desired outcomes have been determined. Reversing these first two steps creates the deadly trap of a self-fulfilling prophecy. In other words, "I've chosen to have a meeting. Since I've already determined that I need a meeting, I'll now decide my reason for calling it and figure out what outcomes I hope to achieve."

Eliminate this trap by sticking to the planning sequence advocated here. First, specify the purpose and desired outcomes of a session. Then, determine if there are ways of achieving the desired outcomes other than bringing people together inside the four walls of a conference room. If the desired outcomes can be accomplished by some means other than conducting a meeting, don't hold a meeting!

A common type of fruitless meeting is when a manager calls a session to be briefed by several people who report directly to the manager but whose work depends little (or not at all) on what each of the others do. While a manager may feel that this is an effective use of her time, the people called to such a meeting will usually resent what seems to them to be a waste of *their* time.

As part of the hundreds of workshops I've conducted on the principles of mining group gold, I've routinely asked the participants, "What percentage of the meetings that you convene, or attend at the request of another person, do you feel are unnecessary?" The responses habitually fall in the 30 to 40 percent range, indicating that far too many meetings are unnecessary.

In my workshops, managers often complain about one huge time waster and energy drain. It's known as the "yearly schedule of preset meetings." One irate manager in a recent session stated that just the day before, he had received from his boss the entire schedule of staff meetings for the upcoming year. This manager's comments were interesting.

"Fifty-two staff meetings—every Tuesday from 7:45 a.m. to 9:45 a.m., whether we need a meeting or not. We've been told to post the list on our walls immediately. So now we've generated a self-fulfilling prophecy. Two months before the New Year, it has been declared that we will hold 52 staff meetings next year, and I guarantee we will. There have been at least half a dozen times so far this year when we should have canceled or measurably reduced the time devoted to our staff meetings. We didn't; we've stuck to our schedule week after week like it was a decree from heaven."

The moral of this story is this: even if a series of recurring meetings is set up in advance, do not get locked in to holding every single one just because its day has arrived. The world will not come to an end if a staff meeting, sales review, or project meeting that was scheduled three months ago is canceled or significantly shortened because of a lack of pertinent subjects or because there is other business that is more important.

Programmers are particularly opposed to sitting in meetings. It confines them and restricts them from doing what they want to be doing. One programmer summed it up best with her comments about most of her unnecessary project meetings: "My train of thought is always along these lines: why am I in this meeting talking about the project when I could be out there coding it or fixing broken code? That is where my real work is."

Especially with staff sessions and ongoing regularly scheduled project meetings, poll your people a day or two in advance and see if they believe that the staff (or project) meeting needs to be held this week. Always remain flexible and adhere to the principle that states: "Regularly scheduled meetings should be held irregularly whenever appropriate."

Alternatives to Group Sessions. The dollar cost figures in Chapter 2 vividly portrayed the high cost of holding even seemingly routine meetings. A great many important matters can be quite satisfactorily shared, processed, and resolved by using alternatives other than the common practice of pulling people away from their desks or in from the field and bringing them together in face-to-face groups or tying them up in virtual (videoconference or teleconference) sessions. Therefore, it is wise to consider all of the following possibilities before rushing off to organize one more potentially unnecessary meeting:

- Telephone calls.
- E-mails (including chain e-mails where inputs are accumulated).
- "FYI" copies of meeting minutes to a select number of people who have a need to know but don't need to attend the meeting.
- Informal hallway conversations ("watercooler" talk).
- One-on-one (or one-with-two) relatively short, to-the-point deskside conversations.
- Voice mail (VMAX).
- Executive summaries of key reports sent out with feedback questions attached, to be answered and sent back to the originator.
- Whiteboards and markers in high-traffic areas.
- Groupware communication providing shared online databases so that employees in different places and time zones can access and benefit from others' thinking to make decisions and perform their jobs.
- Instant messaging, using any number of the current downloadable multiprotocol IM clients or the new Web-based services that are popping up all the time. You can create public or private rooms where you can talk and share media files.
- Internal wiki Web sites that allow users with access to create, modify, and organize page content in a collaborative manner.
- Highly featured intranet Web pages, especially with links to digital videos that employees can view at their convenience—excellent for one-way general information sharing.

When it is *not necessary* to hold a meeting, it is *necessary not* to hold the meeting. Living by this truism in your organization will be money in the bank.

Situations That Usually Require Group Sessions. Still, given the underlying circumstances of the situation, having a face-to-face meeting may be the only way to proceed. A group session offers a variety of viewpoints, the interplay of ideas, and a commitment to action that evolves through group participation rather than from outside imposition. The important common denominator for meetings, as demonstrated by the following list, is that the situation requires collaboration or team commitment. With this thought in mind, situations that require a meeting include the following:

- No one person has sufficient information to make a high-quality decision.
- The team's acceptance of an idea, course of action, or decision is critical to its implementation.
- The topic is complex, and it is critical that everyone has exactly the same understanding of the information and data.
- Conflicting views need to be reconciled.
- The people who are receiving and having to act on the information are interdependent.
- The issue being faced is unstructured; for example, what information is required, where to find it, how to find it, and so on, are unknown but need to be agreed to.
- Information needs to be communicated to and immediately processed among a number of people.
- A synergistic effect to enhance creativity is likely to be produced by bringing a team together to process the issue.
- Ideas need to be brainstormed, or group information-processing tools such as affinity diagrams, fishbone diagrams, decision trees, and so on need to be used.

In any event, if you are convinced that a group session is necessary, you are obliged to plan and facilitate the session in a manner that wastes neither your time and energy nor those of the participants.

Who Should Attend the Session?

Once the purpose and outcomes are defined and it's clear that group action or participation is required, effective planning requires that you carefully consider the question: "Who are the appropriate people to invite to this particular meeting?"

The general principle for choosing group session participants is: select the smallest number of people required to achieve the desired outcomes.

When there are too many cooks in the kitchen, either you don't get the meal out or it takes you twice as long. There may be a good reason for including one or two individuals who may not directly contribute to the achievement of the desired outcomes, but the decision to include them should be a conscious and rational one.

The fatal mistake that many managers and chairpersons make at this stage of the planning process is to use the shotgun approach and invite a "cast of thousands" to ensure that all the right people will be present. This random and indiscriminate approach to selecting meeting attendees does not guarantee the presence of the appropriate people and sows the seeds of a facilitation nightmare.

There is an axiom about meetings that says: "If you want a job done poorly, turn it over to a large group, because performance is inversely proportionate to group size." Cynthia Hymowitz, quoting several businessmen in an article for the *Wall Street Journal*, provides a graphic example of this maxim:

> The more who attend a meeting, the slimmer the chances any work will get done. "Everyone wants some air time—if only to show how persuasive they can be—and meetings with 10 or more participants tend to digress from their formal agendas and run hours longer than they should," says Robert Kelly, a professor at Carnegie Mellon University's business school.
>
> Harry Thompson, president of Gen Corp's reinforced plastics division, took along just two associates for a technical meeting with a customer—only to face a room filled with twenty-five managers. "The issues we needed to resolve weren't that deep, but they had people from every level of the organization, and each of them had to put their two-cents in," he says. The result: the meeting Mr. Thompson figured would last two hours took all day.[1]

Unnecessary attendees, those who have no real interest or stake in the session's desired outcomes, pose a twofold facilitation dilemma. First, this expansion in the size of the group exacerbates the facilitation task. Meeting dynamics are simpler and easier to manage with a group of 5 than they are with a group of 10 or 12. Second, people who are invited to a meeting but are not keenly interested in the desired outcomes tend to be disruptive. In the great majority of cases, these people are not trying to be disruptive and don't realize that they are detrimental to the session's progress; however, facilitation complications develop because of their attendance.

It's only natural for nonessential meeting members to feel compelled to contribute. But because the subject matter is, at best, only of marginal interest to them, these "extra invitees" try to shape the meeting (either consciously or unconsciously) to meet their own needs. They interject thoughts, ideas, facts, and opinions that are irrelevant to the main discussion. They are not working to help accomplish the session's desired outcomes because they are not committed to them.

Often, because they are frustrated with how little they are deriving from the meeting, unnecessary attendees either visibly withdraw (push away from the table, get on their PDAs to read and respond to e-mails, fidget, doodle, or keep leaving and coming back) or develop into irritable, cantankerous participants.

Most of these facilitation difficulties are brought on by a lack of attention to a main planning question, "Who should attend?" If you are preparing to hold a group session, don't stack the deck against yourself by inviting unnecessary people. The selection process may be as straightforward as having your entire staff attend the session, or as complicated as including a few handpicked staff members along with attendees from other departments plus several notables from outside the company. Selection of attendees must never be random. The need to make certain that the right people are at the meeting is amusingly reinforced by Glenn Soden:

> In order to assure maximum results from a reasonable and necessary meeting, a concentrated effort must be placed upon inviting participants with the authority to make decisions. Having unnecessary corporate bodies (corp-ses) at a meeting often means unwarranted discussions and delays. Meetings of the board can become unproductive meetings of the bored. Corporations can end up in a situation similar to that of a British university: A wealthy benefactor's will provided a trust fund of continuing financial support to the university on the condition that the deceased continue as a member of the board of trustees and that the embalmed body be present at meetings. This quiescent attendee was recorded as 'present but not voting.' Nonessential attendees at corporate meetings are useless.[2]

The selection of attendees must never be left to chance. The considerations presented next are useful in helping to ensure that, while a number of people may be contemplated, only those who are deemed essential to the attainment and implementation of the desired outcomes are invited.

Selecting Appropriate Attendees. Meetings without the right people are likely to be unproductive. Meetings with too many people—or people from too many different levels—can also limit productivity. Think small; as Soden pointed out, nonessential people are useless. Unless there is a solid reason for inviting a person to a session, an invitation should not be extended. Few people will feel neglected or overlooked if they are excluded from a meeting that has a desired outcome with which that person has no particular concern. In fact, you may receive thanks for giving the person a gift of time.

The following checklist focuses on justifying each attendee's need to be at the session and thus helps to screen out unnecessary people. An individual should be given careful consideration as a meeting participant only if the person fulfills one or more of the following criteria:

- Possesses critical information, knowledge, or expertise that is pertinent to the subject area under consideration.
- Has a stake in the final outcome. That is, this individual will be directly affected by what is decided, and his commitment is required for successful implementation.
- Has the responsibility for implementing whatever is decided.
- Has the authority and responsibility to make the final decision about what to do.
- Needs to comprehend the situation better in order to reduce her fear of the unknown.
- Is a member of the full staff, task force, committee, or council. (This is a requirement whenever the entire group must get together.)
- Possesses contrary viewpoints that will stimulate discussion, produce critical thinking, and eliminate the dysfunctional behavior of groupthink.
- Needs the developmental experience. That is, this person needs to acquire the knowledge, skills, or processes that are being shared and/or needs to meet and network with the other participants.
- Needs to be present because of his position in the hierarchy or because of the politics of the situation. (This person may not be relevant to achieving the desired outcomes of the particular meeting; however, he

may be very relevant to the success or failure of the overall project. Respect the politics of the situation when necessary.)

- Has the authority and/or influence to act as a credible representative for a number of people, thus holding down the size of the meeting without compromising its productivity.

Remember the simple ground rule: *no justification for attendance, no attendance!* However, anytime you have justified someone's attending a session who is not a regular member, you need to brief that person ahead of time on why she was invited, your expectations for her participation, and any ground rules that the group employs. This prepares the invitee to make a maximum contribution.

Eliminating People from Ongoing Sessions. The use of the checklist just given is not limited to screening and selecting members for newly planned group sessions. It is also an excellent tool for reviewing the membership of all current, ongoing meetings. If you are responsible for conducting such ongoing sessions, use the checklist to justify people's attendance. As many as 30 percent of the current attendees may be eliminated because they are not justified; occasionally, the checklist also could lead to adding another person or two because it points up a previously unrecognized opportunity to strengthen the meeting.

Two questions that I am asked over and over again are, "How do I get rid of someone who has been a regular attendee at my meeting, but who is not really needed?" and "What do I do about the person who insists on coming, against my better judgment?" First and foremost, *eliminating someone from an ongoing session does not mean eliminating that person from the information loop.* This fact must be made clear, as illustrated by the following examples:

- "Bob, I'll make sure you stay on the distribution list for the minutes of the meeting. If you have any questions or issues about what you read, call me directly."
- "Grace, I know Dwight has the same interests as you do. I'll make sure he calls you after each meeting and tells you what took place. Then you can share your views with him."
- "Chuck, feel free to call anyone on the committee if there is something that you want brought up in future meetings."
- "Reynaldo, I'll send you an advance copy of the agenda each month. If there is something that is of great interest to you, we can work out arrangements for you to attend."

Second, be forthright and friendly when discussing the issue with the other person. Since people generally preserve the fiction that they are over-worked and dislike serving on committees and project teams in the first place, it is usually not hard to secure their consent to stay away. Point out that you are, in fact, giving the person a gift of time.

Third, always remain open-minded. If people present sound reasons why their attendance is critical, thank them for their insight and indicate that you're looking forward to their full participation in future sessions.

Finally, if someone who truly is nonessential blows his stack and insists on being involved, back off. If this person has not been an abnormally disruptive force in previous sessions, let him continue attending the meetings.

What Is the Macrocomposition of the Group, and What Is Its Potential Chemistry?

Once the attendance list is firmed up, step back and look at the group from a "macro" perspective. You probably will know many, if not all, of the participants (either personally or by reputation). By taking this macro point of view, you can gain insight into the potential chemistry of the group.

In teaching, counseling, and coaching managers on the principles advocated in this book, I have been surprised by a consistent finding. With few exceptions, managers, chairpersons, and group facilitators totally ignore group chemistry as they plan group sessions. But when this key step is brought to their attention, they invariably see the merit of it and can give personal testimony about situations where ignoring chemistry led to problems that ruined the productivity of a session.

Advance thinking about the group's chemistry is critical. It is a "distant early warning" process that provides premeeting insight into the potential dynamics among meeting invitees and the positive or negative effect that these potential dynamics could have on achieving the session's desired outcomes.

For example, a particular group may be very dedicated, hardworking, and enthusiastic about a session and its desired outcomes; this group could be very productive on a task assigned to run from 4:30 to 6:15 p.m. On the flip side, a 4:30 to 6:15 p.m. task planned for a cynical, unenthusiastic, and disinterested group may be an utterly unproductive exercise.

Assessing potential chemistry does not imply that you must serve as the group psychologist and try to "psych out" the group's behavior. Rather, you should make an effort to anticipate how people might react to the meeting's content and to each other once the session begins. In this way, you will be prepared to deal with any problems that could arise.

One manager, when asked about the chemistry of a task force that she was chairing, gave this humorous response: "Oh, there is a tremendous feeling of togetherness on the task force. Everyone is equally unhappy."

Anticipating group chemistry as a valuable main planning step is reinforced further by the following example. Let's say that a group session includes two attendees with radically different viewpoints on how to tackle a vexing departmental problem. Unfortunately, neither one is particularly open-minded about the other's point of view. Anticipating this situation will not eliminate it, but it does alert you to potentially disruptive behavior and allow you to be prepared to facilitate a sticky situation. This means allowing each member an equal say and making sure that differences are defined in terms of issues, not personalities.

Much tension can be defused if you say something like, "Let me see if I understand the issue here. You, Hal, think that the best way to approach this is to . . . , whereas you, Bette, would like to see us . . . Am I right? Good. Now, as a group, let's list the pros and cons of both proposals."

The following guidelines will help you gauge group chemistry before the meeting begins:

- Have the group members worked together before? If so, what strengths existed in their interaction patterns that should be encouraged now? What should be changed as much as possible?
- Who probably will be enthusiastic about attending? Who is likely to be turned off?
- Which people have had interaction difficulties in the past?
- Who—potentially—could be disruptive, and in what way?
- What is the overall demeanor of the group probably going to be? Aggressive, laid back, fun-loving, serious, emotional, analytical?
- What will be the general degree of support for or resistance to each topic or issue?
- Which people have the greatest influence based on their position, expertise, tenure, charisma, or some other factor? Would any of these people have a tendency to dominate the discussion or take over control of the session?
- Could differences in status among attendees inhibit those who are lower in the hierarchy from being active participants without facilitation encouragement?

For some questions, only a "best guess" estimate may be possible prior to the session. That's fine. Remember, you are not trying to psychoanalyze these people; you are simply looking ahead, anticipating potential trouble spots in the group's chemistry, and preparing yourself to facilitate a problem if it should arise.

You might anticipate that, because of her position and charisma, Lauren will dominate the discussion and push her solutions on the group. So, drawing from ideas presented in Chapter 9, "Facilitating Disruption, Differences, and Confusion: Keeping the Gold Mine Productive in the Face of Obstacles," you plan your methods for dealing with Lauren if she starts to dominate. You're ready and confident. But, guess what? For whatever reason, Lauren turns out to be a model participant. Great! It is far better to be prepared for a problem that never arises than to be unprepared for one that must be handled "on the fly" without any forethought.

What Are the Roles (R) for This Session, and Who Will Be Assigned Them?

Every meeting must have four key role assignments: primary facilitator, secondary facilitators, timekeeper, and minute taker. A fifth role, that of the scribe (or recorder), may not be assigned at every meeting, but when such a person is needed, the scribe is central to the success of the meeting.

Primary Facilitator. The manager, committee chairperson, crossfunctional team leader, or any other person who calls the meeting must, by definition, assume the role of primary facilitator and take responsibility for preparing the PDORA document in advance of the session. The reason is straightforward: it is this person who is interrupting people's work routine and requiring them to congregate around a conference table in an isolated room somewhere. And, by taking that nontrivial action, this person assumes the additional obligations of arriving at the session with the PDORA in hand and undertaking the duty of being the primary person responsible for facilitating that PDORA to a successful conclusion.

As primary facilitator, this person is the one who is most focused on the *process dynamics* of the group session, staying keenly aware of how things are taking place in the session and intervening to preserve the integrity and disciplined use of the processes that he laid out in the PDORA.

Nevertheless, since in most cases the manager, chairperson, or team leader will also want to contribute significantly to the content of the discussion, she must verbally indicate what is happening any time she makes a switch in roles from *primary facilitator* (focused on process) to *manager* (focused on content) or back again. This switching of hats is for the benefit of other participants so that they are not confused about the role the manager is operating in at any time.

Secondary Facilitators. An effective and productive group session cannot be achieved by one primary facilitator—even if it is the boss—trying to direct a herd of wild horses that are intent on ignoring the purpose, desired outcomes, and agenda; resisting any process discipline; making no effort to listen to and understand each other; and trampling on each other to see who can control the session.

Once the identity of the primary facilitator has been clarified, *everyone else in attendance is assigned the role of secondary facilitator.* The secondary facilitators share the responsibility for a productive meeting with the primary facilitator by doing two things: (1) monitoring themselves so that they minimize their own disruptive behaviors, and (2) intervening quickly to facilitate any productivity-robbing activities as soon as they occur.

Typical examples of secondary facilitation, where a person other than the primary facilitator can intervene to help the group process, include the following actions.

- Alerting the group whenever it is straying from its desired outcomes. This can be made easier by setting up a code word that everyone in the group can use to tell the group that it is off course. One group I worked with used the phrase *in the weeds* to indicate that it had strayed from the main path that it had agreed to take. The use of this phrase added some fun to the otherwise tense sessions and helped the members stay focused on their desired outcomes.
- Stepping in to handle the disruptive behavior of another group member (side conversations, domination by one member, rambling, PDA usage, and so on).
- Providing input that the discussion has been reduced to nit-picking irrelevant details and that there is a need to refocus on the broader issues at hand.
- Pointing out that consensus seems to have been reached implicitly, but the discussion is dragging on, and then suggesting that the manager (in the role of primary facilitator) test for consensus by going around the table.
- Halting "the assumed right of infinite appeal." That is, stopping someone from reopening again, without documented justification, a topic that has been thoroughly processed and decided upon by the group.
- Seeking information and opinions from others, especially from quiet or shy members; recognizing or encouraging others; summarizing key

points as a discussion unfolds; testing comprehension when he is not sure what was said or meant.

Other actions may be needed, but these highlight how easy it is to help out with the facilitation activity. The message bears repeating: everybody is responsible for creating a productive group session.

Timekeeper. The timekeeper monitors how long the group is taking to accomplish its tasks and provides regular updates to make members aware of where they are with regard to time spent. Taking the role too seriously by being inflexible and dogmatic will lead to resentment toward you and the process. You are simply performing a neutral service on behalf of the group.

Typically the first warning should come when half of the time allotted to an issue has been used up, followed by a second warning when three-fourths of the time has been consumed, and finally a five-minute warning. At this point, if the desired outcome is not close to being achieved, the group needs to decide whether to continue processing the current topic to its conclusion or stop and move on to the next item.

Minute Taker. The minute taker sits at the conference table and takes notes concerning (1) decision agreements, (2) action item assignments (who has agreed to do what, by when), (3) agreements on the disposition of any topics that have been partially processed, but not completed for whatever reason, and (4) agreements on the next steps arising from this session (including potential agenda items and the time and place of the next meeting, if there is to be one). The minute taker needs to clarify and confirm all of this information by reading it back at the close of the session to ensure that there are no misunderstandings, get it typed up, and e-mail it to all attendees (and other key individuals who were not at the meeting but who have a need to know) within 24 hours at the latest.

Scribe. This role is optional. Depending on the group process that is being used to achieve the desired outcomes, a scribe may or may not be needed at any given gathering. However, when necessary, the scribe is central to the success of the meeting.

The scribe writes on flip-chart pages in front of the group. Her job is to keep track of what is being said in the group by writing it down quickly and accurately on the flip chart. When a page is completed, it is torn off the pad and taped to the wall for all to see and refer to later if necessary. During a discussion, being able to see what points have been made can help individuals analyze what has been contributed so far and build on previous ideas. The scribe should be someone who is skilled at organizing and synthesizing material in a visual form. Spelling and pristine neatness are not major requirements; speed in getting the information recorded so as not to restrict the momentum of the discussion is a key requirement.

Recording notes on a flip chart in no way gives the scribe the right to run the meeting! The only "power of the pen" that the scribe has is to write quickly on the flip chart what people say. The scribe is *not* the primary facilitator; does *not* debate or challenge what people say for the record; and does *not* twist, edit, or in any way alter what is said when it is recorded. If a statement is confusing or complicated, the scribe asks the speaker to shorten it for the record, and then records exactly what is said.

A scribe may not be needed for every session. However, when one is needed, the scribe's role should be reviewed so that there are no misconceptions about what needs to be done. Since this can be a tedious and tiring task, especially if there is a lot of information to record over an extended period of time, rotate the role between two people and change over every hour.

The four main structural roles of primary facilitator, secondary facilitators, timekeeper, and minute taker need to be a routine part of every meeting. The role of scribe should be assigned as needed. If they are performed with spirit and dedication, these roles will dramatically enhance the productivity of a group session. Everyone involved in these roles will feel a sense of ownership and commitment; *the* meeting becomes *our* meeting!

What Is the Agenda (A) Content and the Sequential Flow of Its Topics?

Research has shown that group sessions with a clear-cut agenda tend to be better focused, be significantly more effective, and achieve more specific results than meetings without an agenda.

How many agendas have you prepared or seen that are like the one shown on the next page? More than likely, far too many. The example shown here is not really an agenda at all. It is nothing more than a sheet of paper scribbled out at the last moment by the manager, listing a set of bulleted items with some loose time blocks tossed in, along with the names of topic leaders who may or may not have been notified of this in advance. Its sole function is to serve as the manager's crib sheet. What real impact will it have on the effectiveness and productivity of the group session? The answer is: none!

What are the key particulars of the session? What's the purpose? What are the desired outcomes? What meeting roles do the attendees have? Is

Susan Hart just going to share information on the hiring plan, or is this an information-processing topic with a decision required at the end? Are the topics in priority order? And so on. This all-too-common "agenda" doesn't communicate anything and doesn't provide any mechanism for in-session meeting management.

TYPICAL AGENDA
Agenda for February 11, 201x
8:30 a.m.–11:30 a.m.

15 min.	Introduction	Andy Johnson
45 min.	Cash Flow Analysis Q-II	Joyce Lao
30 min.	Travel Budget	Otto Franz
15 min.	Break	All
60 min.	Hiring Plans	Susan Hart
15 min.	Round the Table	All

The power of a solid agenda cannot be overstated. Think about it. Chefs use recipes, contractors use blueprints, orchestra conductors use scores, and pilots use flight plans. Each of these highly skilled professionals relies on structured documents to help him achieve his desired outcomes. But many meeting leaders try to do their job without an agenda. Why should they be any different? It is not a simple crib sheet providing a list of topics to cover. An agenda is the construction plan for the session. It is the most valuable tool to keep the "group mind" focused, on track, and on time as it pursues achievement of the session's desired outcomes. It is the final building block in your PDORA.

Three Information Elements for Every Meeting Agenda. The three information elements are: (1) information sharing (IS), information discussion (ID), and information processing (IP). Each topic or item placed on an agenda must be categorized as either IS, ID, or IP. Knowing the parameters of each of these information elements, and using them faithfully, will allow you to build an agenda that can be easily facilitated by you and the other secondary facilitators.

1. *Information sharing (IS).* As stand-alone topics, these are "FYI sound bites" of information giving. That is, they are short, simple, relatively noncontroversial bits of information that can be covered in a couple of minutes per person. They are meant to inform others by providing one-way communication.

   When used as a precursor to information discussion or information processing, this form of information sharing can be longer in form and substance, since it is setting the stage for more extensive dialogue and debate. For instance, IS could be a 15-minute formal presentation used to kick off the discussion and processing that will follow.

2. *Information discussion (ID).* These items are higher-order information sharing. This means that once the information is shared, it will stir questions, dialogue, and a sharing of feelings and thoughts. However, all ID topics *must be held to a fixed time limit,* since all the dialogue in the world will not change anything. For example, an announcement that the department head is leaving the company for another job or that the company health-care benefits are being changed for next year will surely raise questions and much conversation among the meeting attendees. However, this discussion must be contained so that it doesn't start eating into the time allotted to other, more important agenda items. No amount of talk on the subject is going to alter anything. Assign 10 minutes to the item and bring it to a close when the time is up.

   Depending on the subject matter, its complexity, and the feelings that may be aroused, more than 10 minutes may be reasonable and needed. Still, the key point is, when the time you have allotted to an ID item has expired, stop and move on. Don't burn any more precious meeting time on a topic where a decision has been made and can't be changed, regardless of how much time the group spends wrangling over it. For the persistent person who wants to keep beating a dead horse, tell the individual that you will be happy to meet her offline and continue the discussion, but right now we are going on to the next agenda item. ID items dragging on and on are gross wasters of meeting time.

3. *Information processing (IP).* These items are the core of an agenda. They involve debate, discussion, mixed opinions, differing ideas, facts and data interpretation, and so on. In other words, some amount of detailed processing of the subject by the full group is necessary. For every IP item, a clearly stated *desired outcome* is a *requirement* before processing begins.

The time limit set by the agenda for processing an IP topic has to remain *flexible*, since it is impossible to know in advance what the team will run into once the processing begins. As the processing nears the posted end time, the timekeeper gives a final time check. The group then decides either to continue processing the item or to table it for a future meeting. If the decision is to continue processing, set a new time limit and readjust the times for the remaining agenda items.

Agenda-Building Principles. While there is no universal format for creating an agenda, there are fundamental principles that, when practiced, can significantly enhance an agenda's development and use. These principles will also be utilized in the next section as we incorporate them into streamlined PDORA template examples for your study and future use.

1. *Prominently display the key particulars.* The standard header for any agenda should include the date of the meeting, its starting and ending times, and its location (building and room number).
2. *Note which participants have been assigned the key roles.* List the four critical roles that must be routinely assigned at every meeting, and note the name of each person who has been assigned one of the roles for the session. The fifth role, that of scribe, is assigned if needed.
3. *Determine the agenda topics and classify them.* Every agenda topic should be assigned one of the three classifications covered earlier: IS, ID, or IP.
4. *Batch information-sharing (IS) items, assign clock times, and handle them early.* Most IS items should be pulled together to be shared at the beginning of the session. Kicking off staff meetings with a 15-minute block of time set for general sharing called "Around the Table" is a good way to get everyone involved and energize the session. If you feel that a specific, stand-alone information-sharing item is more strategically placed if it is in the middle or near the end of the session, that is fine.
5. *Determine whether you have any information-discussion (ID) topics, and set a fixed time limit for each one.* Information-discussion items are used in an agenda to ensure that the group completely understands an issue. Agreement is not the objective; comprehension is. A short introduction of the subject followed by an open Q and A or discussion period among the group takes care of ID topics.

Strategically place special ID items within your agenda. Sometimes what is discussed during an ID item provides important understanding that can be used during the information processing of an associated matter that comes later. Try placing one or two less important ID items at the end of your agenda (before the Wrap-Up phase) that you won't mind dropping if the processing of an important IP issue takes longer than expected. If you get to these final ID items this time around, fine; if not, that's still okay. Above all, stick to your predetermined, fixed time limit for all your ID topics.

6. *Make sure that each information-processing item has its own desired outcome.* Effective planning of a meeting's structure requires that each discrete information-processing item has a plainly noted desired outcome linked to it. The desired outcome is critical, since it defines what should be accomplished after the information processing is completed.

7. *Sequence IP topics to enhance the flow of information.* Arrange processing topics sequentially so that as decisions are made on the early items, those decisions will, in turn, provide relevant input to assist in resolving succeeding issues. If there is a choice, do not start information processing with the most difficult or controversial subject; and, whenever possible, end with a topic that will tend to unify teammates.

8. *Determine clock times for each IP topic.* The guiding consideration should be the desired outcome. The greatest tendency is to *severely underestimate the processing time required* so that you can jam more items into the available meeting time and feel good about how much is going to be accomplished. This approach causes nothing but frustration, as half the agenda never gets completed because the initial items covered all took twice as much time as was initially set. The best advice is for you to be coldly realistic and honest with yourself when setting time frames.

9. *Involve all participants.* Although there may be good reasons why this is not always possible, make every effort to distribute a copy of the agenda at least two working days in advance of the meeting. When creating the agenda, take advantage of every opportunity to obtain input from the meeting participants. This generates a sense of shared ownership and commitment to the session. From the meeting members' perspective, this action moves the meeting from being Tom's session or Rebecca's session to being *our* session.

10. *Write a cover memo to be sent out with each agenda.* A concise cover memo (one page maximum) can clarify, supplement, and/or highlight

the information contained in the agenda. At a minimum, include the following information in your cover memo: (1) provide a distribution list showing the first and last names of all participants, (2) note the names of everyone who is expected to take a lead role in the discussion and analysis of a topic and indicate what data or information they are expected to have available to present at the session, (3) provide a crisp synopsis of the current status for subjects carried over from last time that will be covered, and (4) give clear and concise instructions for any prework sent out with the agenda.

Agenda-Building Tips for Planning Breaks. In today's fast-paced world, managers and other attendees feel a strong need to keep in contact with their job outside the confines of the meeting room. After more than a few hours, people get restless. They begin to feel disconnected from their job and get concerned—often unnecessarily—that the normal flow of work will go awry because of their absence. As a consequence, individuals can be seen operating their BlackBerries underneath the table, checking voice mails or text messages on their iPhones, or leaving the room to hold a brief conference call or to follow up on some "emergency" that came up during the session. Even when participants are trying to be discreet in their actions, these are highly disruptive activities. They cause the session to lose its focus and energy, and the desired outcomes are placed at risk.

I've learned, through the school of hard knocks, that you can't fight the tidal wave of technological gadgets and the overwhelming desire of participants to stay connected. So, you have to go with the flow and plan for it. I've learned that for any session that is scheduled to run for a half day or more, it is imperative to plan a break that is long enough for people to attend to incidental business outside the conference room. On the surface, this may seem like a sacrifice of precious in-session meeting time, but believe me, it isn't. In the long run, you will have a more productive session because people will remain in the room and will be more focused and energized.

So, instead of planning a 10- or 15-minute break for midmorning, plan one for 30 minutes. If the session is to last all day, do the same for midafternoon. Also, give a full hour for lunch. At the beginning of the session, explain your expectations for the break(s). In return for the 30-minute working breaks and the one-hour lunch period, all cell phones,

BlackBerries, iPhones, laptops, and iPads are to be turned off and remain off while the meeting is in session. Hold all breaks as close to the scheduled time as possible, and don't shorten them. However, when the break time is over, restart the session promptly to send the strong signal that both the meeting content and the schedule are important.

Two Types of PDORA

There are only two models that you need to know if you are to build an incisive PDORA document each time. The first is the "Type 1: Nonintegrated, Multitopic PDORA," and the second is the "Type 2: Integrated Steps PDORA." Let's examine each type and provide a template to help you envision these two documents.

Type 1: Nonintegrated, Multitopic PDORA

The Type 1 PDORA is best represented by the staff meeting agenda. Staff-type meetings have only one purpose: "To share and process information relative to topics that are of mutual interest to the entire staff."

Staff meetings cover a wide range of different agenda subjects that usually are discrete and unrelated (or only partially related) to each other. In other words, the agenda topics are nonintegrated. For example, a staff meeting agenda could contain a topic with the desired outcome "department's vacation schedule agreed to," which is unrelated to the next topic's desired outcome, "name for the departmental newsletter selected," which is independent from item three, "new performance appraisal form reviewed." Other sessions that are similar to staff meetings include board meetings like those of school boards, boards of directors, or boards of trustees; field quarterly reviews; various kinds of council meetings; and the like, where any number of dissimilar topics are handled.

Before reading on, look at the template recommended for the Type 1: Nonintegrated, Multitopic PDORA. Notice how the fundamental agenda-building principles were incorporated into this PDORA and how the entire PDORA—the purpose, desired outcomes, roles, and agenda—is completed on just one page. This format has gained acceptance as a benchmark for its supremacy as a simple, yet comprehensive working document for planning a Type 1 meeting structure.

Template for the Type 1:
Nonintegrated, Multitopic PDORA

Key Particulars

Date: June 23, 201x

Start: 9:30 a.m.

End: 12:00 noon

Bldg: #2, 3rd Floor

Room: #305

Key Roles

Primary Facilitator: W. Westlake

Secondary Facilitator: *All*

Timekeeper: S. Dente

Minute Taker: D. Philly

Purpose of Session:

To share and process information relative to topics of mutual interest to the entire staff.

9:30–9:35	*[IS]*	Informal socializing and warm-up
9:35–9:40	*[IS]*	Purpose, desired outcomes, and agenda reviewed (W. Westlake)
9:40–9:50	*[IS]*	Around the Table: Quick Individual Sharing (All)
9:50–10:00	*[ID]*	Changes in corporate travel policy discussed (W. Westlake)
10:00–10:50	*[IP]*	District manager promotion criteria (A. Rosen)
		DO: Set of promotion criteria developed and agreed to
10:50–11:00		*~ ~ Break ~ ~*
11:00–11:30	*[IP]*	Marketing collaterals setback schedule (E. Wynn)
		DO: Two-week setback schedule developed and agreed to
11:30–11:40	*[IP]*	Leadership development training (D. Philly)

DO: *Proposed leadership develop-*
ment plan for Q-lll and IV approved

11:40–11:50   [ID]   Status of call center relocation
                              updated (W. Westlake)

11:50–12:00   [ID]   Wrap-up and critique
                              • Decisions reviewed
                              • Action items reviewed
                              • "Leftovers" dispensed
                              • Session critiques

IS = Information Sharing: short "sound bites" of information. FYIs. Little
     or no discussion.

ID = Information Discussion: higher-order information sharing. Give and
     take. *Fixed* time limit.

IP = Information Processing: core of a session. *Requires* a desired outcome.
     Flexible timing.

Type 2: Integrated Steps PDORA

The best examples of the Type 2: Integrated Steps PDORA are problem-solving and decision-making meetings. These meetings tend to have one or two desired outcomes set forth for the whole session. What then follows is an agenda of *tightly woven, integrated steps that are precisely sequenced* so that when these steps are completed during the session, the stated desired outcomes will be achieved.

In order to solve a particularly troublesome problem or to make a difficult decision, a series of sessions may often need to be convened around a single problem or decision. However, each separate meeting in the series must have a unique PDORA laying out (1) a short purpose statement, (2) a set of desired outcomes for the full session, which are listed at the top of the agenda just below the purpose, (3) assignment of the four standard roles to group members, and (4) an agenda of integrated steps (with clock times) for working through the meeting and achieving the overall desired outcomes.

Since IS, ID, and IP are part and parcel of problem-solving or decision-making sessions, they must be noted next to each agenda step to distinguish the expectations for managing the information flow. Notice too that the desired outcomes pertain to the entire meeting; in other words, the entire agenda is a set of integrated steps focused on achieving a limited number of very specific outcomes.

A cover memo to accompany the Type 2 PDORA is just as critical as it is for the Type 1 Multitopic PDORA. Developing a meaningful PDORA document sets the stage for productive facilitation. A template of a Type 2: Integrated Steps PDORA is shown here.

Type 2: Integrated Steps PDORA

Key Particulars
Date: August 28, 201x
Start: 1:00 p.m.
End: 3:00 p.m.
Bldg: Credit Union
Hall, 2nd Floor
Room: #218

Key Roles
Primary Facilitator: B. Jacoby
Secondary Facilitator: *All*
Timekeeper: C. Snyder
Minute Taker: P. Tabler

Purpose of Session:
To share and process information relative to reducing facility costs.

Desired Outcomes:
• Potential solutions for reducing facilities by $500,000 identified
• Three potential solutions for detailed action planning selected

---

1:00–1:05	*[IS]*	Informal socializing and warm-up
1:05–1:10	*[IS]*	Purpose, desired outcomes, and agenda reviewed (B. Jacoby)
1:10–1:20	*[ID]*	Review and discuss work completed last week (B. Jacoby) • Our agreed-to problem statement • Our finalized list of causes driving up facilities costs
1:20–1:30	*[IS]*	Brainstorm potential solutions to reduce or eliminate causes of rising facilities costs

1:30–1:45	*[IP]*	Clarify items; combine similar solutions into common statements
1:45–2:00	*~ ~ Break ~ ~*	
2:00–2:25	*[IP]*	Discuss pros and cons of solutions; reach consensus on top six to eight
2:25–2:45	*[IP]*	Use criteria matrix to evaluate the six to eight solutions; choose top three
2:45–3:00	*[ID]*	Wrap-up and critique • Decision reviewed • Action items reviewed • "Leftovers" dispensed • Session critiqued

IS = Information Sharing: short "sound bites" of information. FYIs. Little or no discussion.

ID = Information Discussion: higher-order information sharing. Give and take. *Fixed* time limit.

IP = Information Processing: core of a session. *Requires* a desired outcome. *Flexible* timing.

As you look over the template for the Type 2 PDORA, observe the 1:10 p.m.–1:20 p.m. agenda item that specifically links back to what was accomplished in the preceding meeting. This review is especially critical when you are planning and facilitating a series of interconnected meetings to deal with a tough business issue, like reducing facilities costs. The reason is, since your sessions are tightly linked, the quality outputs of the previous meeting will always set the stage for the potential accomplishments of the upcoming meeting. Just one or two poorly run sessions in a series of meetings, resulting in meager or unusable outputs, can derail everything and ruin many days of hard work and time sacrificed away from the job on the part of many people. Planning discipline via your PDORA is an antecedent to meeting success.

PDORA Summary

This section covered two kinds of PDORA: (1) the Type 1: Nonintegrated, Multitopic PDORA, with a universal "boilerplate" purpose statement and discrete, unrelated agenda topics and desired outcomes, and (2) the Type 2: Integrated Steps PDORA, with unique purpose statements, one or two desired outcomes that apply to the entire session, and a content flow of highly integrated steps that focus on achieving the few desired outcomes. Study both carefully and note the similarities and differences between the two types.

Each PDORA is a model for you to follow. You can create a simple Excel template for each type for your personal use. Then you will be in a position to look at a meeting opportunity, match the appropriate PDORA to the situation at hand, and derive a solid, well-crafted document that gets results!

WORKSHEET

Develop written responses to the two items listed below.

1. What do you feel are the main learning points from Chapter 5?

   - Importance of PDORA
   - Understand focus to a meeting
   - Different btwn TS, IO, IP

---

2. Elaborate on why you feel these points are key for you.

 —Don't want to waste time

 —Meetings are expensive

 —Clear understanding of what needs to be accomplished

Notes

1. C. Hymowitz, "A Survival Guide to the Office Meeting," *The Wall Street Journal*, June 21, 1988, p. 41.
2. G. W. Soden, "Avoid Meetings or Make Them Work," *Business Horizons* 27, no. 2 (March–April 1984), p. 48.

Chapter 6

PLANNING THE PROCESS OF A SESSION TO MINE GROUP GOLD: THREE PHASES TO SUCCESS

CHAPTER OBJECTIVES

- To demonstrate the vital role that *process* plays in the success of a group session.
- To provide practical strategies for using simple, but powerful processes to achieve a session's purpose and outcomes.

Introduction

Now that you have prepared your PDORA document to give you a well-organized meeting structure, you must now think about the process side of your session. The question is: "What array of activities should be employed to maximize the group's ability to achieve the session's purpose and desired outcomes?"

Eugene Raudsepp recalls an incident on a golf course that demonstrates the value of a good process in achieving the desired outcomes.

It was the 16th hole in the annual Bob Hope Desert Classic, and the tall, handsome newcomer had an excellent chance of winning. His iron shot fell just short of the green, giving him a good chance for a birdie. Smiling broadly, he strode down the fairway only to stop in dismay. His ball had rolled into a brown paper bag carelessly tossed on the ground by someone in the gallery. If he removed the ball from the bag, it would cost him a penalty stroke. If he tried to hit the ball and the bag, he would lose control over the shot. For a moment he pondered the problem. Then he solved it.[1]

Assuming that the desired outcome in this situation is to hit the ball cleanly without receiving a penalty stroke, what process would enable that? The answer: set fire to the bag. The day was saved. A simple, creative process turned a particularly troublesome situation into a productive one.

Process is crucial to successful task completion within group sessions. Don't sell it short; take time to plan your process. Countless group sessions have been done in because a poorly conceived process—akin to trying to hit the golf ball while it was in the bag—unraveled in the middle of the meeting, with the result that control of the session was lost and there was no way to recover.

The crucial factor in developing any group process is to keep it as streamlined as possible. *Let its elegance be rooted in its creativity and simplicity, not its complexity.* A well-planned process will ease the facilitation task because the process itself will preempt some of the pitfalls and negative situations that might otherwise occur during a group session.

Curtis Carlson and William Wilmot accentuate the need to have a process methodology written down, or at least worked out in your head, as a guide for keeping people engaged and on task in completing the desired outcomes for which they were brought together.

Obviously, just throwing people together on a team, whether face-to-face or virtual, will not automatically result in exponential improvement. Many organizations have team meetings that run all day long but do not have a disciplined process to capture their genius. To leverage the genius of teams, you must have *disciplined processes* led by a champion. Many of us are often asked to attend meetings without any preparation or agreed-to processes. . . . If you cannot list the processes your teams use to leverage the unlocked genius of the team, it will stay locked.[2]

The gold nuggets of wisdom that people bring to every session have to be cultivated, or those nuggets will leave the room still locked in the heads of the people. The process tips, ideas, and techniques presented here are valuable to anyone who wants to cash in on the collaborative genius of teams. These processes are categorized by meeting stage (Start-Up, Move-Out, and Wrap-Up), they are field-tested, they are uncomplicated, they are easy to facilitate, and, best of all, they are effective in moving a group toward goal achievement. They will unlock the creative genius of "setting your paper bag on fire."

The Start-Up Phase: Getting People Involved and Aligned

Excellent meetings almost invariably have excellent beginnings. The climate and mood that infuse the entire session are typically established during the first 15 or 20 minutes. Beginnings must never be taken for granted or disregarded as some worthless rite of passage that the meeting leader must tolerate before getting down to the real business at hand.

The beginning sets the tone. It can help make people feel good about attending because the setting is warm and inviting, or it can make people feel turned off because the opening is disorganized, cold, and unfriendly. A flexible beginning, one that integrates people into the session as they arrive rather than having some wait for others, gives a positive boost to people's initial attitudes about the session. There are a number of ways to kick off a session; five different processes, from unstructured to structured, are presented here to demonstrate the ease with which warm-ups can be done.

Informal Warm-Up Period

Acknowledge the need for an unstructured social warm-up, and allow for it by scheduling 5 to 10 minutes for it on the agenda. A warm-up is going to take place whether you have scheduled one or not, so it is best to "go with the flow."

The informal, unstructured warm-up is especially important for staff meetings and other group sessions where everyone knows everyone else. The informal discussions and bantering that precede many sessions may appear to be extraneous or a waste of time, but in fact, these periods are invaluable, as they serve to create a relaxed atmosphere. Five or ten minutes of informality at the beginning of the session encourages a release of tension, allows business to be transacted, gives people time to collect their thoughts before beginning, and gets the small talk out of the way.

In order for the informal warm-up process to be effective, you and your group members need to discuss its intent. Shared values need to be built so that everyone views the warm-up as a legitimate part of every agenda.

Under no circumstances should the informal warm-up be taken as a license to come to the session 5, 10, or 15 minutes late. The ground rule must be: "Our meetings will start promptly at the scheduled time, everyone is expected to be on time, and the first item on the agenda is a short, informal, social warm-up."

Welcoming Message

A somewhat more structured opening to your kickoff can be orchestrated by using a welcoming message—a flip-chart page, a large piece of poster board, or a PowerPoint slide projected on a screen—that contains both a greeting and beginning instructions for the arrivals. Make sure that the welcoming message is large enough and colorful enough so that the meeting participants can't miss it once they are inside the room. Figure 6-1 shows an example of a welcoming message:

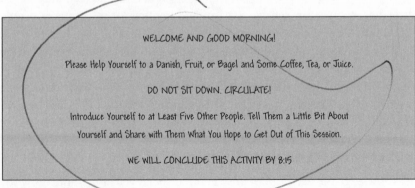

WELCOME AND GOOD MORNING!

Please Help Yourself to a Danish, Fruit, or Bagel and Some Coffee, Tea, or Juice.

DO NOT SIT DOWN. CIRCULATE!

Introduce Yourself to at Least Five Other People. Tell Them a Little Bit About Yourself and Share with Them What You Hope to Get Out of This Session.

WE WILL CONCLUDE THIS ACTIVITY BY 8:15

Figure 6-1 Welcoming Message

Paired Interviews

This process is more structured than the first two and is particularly productive when most of the people at the session will be strangers to one another. As soon as people start to arrive, hand each person a sheet of paper containing a symbol and a set of interview questions. The people then go around looking for the other person who has the same symbol on the sheet as theirs. When they find each other, the pairs with matching symbols proceed to interview each other and record each other's responses on the question sheet provided.

Six or seven questions are plenty. The questions can vary from the thought-provoking to the light-hearted. The following examples illustrate the types of questions that might be asked.

- What is your name, organization, and job title?
- What kind of work do you do?
- In your present position, what has been the toughest challenge you have faced?
- What are the main forces (internal or external) boosting your company's competitive edge in the marketplace, and what are the main forces hindering its competitive edge?
- What can you personally do to help your department become more effective?
- What are the three most vivid memories you have from your childhood?
- What was the make, model, and year of your first car? What happened to it?
- If you had a one-year sabbatical, what would you do with your time? Why?
- If you were the head of your department or group, what changes would you implement? Why?

When the initial interviews are finished, the pairs exchange sheets so that both people now have their own interview answers. The participants then circulate and meet others by sharing the information on their sheets.

Three Ts and an L

This structured warm-up is always good for some laughs and drawing everyone in. Each person writes down three truths about himself and one lie. The lie is mixed in among the truths. When everyone is finished, each participant makes a list from 1 down to the number of people in the meeting. Someone goes first and reads her personal sheet, which mixes her truths and her lie. The other participants write the number of the statement that they feel is the lie next to 1. A second person reads his truths and his lie, and people choose what they think is the lie and write that number next to 2 on their list, and so on. When everyone has had her turn, the answers are graded. Each person, going in the original sequence, now states the number corresponding to his lie. Everyone grades her own paper. A small prize can be given to the person who correctly guesses the most lies.

Coin of the Realm

This opener is quick and easy to conduct. It has minimal structure, yet it can be quite insightful. Participants take a coin from their pocket or purse and look at the date on it. Go around the room, and have each person in turn read off the date on his coin and then recall two personal events that happened that year. The beauty of this warm-up is that it can be used more than once with the same group, since the dates on the coins will be different, and thus the stories that the people tell will be new and refreshing.

The ideas presented here are just the tip of the iceberg.[3] The purpose was to show you a variety of techniques, both unstructured and structured, that you can employ to get people interacting and involved. In planning any process for getting started, the key is to create an activity that encourages open and nonthreatening communication among all participants prior to settling down to the task(s) at hand.

After the warm-up, the next piece of your Start-Up plan must be an agenda item calling for a systematic review of the PDORA. Your PDORA review also needs to include a bit of extra time for people to raise any clarification questions so that everyone is aligned as to "where we are headed" and "how we intend to get there." A good beginning rarely just happens; it requires thoughtful planning. Getting off to an energized and aligned start provides the initial momentum for a productive session.

The Move-Out Phase: Sharing, Discussing, and Processing Information to Achieve the Desired Outcomes

The middle of a group session is where the bulk of the work is carried out. The trick for the session planner at this stage is to plan a process, or a set of processes, that will prompt the group members to share their thoughts, feelings, ideas, and data, and ensure that this information is treated in an organized manner.

Often the sharing and processing of information can be handled in close sequence, as is the case with brainstorming, certain subgroup activities, and force-field analysis.

For example, with brainstorming, ideas are shared in a totally uninhibited environment that is free from criticism. After all ideas have been shared, noted on flip-chart pages, and hung on the wall, the group immediately goes into the processing phase by discussing, refining, modifying, and eliminating the brainstormed items.

With force-field analysis, a list of the positive, driving forces involved in a change situation is created, as is a list of the negative, restraining forces. Once the information-sharing phase is finished, the group moves on to information processing by reviewing, modifying, and eliminating forces on both lists and weighting the remaining ones according to relative strengths. Processing continues by developing a strategy that will maximize the driving forces and minimize the restraining forces.

Just as there are many options for opening a group session, there are many methods and techniques for developing and acting upon information during the middle portion of the session. After gaining experience and confidence in using some of the ideas suggested here, feel free to refine these to meet your own needs or to create other, similar processes.

The approaches provided here are particularly applicable in a wide variety of group situations: staff meetings, problem-solving sessions, communications meetings, task forces, strategy development sessions, and the like.

Structured Prework

Taking advantage of structured prework is one of the simplest and quickest ways in which you can focus the group's energies on the topics that are of greatest concern. When planned and implemented properly, this strategy increases efficiency by eliminating a significant amount of meeting time that is all too often unproductively consumed by boring presentations and messy discussions as group members attempt to comprehend and react to material that they are seeing for the first time.

Given the typical situation, where there is new or freshly revised material, complex issues within the material, and tight time constraints in the session, it is extremely difficult for the group to do any meaningful work on the issues. The attractiveness of the structured prework process is that the burden of reading, comprehending, and developing initial reactions to the material is shifted to each individual outside of the session; this, in turn, frees precious meeting time for the group to do what it needs to do most—process the information together, make decisions, and assign action items. Many managers I've worked with feel, "Any session without action items is nothing more than a social event."

What are the most critical factors to consider when using structured prework?

Give Adequate Lead Time. Whoever assigns prework must ensure that it reaches the participants with enough lead time for them to digest the content thoroughly before they come to the group session. This lead time can be anywhere from a few days to a month or more, depending on the complexity of the material and what activities are required.

Provide Clear Prework Instructions. It is imperative that the participants be given clear instructions as to what they are expected to do with the material before the session. Here are some examples of the kind of instructions that are called for:

- Analyze the attached data and formulate your position regarding the proposed design change. Each unit member will be given five minutes to present his initial position to the whole group.
- Read the results of the District Restructuring Study and respond to the four questions that are attached at the end. We will discuss all four in detail.
- Revise the attached budget figures in light of your new objectives and be prepared to discuss your rationale for any changes. Based on your inputs and our discussion, I will formulate a revised budget for the team to consider at our May 20 session.
- Read the proposed action plan for switching paper suppliers. Note the strengths of the plan, and detail any issues that you believe could jeopardize its successful implementation. All strengths and issues will be processed at the meeting.
- Attached are the old vision, mission, and operating principles for our department. Edit and update all three in light of the significant changes over the past year; we will process your recommended changes and reach consensus on a new set.

Emphasize the Need to Complete Prework. When developing the instructions, be sure to emphasize that failure to complete prework will impair the information-processing activity that is planned during the upcoming session. After sending out your prework, a personal follow-up—a quick phone call or e-mail note—sends a powerful message that you are serious about attendees coming prepared. You'll be pleasantly surprised at the results your little reinforcement message will bring.

Assign Prework Only if It Will Be Used. After emphasizing the importance of coming to the session properly prepared, you must, without fail, make use of the data that the participants have generated or risk losing credibility. Also, an effective tool like structured prework will be rendered useless if participants begin to realize that they can save personal time and effort by ignoring your prework requests because you rarely use the information that you demand from them.

Plan the Process for In-Session Use of Prework. The manner in which the prework will be treated during the session is a critical planning consideration. Techniques described later in this section (present, then discuss; buzz groups; small work groups; introspection, then share) will furnish practical ideas for handling the prework material.

Selectively employing prework enhances the productivity of the group session. The participants come to the session with a deeper insight into the topic(s). Having had time to think about the material and organize their initial thoughts, feelings, and ideas, the group members are primed to spend their time really working on the issues rather than "flailing to understand them."

Present, Then Discuss: Getting the Most from Presentations

One often used, and definitely often abused, meeting process is the presentation and discussion format. This seemingly innocent process gets snarled nearly every time almost before it gets underway. Have you ever been in Ken's spot when making a presentation?

Ken starts to present his information. Five minutes into his presentation, he is interrupted; several other group members chime in; and the whole group gets sidetracked and moves into a phase variously described as "group grope," "random walk," or "dance in a dark room."

Ten or fifteen minutes are wasted as Ken attempts to regain control of the session. He speaks for another five minutes and is interrupted again, and the cycle starts all over.

In this typical scenario, a 45-minute agenda item—15 minutes of presentation followed by 30 minutes of discussion—is extended to two hours of chaos and frustration. Little or nothing is resolved, and the group ends up 75 minutes behind schedule.

This brief drama depicts the debilitating group process that meeting participants often encounter. All is not lost, however. By taking the following planning considerations into account, presentations can be transformed into a potent group process.

Keep Presentations Separate from Discussion. Disciplined facilitation, which ensures that the presentation phase is completed before the debate and discussion phase is allowed to begin, is the cornerstone of success for this process. If the presentation is to last 30 minutes or more, talk to the presenter beforehand and see if she can divide the talk into 15- or 20-minute blocks. Have the presenter give the first block, then open group discussion. Follow with the second block, then discussion; continue with as many blocks as necessary.

Allow Only Clarification Questions during the Presentation. During the presentation phase, clarification questions can be asked (in fact, they should be encouraged) to make certain that people are listening to and grasping the information that is being presented. But do not allow questions to develop into a discussion of the material that is being presented until the presentation is complete. If follow-up questions, going beyond clarification, start being raised, the primary facilitator or anyone acting in the role of secondary facilitator should step in and stop those probing questions on behalf of the presenter.

Develop a Set of Focused Discussion Areas. Before the session at which the presentation will be given, you should do two things:

1. Make certain that the presentation is relevant to the needs of your group, and, if it is, communicate this to the members ahead of time so that they have a general idea of the thrust of the presentation.
2. In conjunction with your group, develop three to six discussion areas that will be the focal points for the discussion portion after the presentation.

Advance planning will help to ensure that the group members extract the most meaning from the upcoming presentation. The focus areas generated by the group members prior to the presentation will pinpoint the parts that are most pertinent to their needs. Whenever possible, informing the presenter of the focus areas ahead of time is helpful because it defines audience expectations and gives the presenter the opportunity to meet these expectations by shaping the presentation accordingly.

Examples of possible focused discussion areas, to assist group member note taking during the presentation and to guide the group dialogue at the conclusion of the presentation, would include things like these.

- What points in the presentation do we agree with or support?
- What points in the presentation do we disagree with or not support? Why?
- How can our group take maximum advantage of the idea that is being proposed?
- What do we want to have happen, as compared to what is actually happening?
- What procedures do we need to put in place to resolve the issue presented?
- What is the impact of the proposed change on our group? What are the opportunities for us? What are the threats to us?
- Based on the information presented, what do we believe our next steps should be?
- What specific feedback or actions are you (the presenter) expecting from us as an outcome of your presentation?

Facilitate the "Present" Phase, then the "Discuss" Phase. The mechanisms for facilitating the present phase and then the discuss phase are straightforward. Before introducing the presenter, distribute the list of focused discussion areas and ask the group members to make brief notes for each of the areas as they listen.

After the presentation, the whole group—with the presenter included as a team member—explores the focused discussion areas one at a time.

Used in the manner described, the present, then discuss approach becomes an excellent group process tool. There is forethought given to what the group wants from the presentation; there is a disciplined flow that avoids interruption, sidetracking, showboating, and so on; people are actively involved during the presentation by asking clarifying questions and/or by taking notes; participants are more active in the postpresentation discussion because they have collected their thoughts on paper; and the presenter—by being asked to sit down at the table with the group—is psychologically made to feel like an ally, a teammate, during the discussion rather than an outsider or an adversary to be shot full of holes.

Two Cases of Presentation Facilitation

The following experiences of Carin, the assistant vice president of strategic planning for a financial services company, provide wonderful insight into the facilitation of presentations. Carin's company needed to close 2 of its 24 district offices, 1 in the Gulf Coast Region and 1 in the Great

Lakes Region. She developed a presentation for each regional staff, which included the region vice president, the six district managers, and the three regional HQ staff members.

Presentation to the Gulf Coast Region. During her presentation to the Gulf Coast Region, Carin made a compelling case for closing a particular district office. She had marshaled her facts, involved the six district managers in the data collection, and made a solid analysis. However, her presentation and corresponding staff decision-making time, scheduled for one hour, turned into a two-hour "slugfest." She said later that it was like being in front of a firing squad. It was a classic case of "killing the messenger bearing bad news."

The presentation started out well enough, but Carin gradually became the focal point for the group's frustration at having to close an office. The staff members started picking her numbers apart, even though they had been heavily involved in generating them. From her individual discussions, she knew that her recommendations had the blessing of some people, but they were not speaking up. In fact, she had counted on the region vice president and one particular district manager for additional strategic arguments to support her case. Instead, they jumped on the bandwagon with the vocal dominators. After two hours of parrying and thrusting, the staff did reach a decision: send Carin back for more information and postpone making a final decision on which office to close until next month's staff meeting.

Presentation to the Great Lakes Region. Carin had to make the same general presentation to the Great Lakes Region staff. Only this time it was different. That vice president, having learned the principles of Mining Group Gold, planned an agenda using the "present, then discuss" approach. Because the staff members had been involved in providing data and assumptions—just like the Gulf Coast staff—everyone had good insight into the direction that Carin's presentation was going to take. The Great Lakes Region staff prepared a set of focused discussion questions to ensure a thorough discussion of her material.

Carin presented everything in 15 minutes, including time for several interruptions with clarification questions. When she had finished, the vice president invited her to sit down at the table and "join us in a constructive debate on the recommendations from your fine presentation." Carin was out of the line of fire. And, even though the debate got heated, the vice president's primary facilitation—and the staff members' secondary facilitation—kept everything under control. Being looked upon as a collaborative member of the staff, Carin felt comfortable relaying adversarial questions to the staff members that she knew supported her.

This helped make the thoughts of others apparent, enriched the discussion, and brought forth a balanced perspective.

Within 45 minutes, the staff had reached a consensus to support Carin's general recommendations with a few modifications. What had taken two hours with no final decision at the Gulf Coast Region had taken one hour and resulted in a consensus decision at the Great Lakes Region. While everything remained on hold and uncertain in the Gulf Coast Region, the Great Lakes Region immediately sprang into action, taking the necessary steps to close the office. People were not left to wonder about their fate and spread more rumors for another month.

In-Session Subgrouping

Any time the group consists of 10 or more people, you will need to give serious consideration to using subgroups for part or all of the meeting. Facilitation complications multiply tremendously with groups this size and larger.

Breaking a whole group into several small groups and providing a basic structure to help them process their assigned task(s) simultaneously is an underused technique. Many groups get caught in the rut of working on every agenda item as a whole group. Not only is this unnecessary, but it is impractical and ineffective.

A great deal of synergy and productivity can be captured with a well-conceived subgroup process. The large group meeting takes on the qualities of a small group meeting. From a planning perspective, the following points are important.

Determine Space Requirements. If possible, subgroups that are going to spend several hours working intensely on a task should have the convenience of a breakout room that provides privacy and comfort. In determining the number of breakout rooms required, keep in mind that the main meeting room can double as one of the breakout rooms.

With shorter activities, however, unless the facility is unduly small, having the subgroups stay in the main meeting room and congregate in the corners of the room (or at each end of the table) is usually very productive. The hum that permeates the room is energizing, there is an air of participation and involvement, and the manager can join a subgroup as an active member while still being available to move from group to group to lend assistance where needed.

Decide on Subgroup Size. The dynamics of group interaction change dramatically depending on how big the group is. The guidelines shown here give an idea of the typical interaction dynamics between members of different-sized groups.

Manage Subgroup Size and Related Dynamics.

- *Twos.* These are not really subgroups because there are not enough members. However, dividing people into pairs and having them carry out an assigned task in partnership is a way to maximize group interaction. As described earlier, pairs are often used during a get-acquainted period or when there is a need to get everyone immediately involved.

- *Threes.* This is the barest minimum that forms a subgroup. It is intimate; everyone can get involved. When members meet in trios to discuss a topic and prepare either a report on their discussion or questions to be offered to the total group, two purposes are served: (1) everyone has a chance to speak, and (2) a degree of anonymity is preserved, since the report or questions come from three people rather than from an individual. As a consequence, greater depth or intensity is often achieved. The one danger with a group of three is that one member can dominate the other two.

- *Fours.* Subgroups of four are reasonably effective. Dividing a group into subgroups of four can be useful for obtaining a sense of the meeting by getting a quick reading on attitudes and reactions within the subgroups before coming to a whole-group decision. Domination by one member is also a risk in a group of this size.

- *Fives and sixes.* A subgroup of five or six is ideal for working on a task. The best results are usually achieved from subgroups of this size. The physical closeness and eye contact aid in communication. Diverse perspectives, supported by a mix of ideas, opinions, and attitudes, promote creative thinking.

- *Sevens.* These groups are quite effective, but are starting to get a little large.

- *Eights and Nines.* The internal structure really starts to break down in subgroups of this size. Coalitions or side conversations often occur. Although results are usually satisfactory, the time required to get these results is longer than with subgroups of five or six.

- *Tens or more.* This size is very unsatisfactory for a subgroup. Communication and coordination become problematic. Subgroups of this size tend to become a drag rather than a value builder. Using 10 or more individuals can be effective for demonstrating how group participants can get in each other's way and negatively affect group accomplishments.

Determine the Composition of Subgroups. Composition will vary depending on the objectives of the specific task. Unless there is a need to do otherwise, the rule of thumb is to make each subgroup a microcosm of the whole group in terms of diversity of experience, knowledge, skills, abilities, and so on. For some situations, however, loading a particular subgroup with people who possess the same strength may be appropriate.

Assessing the potential chemistry within each subgroup is also critical. The considerations outlined in Chapter 5 regarding the chemistry of the group on a macro level are just as relevant for the subgroup on a micro level. For instance, depending on the specific objectives, placing two people who do not get along in the same subgroup may or may not be a good idea.

If the composition is set properly, subgroups can be utilized as small mentoring laboratories where younger, less experienced people can work and learn in partnership with more experienced, "veteran" people as they collaborate on tough business issues.

Develop the Subgroup Activity. If you choose to use a subgroup activity, it will consume part of your in-session meeting time. And since all in-session time is precious, you cannot afford to unleash some poorly conceived subgroup activity that ends up eating valuable meeting time without producing meaningful outputs. There are four aspects to consider when thinking through the development of any subgroup activity.

- What output(s) do I want each subgroup to produce during the simultaneous work sessions?
- What instructions do I need to give each subgroup to be sure that there will be no misunderstandings about their required process and outputs?
- What supplies and materials do I need to have on hand so that each subgroup can complete its assigned subgroup activity properly?
- What whole-group activity will I use to ensure that the outputs of the subgroups are shared, processed, and integrated in a meaningful way?

Use Buzz Groups or Small Work Groups. There are two fundamental types of subgroups: the simple buzz group and the more complex small work group.

1. *Buzz group.* One method of stimulating group effort is the *buzz group*. In teams of three to five, people are asked to interact—to

"buzz"—for a short period of time (usually not more than 5 to 10 minutes) in response to an instruction such as, "Generate a set of pros and cons for the draft of the new absenteeism policy that I just covered. Be prepared to share your reactions with the whole group in 10 minutes."

2. *Small work group.* Small work groups—teams with five to seven members—are larger than buzz groups, they are given more complicated tasks to perform, and they are given more time to perform them—from 30 minutes to several hours.

Assuming you are using three small work groups, you might develop a plan whereby you assign the same task to all three groups. For example, "Brainstorm, consolidate, and prioritize a list of behaviors that a good facilitative leader practices in facilitating a group."

A variation on this approach would be to assign each of the three subgroups a different task to pursue. For example, "Team A is asked to develop a force-field analysis accounting for forces that are both driving and hindering the development of staff talent within our hospital. Team B is asked to develop a set of criteria for objectively evaluating the worth of potential staff development workshops proposed for our hospital. Team C is asked to create a fair method for selecting who gets to attend which staff development workshops during the next calendar year."

With respect to both buzz group and small work group activities, Norman R. F. Maier provides a sound suggestion.

If a specific number of ideas is required, the number of ideas to be reported by each subgroup should be fewer than the number of people in it. This prevents the group product from being a simple compilation of the contributions made by each member. Good information processing requires the resolution of differences, and one way to introduce such differences is to require the group to be selective and integrative rather than additive.[4]

Determine the Necessary Supplies. Determine what supplies and materials are required to complete the subgroup activity, and ensure that they are available to each subgroup when they are needed. At a minimum, you most likely will need to provide a flip-chart stand and paper, watercolor markers (dark colors like black, purple, blue, or brown), and drafting tape.

Develop the Whole-Group Process to Be Used When the Subgroup Activity Is Completed. Once the subgroups' work is completed, there is a need for each subgroup to share the output of its efforts with the whole group. There are a variety of ways to do this.

- The larger group reconvenes, and each subgroup shares its top two ideas or highest-priority items. After that round, lower-priority ideas or items can be added.
- Each subgroup writes its report on flip-chart paper and hangs it on the wall for everyone to review. This makes for a useful interlude, since, in addition to stretching and reading, people can pick up a cup of coffee, leave the room briefly, or get immediate clarification on points of confusion.
- A short stand-up presentation is made by each subgroup followed by a short Q and A period. During the Q and A, the scribe records the main points on a flip chart on behalf of the whole group.
- If there is easy access to a copier, copies are made of each subgroup's report. This information is then distributed to every participant and discussed, and key points are consolidated on flip-chart paper.
- Each subgroup gives its report to a central processing team. The team condenses and synthesizes the results and communicates its findings later in the same session or at the next session.

When planning the whole-group process, keep the sharing and processing activities streamlined, yet interesting for everyone. Try to maximize the number of people who are involved in the whole-group processing activity. The previous examples illustrated a number of ways to do this.

During the information sharing, the primary facilitator should focus on clarification and testing comprehension to make certain that everyone understands what is being presented.

During the processing portion, the primary facilitator works with the whole group to develop a summary that highlights the main points addressed during the general presentations. A good scribe will be a big help during this phase.

Subgroup activities are not idle exercises; therefore, managing the sharing and processing of information at the whole-group level requires careful thought. A poor whole-group plan can ruin terrific work at the subgroup level.

Panel Discussion before the In-Session Subgrouping

Using a panel discussion prior to breaking into small work groups for detailed processing is a strong combination for capitalizing on the collaborative brainpower of a group. The nice thing about this method is its flexibility. This hybrid process can be utilized with a large group, 15 to 40 people, during the panel portion, and then the large group can neatly be broken into small subgroups of 5 to 7 for the working portion.

The essence of the panel portion is to construct a panel of participants from certain zones, regions, or districts or those who represent various disciplines, expertise, functions, or special interests on an issue. The idea is to have the panel members present their various perspectives on the issue, including necessary explanations of new or "inside" information that isn't generally known. All information is shared without resorting to a formal debate before the larger group.

Most panel discussions last from 30 to 50 minutes and can be followed by a general Q and A period with the audience before it breaks into the subgroup processing segment. Questions can be directed to specific panel members or to the panel as a whole. To be most effective as a stage setter for the subgroup activity, the panel needs to be carefully selected. If all members are well versed on the issues under discussion and well prepared, they can provide a most enlightening, entertaining, and informative session that gives in-depth background details and tremendous multiperspective insight into a complex topic as a precursor to subgroup processing.

Once the panel discussion is concluded, the subgroup activity begins—having been preplanned following the guidelines set forth in the previous section.

Introspection, Then Sharing

This final group process technique is an uncomplicated one that can raise the quality of a discussion to a higher level. Instead of asking the group a difficult question and having members immediately launch into a discussion, ask the question first, but have the participants do some silent reflecting before they respond. The purpose is to give all team members time to process an issue mentally, to gain insight into what each personally believes and why, and to assess how others might feel about the subject in question. This individual preparation prior to interacting with others will invigorate the initial group dialogue because people will be primed to interact.

For example, you might ask team members, "What new benefits can we deliver to our customers, and what core competencies will be needed to deliver those benefits?" Then, before they answer, ask the team members to silently reflect for five minutes on two thought-provoking introspection questions: "What are the pluses and minuses of the position you are taking?" and "Who might support, question, or reject your position? What would they say to you about your stance?"

These two introspection questions can be used in any situation where it is important that the participants crystallize the rationale for their position and make an assessment of how others might react to it before discussing and debating the issue in a group. Introspection, then sharing is an elementary process that invariably produces a dynamic group debate.

The Wrap-Up Phase: Planning an Organized Ending That Finishes with Snap

Much like vampires who fade away at sunrise to go to their coffins, too many group sessions tend to sputter to a close because the allotted time runs out and the attendees bolt for the exits to get to their next meeting coffin. So, at this final preparation stage, you must determine the means for ending the session so that there are no loose ends. People need to leave knowing what was decided, who has what action items, how "leftover" agenda items were disposed of, and "what we did well" and "what we did not do so well."

There are four tasks that need to be planned to make certain that the group session finishes with power and impact, as opposed to drifting off into oblivion. Remember, the close of one meeting is often the first step in preparing for the next.

Review the Core Outcomes: Decisions and Action Items

Here is where the role of the minute taker comes into play and adds tremendous value to a meeting. Reading from his notes and supplementing this information by pointing to any flip charts developed during the session that summarize outputs from processing agenda topics, the minute taker first reviews any decisions reached during the session.

For example, the minute taker would say something like: "Decision one, the new software cut-in will not begin until October 1, which is a four-week delay. Decision two, the open financial analyst position is frozen until further notice. Decision three, Allis-Lenerd is selected as our travel agency for the next two calendar years."

Then the minute taker goes over all action items that were assigned during the meeting. Action items specifically spell out *who* is to do *what* by *when*. Action items are read by the minute taker from his notes and reinforced by pointing to flip-chart pages where appropriate.

For example, the minute taker might say: "First action item, Lisa, you've committed to pulling together two exempts and two nonexempts from our department to design our display for this year's American Software Convention by June 9. Right? Second action item, Dylan, you've agreed to have a first color rendering of the full display area for us to study on June 23. Right? Third action item, Josh, you will get bids from three moving companies for us to assess at our June 30 session. Right?"

The "right" at the end of each action item tests comprehension to ensure that the team and Lisa, Dylan, and Josh all see the various action items the same way. If there are differences regarding what was agreed to, these can be brought up and resolved now, or soon after the session. This process ensures that there is no backpeddling after the session ends.

Take Care of Any "Leftovers"

The next task for the minute taker is to call attention to any agenda items that were scheduled but not covered, to deal with agenda tasks that were started but not fully completed, and to take care of "parking lot" items that came up and were deemed important points for the team to consider, but not relevant to the current session. The team, led by the primary facilitator, needs to dispense with each leftover item. There are several options open to the team.

- Adding items that were not covered to the next session's agenda.
- Assigning the items as additional actions to subgroups or individuals to pursue outside of the session, with results reported at a future date.
- Tabling the items for a later time (beyond the next session).
- Dropping the items altogether.

The "straw-man agenda" for the next session is established at this juncture by noting any items that are to be carried over from the current session, plus any new topics proposed for next time. For example, the primary facilitator might state, "So, the one item we will carry over from today's session and include on our next agenda is Strickland's replacement. The two desired outcomes will remain the same: list of potential replacements developed, and an interview list of the top three candidates determined."

The minute taker writes this information in the minutes under the heading, "Next Session."

The primary facilitator goes on, "Does anyone have any new topics to propose for next time? Yes, Desmond."

"We need to process the new 'Customer Relations Workshop' for our call center customer service reps. The desired outcome should be: workshop implementation schedule covering all three call center locations agreed to."

The minute taker also would add Desmond's agenda topic under the "Next Session" heading. The time and place of the next meeting is also set and added to the minutes.

As you can see, the process for handling leftovers assumes that other meetings are going to follow. That is not always the case. Sometimes a meeting is ad hoc, a one-time event. Still, you must dispose of any leftovers to bring about a definitive close to the proceedings. Essentially you have three options. One is to review all leftovers with a decision that all should be dropped. Two, if some items are considered too important to be dropped, those are assigned as action items to team members along with specific people who will be receivers of the outputs to make certain the individuals holding the action items are held accountable for their deliverables. Three, action items are assigned but with the results presented in a different meeting like an upcoming staff meeting, a scheduled quarterly review, a senior staff operations review, or the like which ensures accountability.

Hold a Session Critique

George Santayana, the Spanish poet and philosopher, made an observation about history that relates to meeting assessment: "Those who cannot remember the past are condemned to repeat it." So it is with meetings.

A 5- to 10-minute critique of the entire session, in order to remember the past, is a must if a group is serious about improving its meeting process. Lynn Oppenheim, citing research conducted by the Wharton Center for Applied Research, emphatically underscores this point.

> A set of skills that are valued in organizations which take meetings seriously involve eliciting and providing feedback about the meeting itself. Many of the tasks we carry out provide feedback to us about their satisfactory completion, and meetings should be no exception. Many managers, when asked, say they can tell if a meeting was good or bad. Unfortunately, "good" and "bad" are often global evaluations from

which we learn very little. They may have less to do with what went on in the meeting than what goes on in the organizational context. Feedback about key aspects of the meeting could, if legitimized, stimulate very powerful discussions that would improve productivity within the meeting room and beyond.[5]

There are various ways to hold a meaningful session critique that will lead to more efficient and productive sessions in the future.

Open Discussion. A very simple but effective technique is for the manager to draw a line down the center of a flip-chart page and label the columns as indicated in Figure 6-2 (the Δ is the symbol for change). The manager solicits and records the points offered by the group—including his own—with respect to both questions. The group then reaches a consensus on one or two items from the "do better" side that it most wants to improve next time. The group also concurs on an item from the left side that it would like to continue "doing well." These items are circled. The data from this flip-chart page are included in the minutes so that the "do betters" for next time are documented and a running record that tracks session improvement is preserved.

The two areas for improvement and the activity to continue doing well should be reviewed by the manager first thing at the next meeting. This

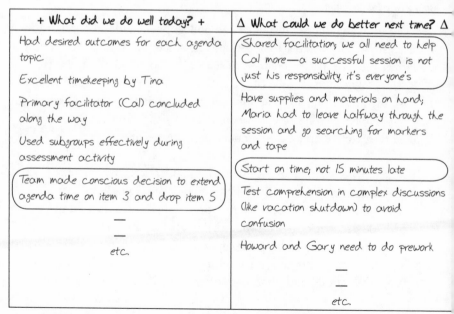

Figure 6-2 Meeting Assessment Results from Open Discussion

will refresh everyone's memory about the session's meeting improvement goals and will demonstrate that the manager is serious about enhancing group session productivity and teamwork.

A few words of caution about the open discussion critique. This is a serious exercise. While environmental considerations may be important, and may require improvements if the team must continue meeting in the same place, the manager cannot allow the chart to constantly fill up with things like "the room was too hot," "the donuts were delicious," "the coffee was cold," "the view was terrific," "the chairs were uncomfortable," "the carpet was dirty," and "Dan's shirt was colorful."

These items don't hit at the things that are going to make for a stronger, more collaborative team. Also, the manager has to facilitate against meaningless, round-worded statements like "we had lots of good discussion," "the agenda wasn't any good," "this was an outstanding session," "there was too much arguing," "we got quite a bit accomplished," and "we need more structure." If statements like this start to be offered, ask the respondent to elaborate. "What, specifically, pleased you about the discussion?" Or, "What aspects of our session need more structure, and in what way?"

The open discussion method requires organized thinking to make it a meaningful session improvement technique. In general, the team will do well to provide direct, specific feedback in these major categories: preplanning, prework, in-session structure, processes, teamwork, facilitation, and action item follow-up.

Session Survey. A second alternative involves handing out a short survey form that contains a series of meeting dimensions. The participants rate the session's effectiveness on these dimensions and then pass their completed form to the minute taker. This person will consolidate the rating results outside the session and publish them in the minutes.

As with the open discussion method, documenting the evaluation in the minutes furnishes a history of the group's progress in improvement on selected dimensions.

The Discussion Assessment Survey (Figure 6-3) is a simple form composed of eight dimensions that focus on group interaction. The Group Session Effectiveness Evaluation (Figure 6-4) is a more extensive instrument containing 16 dimensions closely aligned with both the structural and the interactive aspects of our mining group gold tools, processes, and philosophy.

With proper planning of the meeting's structure and process now completed, what was well begun is now already half done. The next stage is implementation. Part III, "Facilitating Techniques to Mine Group Gold," which includes Chapters 7, 8, 9, 10 and 11, furnishes a host of simple but extraordinarily useful tools and ideas aimed at increasing your confidence and your ability to be a facilitative leader who helps the group achieve the session's overall purpose and desired outcomes.

Session's
Title _____ Date _____ Time _____

Clarity of direction

1. Most of us were
confused about the
purpose and desired
outcomes of this session.

1   2   3   4   5
|___|___|___|___|

We all understood the
purposed and desired
outcomes of this session.

Structure

2. Our discussion went
in several directions at
once.

1   2   3   4   5
|___|___|___|___|

Our discussion was
orderly; no ideas were lost
in the shuffle.

Flow

3. Our discussion required
a great deal of back-
tracking and reorienting.

1   2   3   4   5
|___|___|___|___|

Our discussion moved
forward with succeeding
points building on
previous ones.

Participation

4. Some dominated the
discussion while others
contributed much less.

1   2   3   4   5
|___|___|___|___|

We all shared the floor in
this discussion.

Expression of differences

5. Our disagreeing
produced defensive
reactions.

1   2   3   4   5
|___|___|___|___|

We disagreed without
arousing defensive
reactions.

Listening

6. We didn't listen to each
other very well.

1   2   3   4   5
|___|___|___|___|

We demonstrated that we
were listening to
each other.

Understanding

7. Most of us were
confused about
what went on in this
discussion.

1   2   3   4   5
|___|___|___|___|

We all understood what
was discussed and
agreed to.

Achievement of session's desired outcomes

8. We cannot tell if desired
outcomes were achieved
because they were not
stated or were confused.
Or, if stated, we failed to
achieve them.

1   2   3   4   5
|___|___|___|___|

We fully achieved the
desired outcomes set forth
and clarified for
this session.

Figure 6-3 Discussion Assessment Survey

Session's
Title _____ Date _____ Time _____

1. Were you notified of this session in time to make arrangements and sufficiently prepare for it?

1	2	3	4	5

It was last minute—   Time to minimally   Yes, plenty of time
no time to prepare   prepare   to fully prepare

2. Were the session's key particulars (who was calling the meeting, where it would be held, when it would start, when it would end, and who was invited) clearly communicated in advance?

1	2	3	4	5

No, not   Stated   Yes, clearly stated
communicated,   but unclear   in writing, in
had to track down   advance of the
myself   session

3. Was the session's purpose clearly stated?

1	2	3	4	5

Not stated   Stated   Clearly stated, plus
                               but vague   posted in the session

4. Were the session's desired outcomes clearly stated?

1	2	3	4	5

Not stated   Stated   Clearly stated, plus
                               but vague   posted in the session

5. Was either a predetermined agenda reviewed, or an in-session agenda created, at the beginning of the session?

1	2	3	4	5

Not stated   Vague agenda   Specified agenda

(Continued)

Figure 6-4 Group Session Effectiveness Evaluation

6. Were roles (primary facilitator, minute taker, timekeeper, flip-chart scribe, etc.) defined and assigned at the beginning of the session?

1	2	3	4	5
Not discussed, defined, or assigned		Alluded to, not specifically defined or assigned		Clearly defined, assigned, and posted in the session

7. As the session progressed, was the agenda "managed" by revisiting and modifying: the number of topics; their order; their desired outcomes; and their timeframes based on changing circumstances within the session?

1	2	3	4	5
No, inflexible agenda rigidly adhered to despite need to modify		Somewhat flexible agenda, modified with reluctance		Yes, flexible agenda modified if and when required

8. Were all action items relative to "who is to do what by when" clearly stated before the session adjourned?

1	2	3	4	5
Not stated		Stated, but vague		Clearly stated

9. To what extent were we able to achieve our desired outcomes?

1	2	3	4	5
Don't know because none were stated –OR– (if desired outcomes were stated) we failed to achieve them		Partially achieved		Fully achieved

10. Was the information that was shared and processed during this session useful to you?

1	2	3	4	5
Not stated		Vague agenda		Specified agenda

(Continued)

11. Were you comfortable in asking questions?

1	2	3	4	5
Not at all comfortable		Moderately comfortable		Totally comfortable

12. Were you satisfied that your questions were answered openly and honestly?

1	2	3	4	5
Very dissatisfied		Neither satisfied nor dissatisfied		Very satisfied

13. Were you satisfied with the group's functioning relative to teamwork and cooperation?

1	2	3	4	5
Very dissatisfied		Neither satisfied nor dissatisfied		Very satisfied

14. To what extent do you feel your participation influenced the group's ability to achieve its desired outcome(s)?

1	2	3	4	5
No influence at all		Moderate influence		A great deal of influence

15. To what extent were your ideas/positions understood by the other participants?

1	2	3	4	5
Not at all understood		Somewhat understood		Completely understood

16. To what extent were the ideas/positions of the other participants understood by you?

1	2	3	4	5
Not at all understood		Somewhat understood		Completely understood

Figure 6-4 Group Session Effectiveness Evaluation *(Continued)*

WORKSHEET

Develop written responses to the two items listed below.

1. What do you feel are the main learning points from Chapter 6?

   – THE FLOW OF A MEETING

   – NEED for Informal Session

   – How Important to know on point

   _____

   _____

   _____

   _____

2. Elaborate on why you feel these points are key for you.

   – Know people Interim

   – Doesn't Feel Like a waste of time

   _____

   _____

   _____

   _____

   _____

Notes

1. E. Raudsepp, "Are You a Creative Executive?" *Management Review*, February 1978, p. 12.
2. C. R. Carlson and W. W. Wilmot, *Innovation: The Five Disciplines for Creating What Customers Want* (New York: Crown Business, 2006), p. 180.
3. There are plenty of good ideas for kicking off meetings both large and small. Type "meeting icebreakers" into Google and you will get hundreds of worthwhile hits.
4. N. R. F. Maier, *Psychology in Industry*, 3d ed. (Boston: Houghton Mifflin, 1965), p. 20.
5. L. Oppenheim, *Making Meetings Matter: A Report to the 3M Corporation* (Philadelphia: Wharton Center for Applied Research, 1987), p. 38.

Part III

FACILITATING TECHNIQUES TO MINE GROUP GOLD

Practicing Interpersonal Excellence: Sharing Communication Behaviors within the Gold Mine

- To present a set of shared interpersonal behaviors (IPBs) that are essential to conducting effective group sessions: group task behaviors, group maintenance behaviors, and gatekeeping processes.
- To explain the benefits of practicing these behaviors.
- To provide tips for their successful use and the manager's crucial role.

Introduction

Geronimo, a fierce warrior and the chief of the Apaches who campaigned against the white settlers during the 1880s, was wise and caring toward his tribe. One day a young brave, a handsome, athletic, but self-centered 18-year-old, came to Geronimo and asked what was required for him to become a man in the warrior's eyes.

A few days later, Geronimo received the young brave at the most sacred spot in the tribal burial grounds. They spoke about the kind of life the boy had lived up to that point. Geronimo then served a special tealike drink made from an ancient recipe of herbs and spices. He poured the brave's cup full and kept on pouring. The drink overflowed and soaked into the ground.

After watching for a bit, the brave could no longer contain himself. "Geronimo," he exclaimed, "stop pouring. The cup is overfull. No more will go in."

"Like this cup," Geronimo said, "your mind is full of your own judgments, opinions, values, beliefs, and speculations. How can I possibly teach you how to be a man until you empty your cup first?"

This simple tale serves as a fitting introduction to this chapter on interpersonal behaviors. Like the young brave, our heads are full of judgments, opinions, values, beliefs, and speculations about interpersonal behaviors. After all, since the minute we were born, we have been interacting with others. If there is one thing we can claim to be expert in, it is interpersonal behaviors. We have a lifetime of experience in this activity.

Before reading any further, do as Geronimo would ask, and "empty your cup a little." Make room for some new perspectives and insights into interpersonal behaviors. Make room so that you can look at these interpersonal behaviors through the eyes of a miner of group gold whose intent is to help the group cash in on its collective wisdom.

Setting the Stage

As emphasized in Chapter 3, the manager, acting as primary facilitator, and every other group member must share the responsibility for group facilitation. An excellent starting point for shared facilitation is learning and using the interpersonal behaviors (IPBs) and processes for group sessions discussed in this chapter.[1]

By practicing these behaviors, along with the gatekeeping processes to regulate group participation appropriately, all members can help strengthen the group's ability to share and process information.

In order for any group to be productive, it must direct attention to task accomplishment. That is, the work of different members must be coordinated and combined so that everyone is pulling together to achieve the desired outcomes of the group session. At the same time, the group must also be mindful of the emotional and personal welfare needs of its members. If proper maintenance behaviors are not performed, the survival of the group is threatened, jeopardizing its ability to accomplish its task.

Although these task and maintenance behaviors and gatekeeping processes are a shared responsibility, the primary facilitator must be especially tuned in to them and do his best to role-model them while facilitating.

Before we discuss each of the specific behaviors, look over Figure 7-1 to familiarize yourself with the overall set of behaviors that we will be covering.

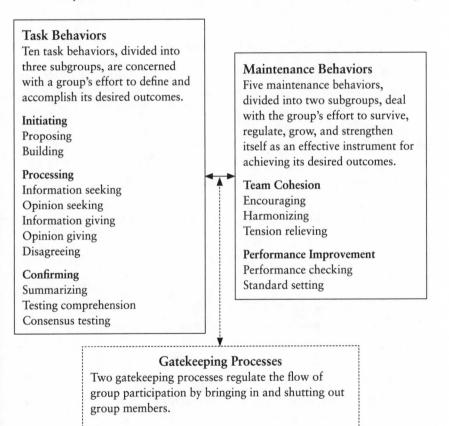

Task Behaviors
Ten task behaviors, divided into three subgroups, are concerned with a group's effort to define and accomplish its desired outcomes.

Initiating
Proposing
Building

Processing
Information seeking
Opinion seeking
Information giving
Opinion giving
Disagreeing

Confirming
Summarizing
Testing comprehension
Consensus testing

Maintenance Behaviors
Five maintenance behaviors, divided into two subgroups, deal with the group's effort to survive, regulate, grow, and strengthen itself as an effective instrument for achieving its desired outcomes.

Team Cohesion
Encouraging
Harmonizing
Tension relieving

Performance Improvement
Performance checking
Standard setting

Gatekeeping Processes
Two gatekeeping processes regulate the flow of group participation by bringing in and shutting out group members.

Regulating Participation
Gate opening
Gate closing

Figure 7-1 The Set of Interpersonal Behaviors

Group Task Behaviors

The task component includes 10 communication behaviors that are concerned with a group's efforts to define and accomplish desired outcomes. To help you understand the various task-oriented behaviors, a definition and several examples of each behavior are provided.

Initiating

Proposing. This is a behavior that introduces a *new* idea, proposition, or suggestion to spark group action. Proposing is vital at the beginning of a session to get the group moving, and it is also indispensable when the group gets bogged down or when it needs to look at another aspect of the issue.

"I suggest we begin by reviewing last year's figures."

"Here's my idea: let's combine Districts 1 and 2 and place responsibility for both within a new position called senior district coordinator."

Building. This is a behavior that takes a group member's previous proposal, suggestion, or idea and then extends, develops, or expands it to enhance its value.

Building on the first suggestion above:

"Then we could compare them with this year's figures and have Chad explain the variances."

Building on the second proposal above:

"Good. That would also allow us to promote Sisler into the senior district coordinator slot for a two-year developmental assignment that will prepare her for the assistant superintendent position."

Processing

Information Seeking. This is a behavior that solicits facts, figures, statistics, or other hard data from others.

"How many 100 percent attendance days did we have at our high school in May?"

"Exactly what would be the year-over-year savings if we did a lease versus buy?"

Opinion Seeking. This is a behavior that solicits judgments, beliefs, or sentiments from others.

"David, what are your thoughts on having the building administrators teach the half-day Disciplinary Procedures Workshop to their own staffs?"

"Ty, do you think Cobb has the ability to upgrade our college relations program?"

Information Giving. This is a behavior that offers facts, figures, statistics, or other hard data to others.

"Our inspection cost alone on those engines is $75 per unit."

"When I worked at TAK, our janitors were responsible for meeting with vendors, testing their products, and determining which cleaning supplies to purchase."

Opinion Giving. This is a behavior that offers judgments, beliefs, or sentiments to others.

"I say hold off on the recall. In my view, these three incidents were nothing more than random, fluke occurrences."

"As far as I'm concerned, we should not accept their current offer. I believe they really want the building; it is only one mile from their main office. They'll come in with a higher offer if we sit tight."

Disagreeing. This is a behavior that provides direct opposition to, or raises doubts and objections about, an issue (*not* about the person who presents it). Technically, disagreeing occurs as a form of information giving or opinion giving; however, since it is such a powerful force—the key to a group's critical thinking—disagreeing is shown here as a distinct task behavior to heighten your awareness of its value.

"I don't buy into Wagner's proposal because it requires a number of my people, who are putting in six to eight hours of overtime per week already, to work Sundays for the next six months on top of that. They will burn out."

"I cannot support having Hornsby observe our team-building session, since he is not a member of our immediate group."

Confirming

Summarizing. This is a behavior that restates the content of a previous discussion or event in condensed form. A summary statement is *not a question*. It does not require affirmation.

"So our plan is set; we will order the machine, train the appropriate personnel, and evaluate the results in six weeks."

"Okay. Our decision, then, is that we will push back introducing the new Social Studies curriculum from the fall to the spring semester because Foxx Publishing can't guarantee delivery of the new textbooks, posters, maps, and DVDs by August 1."

Testing Comprehension. This is a behavior that *poses a question* in order to establish whether a previous communication has been correctly understood. A response back is required.

"Now then, Leroi, are you telling me that you want to be reclassified as a nonexempt because you can make more money with overtime pay than by staying on salary?"

"So, Allison, are you saying that if I get the revisions to you by 2 o'clock tomorrow afternoon, you'll have my report typed by 5 p.m. that same day?"

Consensus Testing. This is a behavior that periodically tests whether the group has reached consensus or whether more discussion of the issue is required. Consensus testing operates by asking each person, in turn, to declare verbally whether or not the individual is on board.

"Do we now have consensus that we will extend this staff meeting for another hour, ending at noon? I'll go right around the table. Christy? . . ."

"Let's see if everyone either can agree with or can agree to support the most popular alternative, which is moving the copier next to the library. I'll start with Tris and go right across the room. Tris? . . ."

Group Maintenance Behaviors

The maintenance component incorporates five communication behaviors that are associated with the operation of the group *as a group*. These behaviors deal with the group's efforts to survive, regulate, grow, and strengthen itself as an effective instrument for achieving desired outcomes. A definition plus several examples of each behavior are given here.

Team Cohesion

Encouraging. This is a behavior that supports, agrees with, or recognizes the contributions of others.

"Carol and Janice, your budget presentation to the school board was incisive, well organized, and documented to the hilt. You've both proven that you are ready for more difficult assignments."

"Great point, Ed! You're right, we can do it together. It's risky, but I know we are capable of working out our mission, goals, and operating principles as a team."

Harmonizing. This is a behavior that attempts to reconcile disagreements or conflict by mediating differences between group members, pointing out the strengths of alternative solutions, or searching for common elements of agreement in opposing positions.

"I don't see this as an either/or issue. We can have both! We can take 20 percent of the budget surplus, and with matching funds from the state, we can remodel the old fire station and turn it into a centrally located day-care center. Then, we can take the remainder of the surplus and build a larger, more up-to-date fire station."

"We are all in agreement that more privacy is necessary for the 10 of you, but permanent walls are inflexible and costly. Eight-foot dividers and soft background music should accomplish the same results. And you will have a lot more privacy than all of you have now sitting in a common 40-by-40 room."

Tension Relieving. This is a behavior that eases tensions and increases group members' enjoyment by joking, suggesting breaks, or proposing fun approaches to group work.

"Whew, that was difficult! Let's take a 15-minute break and get our blood circulating again."

"Why don't we hold our next all-day staff meeting at the cabin in Webster Park and then have a picnic when we're finished?"

Performance Improvement

Performance Checking. This is a behavior that suspends task operations in order to examine where the group stands in relation to achieving its desired outcomes, to determine how the team members feel about the group's progress in attempting to accomplish its desired outcomes, to air feelings and conflicts, or to evaluate the session at its conclusion.

"I would like to stop our process for a few minutes. Willie, Mickey, and Duke, all three of you are certainly upset over the criteria we are generating to select a replacement for Gehringer. Our group really can't move forward unless we understand what your reservations are. If you'll share your concerns with the group, I'll write them on the flip chart so that the three of you will know that the rest of us truly understand where you're coming from and why."

"Performance check, please! We said that we would complete our force-field analysis by 3:30; it's now 3:20, and we have at least another 45 minutes' worth of work to do. Our energy level really is dragging. I believe we need to pause and discuss where to go from here."

Standard Setting. This is a behavior that expresses standards for the group and applies these standards to improve the quality of the group process.

"We're into groupthink. If we're going to make the best possible decision, we must increase our critical thinking and hold a candid debate on the consequences of waiting six months before going to market versus launching now."

"Before Aaron begins, I would like to remind everyone of our ground rule for getting the most out of presentations. We'll allow Aaron to complete his presentation before we discuss its content. Ask only clarification questions during his presentation."

Gatekeeping Processes

Unlike the task and maintenance behaviors, the gatekeeping processes do not have content per se. That is why they are shown in a dashed box in Figure 7-1. The two processes of gate opening and gate closing can occur only in conjunction with a task or maintenance behavior. In other words, the content for the gate-opening and gate-closing processes is provided by the actual task or maintenance behavior being enacted at that point.

When individuals gate-close each other's verbal communications, they often do so by verbally interrupting. These interruptions cannot occur in a vacuum. They occur because someone has utilized a task-oriented behavior such as proposing, giving information, giving opinions, disagreeing, and the like. They can also occur because someone has introduced a maintenance-oriented behavior, such as encouraging, harmonizing, or performance checking, to bring about the gate closing.

The same holds true for gate opening. The only difference is that behaviors such as seeking information, seeking opinions, testing comprehension, consensus testing, performance checking, and tension relieving are used for bringing others in rather than shutting them out.

Regulating Participation

Gate Opening. This process uses a task or maintenance behavior as a means for directly including another individual in the discussion or for increasing that individual's opportunity to contribute to the discussion.

"Jeanne, where do you think we ought to take Lopez for dinner when he visits?"

"Barry, we haven't heard your thoughts on changing from a seventh- and eighth-grade middle school to one covering grades 7 through 9. What's your position?"

Gate Closing. This process uses a task or maintenance behavior as a means for directly excluding another individual from the discussion or for reducing that individual's opportunity to contribute to the discussion.

John: "How do you feel about our office move, Brett?"

Brett: "Well, from my perspective, I'm hopeful . . ."

Kathi: "John, I've told you a hundred times that we'll be the forgotten group in that remote location!"

Kathi has gate-closed Brett to insert her opinion.

Terry: "Steve, do you have the figures?"

Steve: "Yes, we sold 451 units in . . ."

Jesse: "And as always you double counted the . . ."

Terry: "Please, Jesse, Steve's talking. Let's give him time to finish his review."

In the first part of this interaction, Jesse disruptively gate-closed Steve, who was beginning his review. However, in the spirit of secondary facilitation, Terry productively gate-closed Jesse to restore Steve as the rightful "owner of the airwaves" so that he could complete his task.

A synopsis of all task and maintenance behaviors and both gatekeeping processes is shown at the end of this chapter as a "quick review" learning aid.

Interpersonal Behavior Data

Figure 7-2 summarizes the results that I obtained from observing and checking off IPBs as they occurred in meetings. I did this to get a sense of the proportional use of each IPB and see if there was some optimal proportion. I soon discovered that there is no universal proportion; they all have their time and place. The optimal proportion for any single meeting depends on the content and structure of the PDORA. Different proportions will result from the specific purpose, desired outcomes, roles, and agenda that are laid out. The mix of proportions will affect the flavor and tone of the session. Still, the results shown in Figure 7-2 can be used as a rough benchmark of the proportional tendencies of IPBs over a large population of meetings where the desired outcomes essentially were met.

Looking at a few percentages, it is interesting to note that while all task-oriented behaviors (at 84 percent) drive a meeting, it is the five processing behaviors (at 56 percent) that are the core of the task focus. However, the critical role that proposing plays (at 11 percent) as the group's wellspring of ideas is shown by its ranking as the third most utilized IPB of the 10 task behaviors.

Maintenance behaviors (at 16 percent) are utilized much less than task behaviors. Yet, when they are used at the right time and place in a session, they are invaluable in helping the team stay together. Encouraging (at 8 percent) is easily the most frequently used maintenance behavior and is a powerful one for keeping individuals motivated and involved.

1. These guidelines summarize the results of participant interpersonal behaviors from roughly 150 staff meetings, problem-solving sessions, and decision-making sessions observed by Tom Kayser where at the session's conclusion, the attendees felt the desired outcomes had been achieved.
2. Percentages are approximate and assume a base of one to two hours of interaction.
3. Caution should be used in applying these general guidelines to a single person's contribution to one discussion of short duration—30 minutes or less. However, behaviors noted for several short sessions could be compiled to simulate a larger base.
4. Percentages are useful when contributions of members over a number of sessions are combined and the results are used in conjunction with DOs to determine effectiveness.

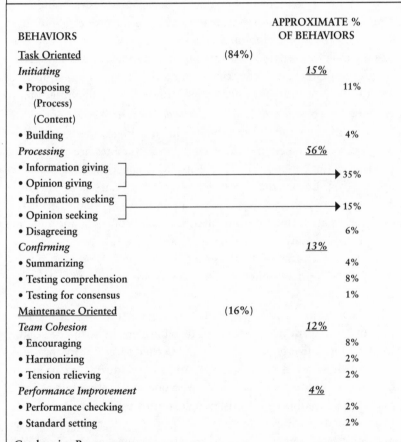

BEHAVIORS		APPROXIMATE % OF BEHAVIORS	
Task Oriented	(84%)		
Initiating		*15%*	
• Proposing			11%
(Process)			
(Content)			
• Building			4%
Processing		*56%*	
• Information giving			
• Opinion giving		→	35%
• Information seeking			
• Opinion seeking		→	15%
• Disagreeing			6%
Confirming		*13%*	
• Summarizing			4%
• Testing comprehension			8%
• Testing for consensus			1%
Maintenance Oriented	(16%)		
Team Cohesion		*12%*	
• Encouraging			8%
• Harmonizing			2%
• Tension relieving			2%
Performance Improvement		*4%*	
• Performance checking			2%
• Standard setting			2%

Gatekeeping Processes
Gate-opening and gate-closing interventions each occurred roughly 3 percent of the time as a specific task or maintenance IPB to bring in a person or to shut out (by interrupting) an individual.

Figure 7-2 Observation Data of IPB Use in Group Sessions

Benefits of the IPBs

While many benefits will accrue to a group that learns, understands, and routinely practices the interpersonal behaviors described in this chapter, the five following benefits are notable:

1. *Teamwork is enhanced.* Using the behaviors outlined here increases the collaborative capacity of team members. This is a major payoff. Lack of good interpersonal skills among those participating in a meeting can carry a huge price tag, as just one person can interfere with the ability of the entire group to achieve its desired outcomes. Collaboration is a vital part of teamwork, and the proper use of these communication behaviors and processes fosters collaboration. Proposing, building, seeking information and opinions, encouraging, harmonizing, performance checking, standard setting, and gate opening are all root behaviors for improving teamwork and collaboration.

2. *A climate of openness and trust is nurtured.* Another key benefit arising from practicing good interpersonal behaviors in group sessions is the development of an environment in which teammates are encouraged to identify and communicate problems. Messengers bearing bad news are not shot. Rather, they are welcomed so that issues can be resolved as early as possible, not kept covered up until they precipitate a major crisis. A positive climate is nurtured because proposing and building are promoted, any personal attacks are stopped immediately, differences are harmonized by the group, and the gate is opened to bring in others—especially quiet members so as not to miss their thinking on the issues.

3. *Listening is improved.* Listening and understanding are greatly improved as team members come to recognize the value of seeking information and opinions from one another to get everyone's gold nuggets of wisdom on the table. And if seeking information and opinions is increased—rather than everyone constantly offering information and opinions—then listening carefully to the speaker in order to summarize various points of view accurately, test comprehension, and build on another's idea or proposal becomes an expected obligation for every group member in attendance.

4. *A fuller understanding of the subject is developed.* An additional benefit derived from appropriate use of the IPBs—besides the listening that they prompt—is that the IPBs help to ensure that debate and discussion are objective and orderly, and that they lead to logical

conclusions. Mistakes resulting from misunderstandings or incomplete information are minimized. Seeking information and opinions and then listening carefully to what is said, disagreeing over issues without being disagreeable by personally attacking others, testing comprehension, summarizing, and testing consensus all play important roles here.

Disagreeing is especially important in gaining a fuller understanding of a subject, especially one that is controversial or complex, because disagreeing is the key to the group's critical thinking. Disagreeing prevents groupthink, where the main goal of team members is to be agreeable and not to make any waves by challenging the points that others bring up or by making proposals that are outside the mainstream thinking of the group.

5. *Decision commitment is solidified.* The fifth payback, from the whole team practicing the behaviors associated with the task, maintenance, and gatekeeping actions, is commitment. The use of proposing, building, seeking information and opinions, encouraging, harmonizing, performance checking, and gate opening involves everyone in the group's deliberation. These IPBs fully engage the teammates. When they are fully engaged, people are encouraged to speak up and help shape the final decision, which, in turn, produces a greater commitment to the final decision along with a greater chance of a successful implementation.

Pat Williams, senior vice president of the NBA Orlando Magic, makes a fascinating point related to the power of listening and its impact on others:

> It's interesting to notice that the word *listen* is an anagram for *silent*—same letters, different order. Perhaps there is a subliminal message there. If listening doesn't come naturally to you, then remember that you must be silent to listen—you can't be a good listener while you are doing all the talking. When you take time to look someone in the eye and say, "I'm listening," you empower that person in a way that goes beyond words.[2]

Tips for Successful Use

Balance Is Required. In order for a group to define and accomplish its desired outcomes, a balance between the task and maintenance behaviors must be sustained. In addition, the gatekeeping processes must be employed at times to bring in individuals who are quiet and to shut out, in a productive way, individuals who are interrupting and/or dominating the group session.

There is no right or wrong answer regarding the proper mix among the task, maintenance, and gatekeeping components. All are important. Some group sessions benefit from emphasizing certain behaviors over others. The best balance will vary depending on the particular content of a PDORA and the circumstances influencing its creation.

For example, a session that was set up to brainstorm ideas would have an extremely high percentage of proposing and building IPBs, which would be perfectly appropriate for that kind of meeting. On the other hand, a meeting that was convened to unveil and explain a departmental reorganization to an audience of employees would be heavily laden with information and opinion giving, which also would be fitting given the desired outcome of that session.

Stop Task and Invoke Performance Checks. Another noteworthy point regarding the use of the task-oriented and maintenance-oriented behaviors is that at any time during a group session—especially when the task is a difficult, complex one—the group may be forced to do a performance check to get back on task. Or a performance check may be necessary to confront group maintenance problems. Quite often this entails working through the "feelings" stage of the "feelings, facts, solutions" sequence covered in Chapter 10.

The central idea, however, is that when issues arise, an effective group stops its task-oriented process, calls attention to specific problems with the group processes, and takes action to reduce or eliminate these stumbling blocks. After this is done, the group can refocus—often with greater unity—on achieving the desired outcomes it has set for itself. The manager and all group members must share the responsibility for recognizing the need, and for taking the initiative, to call for a performance check.

Moderation Is the Key. Finally, moderation is critical to successfully performing any of the described behaviors and processes. The strength and utility of any of them will be impaired if it is used too much or too little, or if it is used to thwart the group from reaching its desired outcomes.

The Manager's Crucial Role

Attaining a reflexive, or unconscious, ability to use these group behaviors takes time and patience, since, in many cases, the manager and the group members will be required to practice behaviors that are new and/ or awkward for them. The discussion that follows outlines key steps for instilling excellent interactive skills in a work team.

Role Modeling

The degree of success your team will have in routinely performing the behaviors associated with the task, maintenance, and gatekeeping functions will depend to a large extent on you the manager (or in the case of committees, task forces, or quality improvement teams, you the designated chairperson or team leader).

As the head person with the formal authority to run the team, you will be watched by your team members. They will take their behavioral cues from you. Therefore, you need to initiate and role-model the use of these behaviors via personal action because doing so will legitimize the IPBs for everyone else on the team. But in doing so, keep in mind that the *priceless ingredient is the honesty and integrity with which you perform the IPBs.* This priceless ingredient is your ticket to success in building team relationships and will communicate far more about your integrity than how precise you are in executing them.

In working with teams at all organizational levels, my personal experience validates the following principle over and over: group members invariably will respond more positively, and with greater openness, to a manager (or any group member, for that matter) who makes unpolished but sincere attempts to practice the interpersonal behaviors, as opposed to the manager who mechanically performs them well, but does so with an aura of hidden agendas, double meanings, and self-serving manipulations.

Encouraging

As well as making a genuine effort to role-model, it is also imperative that you use the maintenance behavior of encouraging to stimulate all members to use the interpersonal behaviors and processes with sensitivity and authenticity. Each effort that a group member makes to carry out some of the more troublesome behaviors, like summarizing, disagreeing without getting personal, testing comprehension, standard setting, tension relieving, and productive gate closing, must be recognized immediately with positive feedback.

This recognition does not need to be given with a lot of fanfare. Giving simple, straightforward acknowledgments throughout the group session is all that is required.

"Thank you, Earl; that was a crisp summary of some complex issues."

"That was a difficult topic to reach consensus on, but we were able to disagree without getting personal—that was a big plus."

"Ellen, your testing of comprehension on those two key items short-circuited a major misunderstanding that was developing between us. Nice going."

"You're right, Brady, we did agree as a group to spend 10 minutes at the end of each session reviewing our group processes. Thanks for reminding us."

"Good point. We certainly could use a break now."

Unsuccessful attempts by group members to enact the behaviors and processes should not be punished; instead, they should be used as a learning experience. This point can be illustrated by the following example.

Assume that the group is confused and that an individual attempts to summarize the various issues in order to clarify the situation and reduce the confusion; however, the person's summary takes an inordinate amount of time, is convoluted, and does nothing to reduce the confusion. At times such as this, you have a tremendous opportunity to "make lemonade out of lemons."

Thank the individual for making an attempt to help reduce confusion, highlight at least one point from the person's comments, and then ask if anyone else has other thoughts on the subject that is being discussed.

"Norm, thanks for trying to help us determine the main issues concerning our sales strategy. Your point about the impending reorganization is critical. Does anyone else have other thoughts that would help summarize the key issues?"

Coaching

Remember the priceless ingredient: the honesty and integrity of the interaction is more important than the skill in doing it. Nevertheless, using the previous example, a little private postsession coaching would be valuable to Norm, to help him do a better job of summarizing next time. The basic process is a very simple and nonthreatening one. At the first appropriate one-on-one opportunity, you should help the individual review what he did, what the results were, and what he might do differently next time.

Above all, the group member should be urged to try out the behavior again—and again!

As your team matures, or if there are team members who understand the priceless ingredient and have already refined their abilities to use the IPBs effectively, the responsibility for practicing these behaviors must be shared. You should never be expected to do it alone.

A Few Classic Examples of Humorous IPB Use

What follows are several interactions that I have been party to over the years in which a variety of the interpersonal behaviors were used quite humorously.

In one lively discussion I was participating in, Mary started to speak, but after saying only two words, she was gate-closed by Eric. Actually, they both started to speak at the same time, and Mary stopped. Eric noticed what had happened and, after pausing for a second or two, recovered beautifully. Looking directly at Mary, he replied in the sincerest tone, "Not to gate-close you Mary, but let me build on what you were about to say!" It took several minutes for the laughter to die down.

At a project team meeting, Art, a new member of the team, was extremely vocal. He had opinions about everything. Some of his ideas were good, but many others bordered on babbling. I could see that Bill, the project team leader, was getting irritated. Finally, in a firm but friendly tone of voice, Bill said, "Art, I'd like to bring you in; you've been silent for two minutes." Art was about to respond, but before he could say anything, Bill continued: "However, we are out of time on this topic." Everyone had a good laugh. Art got the message. Then, at the meeting's conclusion, Bill held a short coaching and counseling session with Art to iron out expectations regarding Art's behavior at future meetings.

This next anecdote is a perfect example of the maintenance behavior of tension relieving. I was facilitating a senior-level task force that was trying to decide whether a particular part should be made at our Webster, New York, manufacturing facility or be produced offshore in the Pacific Basin. This was a complex, very serious issue, and the atmosphere was all business. After three hours of presentations and discussions, the task force chairman announced, "Well we finally have defined two specific alternatives. Now, before I do the consensus testing, I'd like to summarize. What you've told me is: alternative one will lead to despair and utter hopelessness, and alternative two will lead to total extinction! Members of the task force, let's pray that we have the wisdom to decide correctly."

At that instant, the roof came down. The whole atmosphere lightened up, and even though consensus was not achieved immediately, the group was sparked to a greater effort. At the next session, the task force all agreed on a win-win course of action.

The following interaction is a prime example of seeking and giving information. Rochester, New York, winters are nasty. In mid-February, a manager there received an e-mail from one of her team members, who was on a business trip, seeking information. The e-mail read, "Stuck in Hawaii for several days due to a tropical storm. What should I do?" The manager sent back an e-mail giving information: "Start vacation as of yesterday."

This exchange demonstrates process checking in action. In this particular meeting, one person kept prefacing every one of his statements with things like: "This may be a dumb idea . . . ," "I know this is a stupid thing to say . . . ," or "I may be an idiot for proposing this . . ." After a while, Karen called for a process check and said, "Dale, remember there's no room for personal attacks on this team, so quit attacking yourself." Point made, and we all got a good chuckle out of it.

This final apocryphal story was related to me by a manager attending one of my workshops, but it certainly provides a humorous example of testing comprehension. The president of a company addressed the employees of the plant. "I know all of you are worried about your jobs now that we have restructured and installed all of our computerized robots. I can understand that you are quite concerned that these robots will eliminate your jobs. Well, I'm happy to say, that won't happen. This company values its human assets. Not only will no one be let go, but you will only have to come to work on Thursdays. Think of it! You will only have to work on Thursday to receive a full week's pay!"

From the back of the room an employee asked, "Are you saying we have to work *every* Thursday?"

Chapter 7 Summary

GROUP TASK BEHAVIORS		
Behavior	Definition	Example
Proposing	Initiating a new idea, proposition, or suggestion to spark group action	"Let's start by introducing ourselves."
Building	Taking a group member's proposal, suggestion, or idea, and then extending, developing, or expanding it to enhance its value	(Building on the proposal above) "And then tell one wild or crazy thing we've done in the last 12 months."
Information seeking	Soliciting facts, data, experiences, or clarification from others	"What would it cost to ship this package overnight?
Information giving	Offering facts, data, experiences, or clarification to others	"$16.75 and it will be there by noon tomorrow."
Opinion seeking	Soliciting values, beliefs, or sentiments from others	"What do you think about Shurgot's chances of winning the election?"
Opinion giving	Offering values, beliefs, or sentiments to others	"Unless Shurgot takes a more liberal view on tax reform, I don't think he has any chance of winning."
Disagreeing	Providing direct opposition to, or raising doubts about, an issue—not the person	"No way, we'll have to find an area other than travel to cut expenses."
Summarizing	Reiterating the content of previously shared dialogue in condensed form	"So, what we'll do then is: take legal action; take it before May; and, issue a writ in the chairman's name."
Testing comprehension	Posing a question in order to establish whether a previous communication has been correctly understood	"Are you saying that I can use the yearly dividends from my policy to increase the death benefit on Marianne's policy?"
Consensus testing	Periodically testing whether the group has reached consensus or whether more discussion of the issue is required	"Alternative six seems to be everyone's favorite, let's see if we have consensus. Ed . . ."

GROUP MAINTENANCE BEHAVIORS		
Behavior	Definition	Example
Encouraging	Supporting, agreeing with, or recognizing the contributions of others	"Excellent point, Wayland, I wish I had thought of it."
Harmonizing	Reconciling disagreements and conflict by mediating differences between group members, pointing out the strengths of alternative solutions, or searching for common elements of agreement in opposing positions	"Ed's proposal costs us $50,000 but could be completed within four weeks. Don's idea costs us $45,000 but would take six weeks to complete. Both are within budget and schedule constraints. The key tradeoffs are . . ."
Performance checking	Suspending task operations to tend to internal group processes	"We're definitely confused. Let's stop for a moment and reaffirm what this decision *is* and *is not* about."
Standard setting	Expressing standards for the group and applying these standards to improve the quality of the group's process	"From now on, all staff meetings begin at 8:00 a.m. sharp."
Tension relieving	Easing tensions and increasing the enjoyment of group members by joking, suggesting breaks, or proposing fun approaches to work!	"This meeting has gone on long enough in this conference room. Let's finish it over margaritas at the Red Onion."
GATEKEEPING PROCESSES		
Process	Definition	Example
Gate opening	Utilizing a task or maintenance behavior to include another person in the discussion.	"Ashley, you've been quiet, in what other areas might we cut costs?"
Gate closing	Utilizing a task or maintenance behavior to exclude another person from the discussion.	(Sandi) You turn left at the first light . . . (Luke) No, go to the third light, hang a left and then . . . Luke has gate-closed Sandi.

WORKSHEET

Develop written responses to the two items listed below.

1. What do you feel are the main learning points from Chapter 7?

UNDERSTANDING

• GROUP TASK BEHAVIORS

• GROUP MAINTENANCE BEHAVIORS

• GATEKEEPING PROCESS

2. Elaborate on why you feel these points are key for you.

- HOW TO KEEP A MEETING FLOWING

- DURING GATE CLOSING & OPEN GATE

- REMOVE PERSONAL OPINION

Notes

1. The IPB model presented in this chapter draws from the following excellent base of research:

- K. D. Benne and P. Sheats, "Functional Roles of Group Members," *Journal of Social Issues* 4, no. 2 (1948), pp. 42–47.
- R. Likert, *New Patterns of Management* (New York: McGraw-Hill, 1965), pp. 162–177.
- J. K. Brilhart, *Effective Group Discussion* (Dubuque, Iowa: William C. Brown, 1967).
- A. G. Athos and R. E. Coffey, *Behavior in Organizations: A Multi-dimensional View* (Englewood Cliffs, N.J.: Prentice-Hall, 1968), pp. 115–127.
- N. Rackham, P. Honey, and C. Colbert, *Developing Interactive Skills* (Guidsborough, Northampton, England: Wellers Publishing, 1971).
- D. W. Johnson and F. P. Johnson, *Joining Together: Group Therapy and Group Skills* (Englewood Cliffs, N.J.: Prentice-Hall, 1975), pp. 18–30, 40–42.
- L. P. Bradford, *Making Meetings Work* (La Jolla, Calif.: University Associates, 1976), pp. 35–46.
- P. S. Goodman and E. J. Conlon, "Observation of Meetings," in S. E. Seashore et al., eds., *Assessing Organizational Change: A Guide to Methods, Measures, and Practices* (New York: John Wiley & Sons, 1983), pp. 353–367.
- W. G. Dyer, *Strategies for Managing Change* (Reading, Mass.: Addison-Wesley, 1984), pp. 127–133.
- "Building a Team through Effective Meetings," *Trainer's Workshop: A Publication of the American Management Association* 1, no. 5 (November 1986), pp. 22–33.
- E. H. Schein, *Process Consultation: Its Role in Organizational Development*, Vol. 1 (Reading, Mass.: Addison-Wesley, 1988), pp. 49–56.

2. P. Williams with J. Denny, *Extreme Dreams Depend on Teams* (New York: Center Street, 2009), p. 207.

Chapter 8

FACILITATING GROUP COLLABORATION: MINING THE COLLECTIVE WISDOM OF THE GOLD MINE

- To discuss proper use of the indispensable facilitation tool—the flip chart.
- To discuss facilitation concepts and provide tips and techniques for both initiating and maintaining an open, collaborative climate.
- To discuss the importance of concluding along the way to enhance productivity.

Introduction

Herbert Simon, former distinguished professor of psychology at Carnegie-Mellon University and a leading force in the development of contemporary organization theory during the 1960s and 1970s, often recounted a story about Louis Agassiz.[1]

When Agassiz, the great biologist, acquired a new graduate student, his first concern was to train his student to see. His standard procedure was to confront the student with a pickled fish laid out on a plank and ask her to observe the fish until she could describe it accurately. When the student, after some minutes of looking, reported to Agassiz, she was cross-examined thoroughly and persuaded that there were many things about the fish that she had not seen. Agassiz sent his student back to look again, and the cycle was repeated many times. After some days, or weeks, the new graduate student would finally pass the initiation and satisfy Agassiz with her description. The graduate student could now see a specimen the way a biologist sees it.

Like Agassiz with his graduate student, this chapter will help you see group interactions as a facilitator sees them. You will see group dynamics in a different light; you will understand how to take charge and successfully guide a group through the use of facilitation behaviors.

The Flip Chart: An Indispensable Tool

Before proceeding with the discussion of specific techniques and methods for facilitating group sessions, a word about the humble flip chart is in order. While everyone seems to be interested in creating high-tech computer-generated presentations, the flip chart still continues to be the most effective presentation medium of all. *No group session should be conducted without flip charts!* They are the main physical tool in successful facilitation. Write on flip charts with dark (black, purple, blue, green, or red) watercolor markers that will not soak through the paper. Post flip-chart pages with drafting tape, since this will not peel paint or wallpaper when it is removed.

Importance of Flip Charts

There are five significant advantages to using flip charts throughout the entire group session. Flip-chart pages

- Activate the collective brainpower of a group. By using flip charts, you become much less the boss and much more a facilitative leader, since you are eliciting, building on, and recording the knowledge of the group, not controlling it.

- Allow important data or information to be preserved and displayed during a session.
- Provide a common data or information base that the group can refer to and work from.
- Provide immediate feedback to group members that their ideas, comments, and proposals have been listened to, understood, and respected by writing them down.
- Provide a portable postsession written record that can be given to another person for consolidation, transcription, and distribution. Or, better yet, with the proliferation of laptop computers, it is quite possible to have a participant in the session key in the most relevant flip-chart pages and send them to the minute taker, who then includes them when the minutes are e-mailed.

Tips for Using Flip Charts

The following ideas will help you use flip charts as an integral part of every group session.

- Print. Use upper- and lowercase letters. Be quick; don't slow the momentum of the group.
- Write what people say. Don't change their words without getting their permission.
- Take turns being the scribe. Scribing is challenging and important work. Rotate the job between two people every hour during long sessions with lots of writing.
- Avoid having the primary facilitator do any scribing. It is difficult to be an effective facilitator, with all its nuances, while scribing.
- Keep all information visible. Each time a flip-chart page is filled up, tear it off and tape it to the wall. Information that is recorded on a page and then "flipped over" the top of the pad is essentially lost and is useless for the rest of the session.
- Make it clear to others when you, the manager, are contributing your own thoughts, ideas, and opinions to the flip chart as a team member. This is the concept of role splitting.
- Summarize complicated ideas. Have people summarize their own ideas and then write their summaries.
- Assign the scribe role to aloof or indifferent members to involve them more in the group process.

Establish and Use a Flip-Chart "Parking Lot" for Every Session

Institute and use a "parking lot" for proposals, information, and opinions that are worth preserving so that they are not lost, but that are not directly related to the immediate discussion.

Set up your parking lot by tearing off a sheet of flip-chart paper before the session begins, taping it to the wall, and labeling it "Parking Lot." Add thoughts and ideas from group members to it throughout the session. Review the parking lot periodically and use any of the information whenever it becomes relevant to the discussion. At the conclusion of the meeting, sort out which remaining pieces of information should be retained for the next session, which should be taken as action items by an individual or a small subgroup to complete between this meeting and the next, and which should be dropped.

Initiating an Open, Collaborative Climate

Return for a moment to Figure 4-1, "A Map to the Gold Mine," in Chapter 4, page 41, to orient yourself as to where we are on the map before we move ahead with Chapter 8. At this juncture, you have taken the time to plan the structure and process of the forthcoming group session; your preparation is over, and the team is in the conference room. Now it is time for you to facilitate the event. You have completed your short warm-up and reviewed your PDORA document, including answering any questions about it. The art of excellent facilitation now continues with the way in which the topics for discussion or analysis are introduced. The manner of presentation is crucial because it sets the mood, positive or negative.[2] If process obstacles are to be avoided, you must approach each issue in a way that stresses the constructive aspects of the situation.

By setting the stage properly each time you undertake a new initiative in a meeting, you are laying the foundation for a productive interaction by helping group members feel comfortable so that they *want* to collaborate, and instilling in them a *need* to collaborate because they recognize the issue as important and worthy of their time and effort to work through. Your ability to do this each time provides the necessary setting that establishes the collaborative spirit; getting off on the wrong foot with an unenthusiastic beginning will be compounded as the meeting moves forward.

Figure 8-1 highlights the guiding principles that can be used to initiate an open, collaborative climate while significantly reducing the chances that apathy, destructive conflict, indifference, confusion, or other negative situations will arise.

1. Present the issue so that the focus is on the situation, not on behaviors.	2. Present the issue so that it encompasses common interests. • Degree of group control • Fairness • Goal congruence
3. Initially, share only primary information. • Provide background information • Present only information needed to clarify and describe • Set expectations • Delineate the range of freedom	4. Be succinct.

5. WAIT!

Keep the door open for team members to explore the subject matter freely rather than restricting the discussion by imposing your will or setting a predetermined direction for the exploration.

Figure 8-1 Guidelines for Initiating an Open, Collaborative Climate

Present the Issue So That the Focus Is on the Situation, Not on Behaviors

There are a number of sound reasons for stating the issue in situational rather than behavioral terms. To begin with, it is usually easier and less frustrating to change situations than it is to change people. Formulating and presenting an issue in terms of behaviors immediately locks in a limited and biased perspective: the *people* are to blame.

On the other hand, formulating and presenting an issue in terms of the situation immediately expands the number of possible solutions. A situational focus virtually eliminates the possibility of the "personal attack, defend, counterattack" spiral that easily can consume and destroy a group session before it really gets underway.

Focusing on the situation does not imply that any discussion of behavior change is to be avoided. As a matter of fact, some issues, such as skill deficiencies, disruptive meeting behaviors, and disciplinary actions, can be stated only in behavioral terms. On those occasions where a behavioral focus is warranted, be sure to focus only on the specific behavior that needs changing; don't get into questioning the individual's attitude or personality. Be alert to, and resist, the common tendency to jump immediately to a behaviorally oriented initial statement.

Because of its importance in generating active participation, you should work out the initial disclosure of an issue before the group session. Here is one example that demonstrates the difference between presenting an issue or problem in terms of behaviors and highlighting the situation.

The print shop of a mid-sized city school district consistently misses deadlines. The manager of internal services could present the problem to an employee problem-solving team in *behavioral terms* by asking, "What can be done to motivate you people to work faster?"

In *situational terms*, the manager could ask, "What can be done to improve the efficiency and effectiveness of our print shop operation across our two shifts?"

Behavioral statements tend to be judgmental; they "point the finger" at group members. Situational statements are descriptive and impersonal; they seek to generate collaboration among group members—including the manager.

Present the Issue so that It Encompasses Common Interests

This guideline increases the group members' motivation to embrace the issue at hand, since the effectiveness of a session is influenced by the amount of interest the issue stimulates.

Making an issue appealing means showing group members how they will benefit from taking a hard look at the issue or what they will gain from spending the necessary time to solve a problem. Drawing the members together by emphasizing common interests enhances the likelihood of group cooperation in reaching an acceptable solution that everyone can support. There are at least three powerful ways to present an issue so that it conveys mutual interests.

Degree of Group Control. Emphasizing the degree of control that the group has in resolving the issue is one way to demonstrate mutual interests. Even if the group is split into two or three camps, helping members realize that they have what it takes to solve the problem—or, at the very least, to develop a set of recommendations that will be given full attention by higher management—absolutely will increase the members' motivation to tackle it. The greater the degree of control, the greater the motivation to solve the problem. Having control of one's destiny is a significant motivator.

Returning to our earlier example, the internal services manager could go on to underscore the print shop's degree of control by saying something like, "Improving the efficiency and effectiveness of the print shop is critical to our ability to service the school district. The five of you will have full access to all records. I've made certain that you can talk to anyone, including the superintendent, and I've assigned Dorothy to the project to provide clerical and administrative support. Nothing is sacred about the way we've done things in the past. With 104 years of experience among you, I'm confident that you can do the job. You're our best hope to lick this one."

Fairness. Another approach for creating common interests is to state the problem so that it stresses fairness for all concerned. Volatile issues such as budget cuts, downsizing, reengineering, restructuring, relocation, and merit increase plans can be defused, and motivation built for a collaborative effort, if the issue emphasizes fairness.

Stress fairness with statements similar to this: "Since headquarters has mandated that our division must cut its budget by 10 percent, what would be a fair method for determining who pays what portion of the budget cut?"

Congruence between Personal and Organizational Goals. Setting forth the issue so that the team members' personal goals are congruent with organizational goals is another technique for stimulating interest. For example, the manager could present this issue in the following manner: "The reorganization has caused a five-week slip in our schedule for the introduction of our TOM-67 model boat at the February 1 boat show. How can we recover those weeks? If we make the show, we'll get our bonus."

Initially, Share Only Primary Information

Another ingredient in building an open, collaborative climate is for you to share whatever relevant knowledge and situational facts you have regarding the topic or issue. However, in doing so, you must be careful to supply this information without interpreting it or suggesting how it should be used. The initial information given to the group is critical, since it provides the members with their first impression of what they are undertaking.

This is not a time for hidden agendas. It is a time for stating the facts honestly so that the group will have the best chance of getting off to a good start in attacking the issue. Properly supplying essential information involves the following four considerations, which should be given some forethought prior to the meeting to ensure that you do not inadvertently go overboard with your remarks and carve out "reality" as you believe it to be.

- *Provide background information nonjudgmentally.* Primary historical or background information must be presented in a descriptive, nonevaluative manner and without suggestions as to how the data should be used. Interpretation and evaluation come later, when all members of the group, including yourself, mutually process this information.
- *Present only the information needed to clarify and describe the situation.* This is just the beginning of the group activity. More detailed information can be introduced later in the discussion as the need arises. This prevents overwhelming the group with too much too soon.
- *Set expectations.* Alert the group members to what they should do in order to process the issue. For example, should they simply clarify the data, hold a limited discussion, provide their reactions, generate several alternatives or recommendations, hold an extensive discussion and analyze the problem, solve the problem, make a decision, or do some combination of these alternatives?
- *Delineate the range of freedom.* Inform the group of what it can and cannot do in working the issue. This information is valuable because it provides a perspective on situational constraints and on the group's authority to act on the problem. It curbs the all-too-familiar situation in which the group assumes that it has more latitude than it actually does—and is frustrated when its decisions cannot be put into effect.

In closing, there are no precise rules for determining the amount and type of information that it is essential that you share initially. You will have to make that determination based on the maturity of the group members in combination with the nature of the subject. However, the four points just covered are proven guidelines to help you stay focused while setting the table for the team.

Be Succinct

Less is better. Take no more than 15 minutes to present whatever information you deem necessary, using the 3 previous steps as your outline. If a compelling overview cannot be given within that time, you're probably being too long-winded. Remember, more facts and information can be added as the group session unfolds. Be brief so that the group can get down to its main business: working the issue to achieve the desired outcomes.

The key to being succinct is forethought. My experience indicates that many managers are prone to needlessly long descriptions of situations, issues, and problems because they have not prepared an incisive narrative in advance. Drawn-out initial comments tend to lead to only one thing: confusion. When I help managers plan meetings, I limit their initial stage-setting remarks for an issue to an absolute maximum of 10 minutes and 3 PowerPoint slides.

Thus, to prevent confusion, do your planning homework, have a concise introduction of the issue prepared in advance, present your introduction clearly, and avoid attempts at restating the issue.

Wait!

To initiate a truly collaborative atmosphere, you must resist the greatest temptation of all: influencing the thinking of the group. Using Robert Lefton's term, the manager must avoid becoming a "promotional leader."

> A promotional leader leaks his or her own ideas to subordinates before they've had a chance to state theirs. ("I think we ought to revamp the entire plan, but right now I'd like to hear what you think.") Nothing will do more to stifle discussion and squelch candor. Once people know what the boss thinks, the whole discussion is likely to shift in the direction. . . . [T]eam leaders often use promotional leadership as a subtle means of ensuring that no real discussion takes place. They can make a show of open-mindedness, while guaranteeing that the discussion won't get out of hand. ("I'm absolutely convinced we should close down the Eureka operation, but of course we won't do it until you've had a chance to speak your minds.")[3]

Therefore, the fifth and final guideline for initiating a collaborative climate requires that you stop and hold back your thoughts, perspectives, value judgments, or favored actions.

One reason that you can have trouble holding back has to do with control. At the outset, you are in control of the session. By waiting, you are, in effect, relinquishing full control and sharing it with group members by giving them an opportunity to focus attention on areas that are important to them. The line of discussion generated by the group may be difficult for you to hear, yet these matters may be the very ones that require debate in order to make a high-quality decision that the whole group can support.

From the manager's perspective, holding back does trade off total control for shared control; however, this is one of the keys to initiating a collaborative climate.

Even if you are asked for an opinion early on, you should practice the art of facilitation in a positive manner by saying something like, "Ron, I do have some thoughts as to how we can safely dispose of our hazardous wastes. However, I'm not convinced that I have *the* answer. For now, I prefer to facilitate the rest of the group to be sure that everyone's ideas can be heard without their being influenced by my thoughts. I'll be happy to share my ideas later on, and when I do, remember that they carry no more weight than anyone else's."

As you can see from this example, the leader's views should be woven into the general group discussion as the processing of the information and data unfolds.

Zenger, Folkman, and Edinger, in their book *The Inspiring Leader*, buttress what has been presented in this section:

> [I]nspiring leaders refrain from dominating the conversation. They encourage ideas to come from others in the group rather than being the one who always provides them. The best leaders never speak first on a complex topic unless it is simply to frame the issue. If the leader goes beyond that to express a strong point of view, that most often has a chilling effect on others speaking up and saying what they truly believe. By holding back and speaking at the end, the leader encourages others to speak. They then say what they truly believe. This avoids the frequent posturing that sometimes occurs that is primarily geared toward gaining the approval of the leader.[4]

The recommended approach, then, for initiating an open, collaborative climate requires that you introduce the issue by following the first four guidelines outlined in this section. Subsequently, having done that, you must wait and keep the door open for members to explore the subject matter freely instead of restricting the discussion by masterminding it.

Maintaining an Open, Collaborative Climate

Once an issue for processing has been properly introduced, the nonpromotional, facilitative leader—with solid secondary facilitation support—needs to keep the processing momentum moving along by maintaining the open, collaborative climate. If members are to participate willingly and constructively in a group session, they need to feel that their thoughts, ideas, opinions, and proposals are genuinely wanted and needed by the manager and the rest of the group members. The atmosphere must be such that everyone feels comfortable in putting his viewpoints on the table.

"Feeling comfortable" is not a result of participating in agreeable, superficial, flattering, frictionless meetings that tend toward groupthink. Rather, it is a result of knowing that one's ideas and opinions will be respected and given a fair hearing, and, above all, knowing that *issues* will be attacked—not people.

Group members understand that tough problems and issues require healthy debate, in-depth exploration of pros and cons, constructive criticism, disagreements, and challenges to people's positions. The leader encourages this type of participation because it is the key to the group's critical thinking. Losing even one person's contribution can be unproductive for everyone.

By being patient, using the group task functions of information seeking and opinion seeking to involve all group members, and employing the maintenance behavior of encouraging to recognize constructive participation, you can facilitate a great deal of positive interaction and markedly reduce the chances of missing valuable contributions of group members.

Figure 8-2 shows the circular process between excellent questioning techniques to stimulate contributions and the follow-on positive reinforcement that recognizes team members' constructive participation. This positive reinforcement then engenders increased willingness on the part of other participants to get involved by asking and responding to questions.

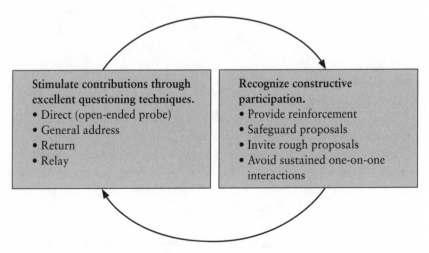

Figure 8-2 Guidelines for Maintaining an Open, Collaborative Climate

The creative momentum of an open, collaborative climate is sustained in group sessions by this ongoing flow between solicitation and recognition.

Stimulate Contributions

Questions are the main tool for information seeking, opinion seeking, and testing comprehension. Questions are a primary force for sustaining a participative climate. Used well, questions can invigorate a group session and help drive it toward the achievement of its stated desired outcomes. Used poorly; they can stop a meeting dead in its tracks.

To stimulate and maintain collaboration, you need to ask questions that are nonthreatening, yet specific enough to bring about a spirited response because they cannot be answered in just two or three words or with a curt yes or no. Closed-end questions, like the ones in the following list, that elicit only cryptic answers do nothing to create collaboration.

"Is floor plan A better than floor plan B?"

"Do you ever read the CEO's monthly *State of the Business* newsletters?"

"In what order would you rank the four candidates to replace Lynn as principal?"

"Is there a possibility of a layoff in our division this year?"

Questions become threatening when they are seen by the recipient as judgmental or personality-focused, or as an attempt to dig for information that the person does not want to divulge. Threatening questions can be perceived as an attack; this brings about defensiveness and the possibility of a counterattack, which can destroy the session.

Frequently, threatening questions seem to press group members to reveal their own inadequacies. Most people don't like to do this, especially in a group setting.

Finally, threatening questions tend to make people feel as if they are getting the "third degree." An excellent tip-off that your questions are perceived as threatening would be guarded, clipped responses that keep coming during a succession of exchanges. These examples are threatening questions that embarrass the participant on the receiving end and are guaranteed to create a frosty, noncollaborative atmosphere.

"How in hell could you have left out the conclusions section of this proposal?"

"Bruce, what excuse do you have this time for being unable to get the packaging problem fixed once and for all?"

"Does anyone else have trouble understanding the three simple alternatives we are attempting to vote on?"

"Do I need to put all your assignments in writing so that you'll know what is expected?"

Good questions raise issues that require an expansion of thought and a consideration of the situation that is being examined. You can produce an open-ended question that requires the receiver to elaborate on the problem or issue at hand if you nonthreateningly use opening phrases or follow-up statements like these: "What do you think about . . . ?" "Tell me about . . ." "Why do you feel . . . ?" "What is your take on . . . ?" "Tell me more." "That's interesting; please elaborate." "Can you amplify that with some examples?"

By simply asking nonjudgmental, open-ended questions, you can orchestrate a rich and highly interactive discussion focused on achieving the desired outcomes. There are four major questioning techniques at your disposal; all four are illustrated with examples of nonjudgmental, open-ended questions to show the potency of good questioning in maintaining an open, collaborative group session.

Direct Question. A direct question is aimed at a specific person to obtain his input into the subject that is being discussed. Direct questions offer an excellent opportunity to use an open-ended probe. The direct question is also used for testing comprehension to ensure that the receiver has understood the content of the speaker's message.

"Dick, what is your take on slipping the schedule by 30 days?"

"Jim, we haven't heard from you yet. What do you think about the mission statement as it stands now?"

"Megan, are you saying that you are not interested in an international assignment unless it is a manager's position and for a maximum of three years?"

General Address Question. This is an open-ended question that is pitched to the whole group so that anyone can volunteer a response. General address questions can spur a great discussion.

"What are we missing here? Is there some angle we haven't yet discussed?"

"What do you think, team—where can we cut expenses in order to fund this item?"

"Is there anything simmering below the surface that we need to talk about?"

Return Question. A return question is one that is returned to the person who asked it. This is especially effective when the person asking the question appears to have more to say than the question indicates.

"Kristen, you asked how to attack the problem; where would you start?"

"Stan, that's an interesting question; what is your analysis of the situation?"

Relay Question. A relay question is one that is deflected to another person. This is an excellent technique for gate-opening for noncontributors or for giving the person who has the data a chance to respond to the question directly.

"Joey, you've been working in distribution for a while; how would you respond to Alyssa's question?"

"Tim, that's a tough question for me to answer. Newt, you're the financial expert; what are your views on the payback issue that Tim has raised regarding the Chadwick project?"

Recognize Constructive Participation

The second dimension that is critical to the maintenance of a collaborative climate is positive reinforcement of constructive participation by each member of the group. This recognition is important because people tend to repeat behaviors that are reinforced. Recognizing members for their involvement in the group session makes it clear that you value their participation and that it does not go unnoticed.

Essentially, positive reinforcement motivates more people to share more ideas and opinions with the whole group. With more information on the table, the group creates a more extensive database, which, in turn, increases its opportunity for building half-developed ideas into realistic solutions.

There are four useful behaviors that you need to practice routinely to increase your effectiveness in recognizing constructive participation.

Provide Reinforcement. The impact of positive reinforcement is strengthened considerably when it is communicated verbally and augmented nonverbally with expressions and gestures. Be certain, however, that the verbal message that you deliver is congruent with your nonverbal cues. If it is not, the reinforcement is ambiguous. Studies have shown that, when faced with ambiguous messages, the receiver typically derives the meaning of the message from the nonverbal cues.

For example, if you are doodling on a legal pad, fidgeting in your chair, and trying to stifle a yawn while you say, "Thanks, Sylvia, for your ideas on correcting the billing problem. I appreciate your contributions; please keep sharing your suggestions with us," Sylvia will conclude that you couldn't care less about her contributions.

To provide the most credible and unambiguous positive reinforcement, you need to fortify your encouraging verbal statements with congruent expressions and gestures. The following examples illustrate the point:

- *Verbal reinforcement:* "Good"; "That's right"; "Thanks, that was very enlightening"; "Excellent point"; "You sure clarified that mess"; "Well said"; "Thanks, that helps"; "I think you're on the right track; tell me more."
- *Augmented by expression:* Smiling, showing a look of interest, or showing a look of concentration.
- *Augmented by gestures:* Giving a positive head nod, leaning forward, giving the "A-OK" sign, or giving a wave of the hand to signal the person to keep talking.

Zenger, Folkman, and Edinger, citing research covering 60 leadership teams performing their annual strategic planning, problem-solving, and budgeting activities, reveal the immense influence that positive reinforcement has on team success:

[A] startling discovery was the one factor that was twice as powerful as anything else in predicting the teams' success was the ratio of positive comments (approval, suggestions, praise, appreciation, compliments, and overall support) to negative comments (pointing out faults, disparagement, criticism, or disapproval). The ratio of positive to negative comments in the highest-performing teams was 5 to 1, in medium performing teams it was just below 2 to 1, and in the lowest-performing teams it was roughly 1 positive for every 3 negative.[5]

Safeguard Proposals. Not every idea or proposal put forth by a group member is going to be worthy of a detailed analysis. However, making sure that proposals and ideas are heard and understood by the whole group is a top priority for any manager who is attempting to mine group gold.

The value of the safeguarding action is threefold. First, it decreases the chance of prematurely rejecting an idea whose merit is not immediately obvious; second, knowing that their propositions will at least be heard and understood encourages group members to offer suggestions more freely; and third, the group can add to an infant idea and ultimately develop it into a mature solution. Remember, a good idea doesn't care who had it!

Without protection, far too many good ideas are squashed. You must constantly be alert for the "idea killers." The difficulty in protecting proposals is that idea killers are so common that they are invoked without anyone, including the manager, ever noticing the damage that is being done to group productivity. Here are some common examples of idea killers:

"We've always done it this way."
"We're not ready for that yet."
"It goes against established policy."
"Don't be ridiculous!"
"It's a good idea, but . . ."
"The higher-ups will never go for it."
"If I thought that would work, I'd have done it six months ago."
"Our business is different."
"I wouldn't go there if I were you."
"No way, not here."
"We've already tried that."
"Let's put it on the shelf for now."
"You're joking, of course."
"That will never work."
"Now that's a career-threatening suggestion if I ever heard one."

Idea killers are really death sentences for ideas—certain death for an idea that goes against the existing way of doing things. Saving ideas from being murdered by actively protecting proposals requires you to be alert for idea killers and intervene when a group member fires one across the table. The intervention should be firm, swift, and simple.

"Whoa, put your guns back in their holsters; there are at least two things about Martin's unique approach that are worthy of further exploration."

"Hold it, please; before we bury Irene's proposal, let's take a few minutes to understand how it might apply."

"Let's not be too hasty; we've covered the negatives, but what about the positive aspects of Hal's idea?"

Invite Rough Proposals. This activity is closely aligned with the previous one. As facilitator, you cannot afford to have people holding back because their proposition is hazy in their own minds. If you wait for, or only accept, fully developed and well-thought-out ideas, many viable proposals and solutions may never surface. Whenever you get a sense that a group member has something to propose but seems reluctant to do so, or when a person starts and stops a proposal because she feels that it is an inferior one, that is the time to be a gold miner.

"Teddy, a rough idea often sprouts into a big idea; we want to hear your whole proposal so that we can take a crack at improving it."

"Don't worry about not having everything buttoned up, Anne; your input is invaluable."

"Ryan, maybe you don't have the final answer, but let's hear what your idea is, since it may move us that much closer to a solution."

Avoid Sustained One-on-One Interactions. Fundamental to the facilitation process is the precept that you are facilitating a group, not one or two people. The job of the facilitator is to involve everyone present in the achievement of the group's desired outcomes. The bulk of the dialogue must be among the group members, not a sequence of one-on-one exchanges between you and just one or two of your team members.

Getting involved in a prolonged facilitator-to-participant dialogue can sidetrack the session hopelessly, cause other members to tune out, and bias the direction of the entire session. This is especially true if the person who is interacting with you has a great deal of authority or influence.

You must direct the discussion in such a way that it is shared by the entire group. The following techniques help accomplish this goal:

- Disengage with the participant who is attempting a one-on-one dialogue by looking away or shifting your body position.

- Ask general address questions and encourage input from a variety of people.
- Use relay questions from you to other group members. This is an especially good technique because it breaks the participant-to-facilitator link and brings in another group member.
- Ask direct questions aimed at nonparticipants.
- Be candid; clarify your role. Say something like, "I want to take a moment to remind everybody that while I'm facilitating, my role is to stay tuned to the group process and reduce obstacles to good group functioning. I'm not the central communication hub. I'm not heavily involved in information processing."

If you need to add to the content of the discussion or challenge the ideas or opinions of others, you must "switch hats" to do so, and then return to the role of facilitator. Long dialogues with one or two people typically occur when you are swept up in the content of the session and forget to move back into the facilitation role to break off the discussion.

Conclude Along the Way

The final major action for maintaining an open, collaborative climate is to conclude along the way. Each significant conclusion that can be made along the information-processing journey acts as a "success marker." It signifies progress and motivates further participation by group members.

Therefore, don't wait until the session's wrap-up to summarize and generate conclusions for the first time. Besides the motivational aspect, the productivity of a group session can be increased if the manager, working from the facilitator's role, helps the group reach conclusions throughout the session.

The task behavior of summarizing is an activity that should be performed repeatedly as progress is made through the agenda. Developing summarized conclusions along the way is important because it keeps the discussion focused. Summarizing cuts down on confusion and on the tendency to wander off into irrelevancies. Also, if you wait until the end of the session to summarize everything, the sheer volume of information that is processed during most meetings makes developing meaningful conclusions very difficult, if not impossible. You should facilitate a conclusion as follows:

- After each topic, agenda item, or task is brought to a close
- Periodically as a long and complex topic is being addressed

- Any time there is a question about what has been decided
- Just before a decision is to be made, to set the stage for the decision-making process
- Just after the decision is made, to ensure that everyone understands what was decided

The method for facilitating a conclusion will vary, depending on the topic and the desired outcome. There are several options open to you for managing the periodic conclusion process:

- The person responsible for the minutes can be asked to read aloud her notes regarding the item or task that was just finished. Check this with the group to make sure that everyone is in accord.
- A volunteer from the group can be asked to provide his thoughts about the topic's conclusion. Ask the rest of the group members if they agree.
- Acting as a facilitator, state your sense of the discussion and the conclusions that were reached. Ask the group members if they concur.

Throughout an ongoing meeting the final conclusion for any agenda item that is being brought to a close should be written on a flip chart by the scribe, checked with the group to make sure that the wording is correct and complete, and posted on the wall for later reference.

A Final Word

Chapter 8 set forth the center-line process for facilitating any group session. After completing the start-up activities, the hard-core meeting action then takes place during the move-out phase. It would be terrific if all you had to do as a facilitator was roll through the center-line scenario, practicing tools and processes for initiating an open, collaborative climate; maintaining an open, collaborative climate; and concluding along the way.

While this may happen on some occasions, there will be other times when you are pulled off the center-line into the weeds and have to contend with disruptive behaviors on the part of some group members, conflict among a few others, confusion among another subset, and/or strong feelings from a few more. Don't despair; there are some sound practices for dealing with all of these, which will be covered in Chapters 9 and 10.

WORKSHEET

Develop written responses to the two items listed below.

1. What do you feel are the main learning points from Chapter 8?

   — Paur of fire only

   — Avoid idea kills

   — Acto Be a Playacts Advocte

2. Elaborate on why you feel these points are key for you.

   — Use of fire um

   — Dont stop the momvm

Notes

1. A. J. Melcher, *Structure and Process of Organizations: A Systems Approach* (Englewood Cliffs, N.J.: Prentice-Hall, 1976), p. x.
2. This section builds on the classic work of N. R. F. Maier, *Problem Solving Discussions and Conferences: Leadership Methods and Skills* (New York: McGraw-Hill, 1963), pp. 74–97. See also F. C. Miner, Jr., who presents his Problem Centered Leadership (PCL) research findings in the article "A Comparative Analysis of Three Diverse Decision Making Approaches," *Academy of Management Journal* 22, no. 1 (1979), pp. 81–93.
3. R. E. Lefton, "Communication: The Eight Barriers to Teamwork," *Personnel Journal*, January 1988, p. 18.
4. J. H. Zenger, J. R. Folkman, and S. Edinger, *The Inspiring Leader: Unlocking the Secrets of How Extraordinary Leaders Motivate* (New York: McGraw-Hill, 2009), p. 143.
5. Ibid., p. 139.

Chapter 9

Facilitating Disruption, Differences, and Confusion: Keeping the Gold Mine Productive in the Face of Obstacles

CHAPTER OBJECTIVE

- To discuss facilitation concepts and provide tips and techniques for handling disruptive behavior, differences, and confusion effectively when they arise in group sessions.

Introduction

Again, go back to Figure 4-1 and look at the "map to the gold mine." It is a fact of facilitation life that you will run into problematic group situations that take you beyond the center-line design. This chapter covers three very common occurrences: disruptive behaviors on the part of one or more group members, differences between two or more teammates that start to become destructive, and confusion regarding "where are we going?" and/or "what should we be doing?" The final troublesome area, facilitating feelings, will be covered in Chapter 10.

Every meeting will have a mix of personalities. Very few sessions are made up entirely of people with the same behavioral characteristics; in addition, depending on the nature of the issue, its impact on each person, and a host of other factors, people vary their behavior throughout a meeting. Thus, as the session flows on, an individual can move from being quiet to being argumentative; another can shift from being helpful to being confused; someone else can change from being alert and involved to being disruptive or indifferent. Two members may be upset by what happened in the previous meeting that they attended; another may be preoccupied with an impending job offer. The combinations are endless. Doyle and Straus vividly portray meeting personalities as jungle animals:

> Sometimes as you stand in front of an energetic group, you can feel as if you are standing in the middle of a jungle path with all kinds of animals rushing to a water hole. Loud, assertive beasts are pushing their way past others; sleek, speedy animals dart back and forth; timid animals wait with watchful eyes for a chance to move without being crushed. And then there are the fierce animals, more hungry rather than thirsty, ready to leap upon the unsuspecting fellow traveler.[1]

Operating as primary facilitator, you have the task of keeping all these animals, regardless of their personalities or present dispositions, working together toward the achievement of the session's desired outcomes. You should not expect, or even attempt, to change people's personalities; on the other hand, you must influence their behavior.

Dealing with Disruptive Behavior

Experience shows that much of the disruptive behavior in group sessions is unintentional. For slight indiscretions that occur only occasionally and don't put the group's effectiveness or productivity in jeopardy, the best policy is to let them slide. When a negative behavior requires confrontation, you'll have to correct the behavior without embarrassing the person, creating an uncomfortable scene, or inhibiting collaboration.

Disruptive behaviors take many forms: rambling, arguing, gate-closing, dominating, side conversations, and more. These dysfunctional behaviors may occur because preparation for the group session has been inadequate or because facilitation is slipshod. Your upfront clarification of the purpose and desired outcomes, along with a close rein on the agenda, will help keep the group focused on tasks and reduce disruptive behaviors.

General Guidelines

Even with careful preparation, some troublesome behaviors may crop up. It is often possible to help difficult group members channel their energies in more productive directions. Here are a few general techniques to help facilitate disruptive behavior.

Firm but Friendly Confrontation. Because a lot of dysfunctional behavior is unintentional, dealing with the problem is not as difficult or as threatening as it might seem at first glance. Many times, calling attention to the behavior in a firm but friendly manner is all that is required. To confront a bothersome individual effectively, use the following little three-step process, which provides a simple, highly effective method for handling most situations.

1. Zero in on the negative behaviors; do not label or classify the individual. Personal labeling leads to defensiveness and provides the ingredients for an emotional explosion.
2. Highlight the impact that the disruptive behavior is having on the group. As mentioned earlier, many times the offending person is totally unaware of the problem that his behavior is causing. Once he is made aware of the negative impact that he is having on the session, the person is only too happy to stop.
3. Suggest different, more functional behaviors. This gives the disruptive person an easy way to save face by steering him in a direction that will lead to more productive contributions.

These three guidelines can easily be incorporated into a concise statement that confronts the offender without attacking or belittling him.

"Jacob, continually evaluating the group's ideas while we're brainstorming slows us down and discourages others from being totally open with their ideas. There will be plenty of time in our next session for everyone to analyze what we're coming up with here. Please hold your evaluations until then."

"Marcia, using your BlackBerry in this meeting is distracting to me and I'm sure to others. We need you to be mentally present and actively involved in contributing your ideas for fixing this software glitch. You'll have time during our break to handle your other business."

Move swiftly on after making your point. The last thing you want is to make it seem to be a point-scoring session, where you become the winner and the difficult person becomes the humiliated loser. All this will do is cause the difficult person to ratchet up her disruptive behavior to an even more extreme level. In confronting counterproductive behavior, model a direct, firm, but friendly style that group members can emulate.

Encourage Shared Responsibility for Handling Difficult Members. In the spirit of secondary facilitation, if the group is encouraged to share the responsibility for successful facilitation, negative behaviors will decrease. Peer pressure, especially when it emanates from several different people, is a major deterrent to disruptive group behavior. Group censure puts pressure on disruptive members to modify and control their behaviors to meet the group's behavioral norms.

Use Nonverbal Cues. Making eye contact, sending a glance of dissatisfaction, moving in close, placing a hand on someone's shoulder, stopping in mid-sentence, and giving a negative head nod are all ways to communicate displeasure nonverbally and halt disruptive behavior.

Acknowledge Acceptable Behavior. Try to catch the person doing something right. People often engage in disruptive behavior to draw attention to themselves; to some extent, this behavior can be altered through positive reinforcement. The power of positive reinforcement was shown in Chapter 7 to be a major driver of high team performance. This process takes time; you won't see a dramatic improvement in a short period. Still, watch for acceptable behavior and comment on it; people tend to repeat behaviors that are encouraged.

"Excellent point, Karl. I agree that we should put the artwork out for bid rather than accepting the price from our internal art services group. By the way, thanks for being on time today so that you were here to share your ideas on this. If you hadn't been here, we might have made a costly mistake."

Talk Privately with Repeat Offenders. If these techniques fail to keep disruptive behavior from being repeated, a private conference is in order. A one-on-one discussion, where you present your concerns and hear the disruptive member's views, provides a confidential forum to discuss feelings and needs and to work out an acceptable solution.

Use the three-step firm but friendly confrontation approach for this discussion, and remember to focus on the behavior, not the person's personality or past history. This strategy preserves the member's sense of dignity and conserves precious session time.

Handling Specific Problems

The Late Arriver. When they arrive late, some people make a grand entrance, while others try to be as unobtrusive as possible. In either case, there is disruption: the door is opened, someone moves through the room, people have to clear space at the table, a jacket is removed and hung on the back of a chair, a briefcase is snapped open and shut, papers are shuffled. The momentum of the meeting has been interrupted. *If it is a rare occurrence, ignore it.*

To be able to censure late arrivers, however, you must be disciplined about starting your meetings on time. Build a reputation for prompt starts. If you do, people will know that when you say 9:30, you mean 9:30, not 9:40 or 9:50! They will put forth a greater effort to be on time, and those who come in after the start time will *always* know that they will be late.

If the person is a chronic latecomer, don't confront him when he enters the room or publicly during the meeting. During a break or after the session, ask the person why he is late so frequently. Don't lecture or talk down to the person. Follow the three steps of the firm, but friendly, confrontation model presented earlier.

Never stop your meeting and review what has taken place up to that point in order to bring the latecomer up to date. This only reinforces the lateness habit: "Why be on time? I can come late and still not miss anything." Instead, simply mention the topic being discussed, point to any flip-chart notes on the wall, and provide any handouts that the others have. Say something like, "Sam, while you quietly review the flip charts and the handout, I'm going to continue facilitating the group discussion."

If the person is central to the information processing and a review of foregoing information is essential, call a break and do it quickly. Try to avoid using the whole group's time for the benefit of one or two people.

Talk about lateness with the whole group. See if shared values can be built around being on time. Help the group decide how it wants to deal with latecomers (many groups develop a schedule of fines based on the number of minutes late).

When a person is late for the second or third time in a row, use the silence technique. As the individual enters, pause, look at the person until she gets settled, then pick up the discussion right at the point where you were interrupted. Afterward, confront the person privately and work out a mutually acceptable solution to correct the chronic lateness problem or drop the person from your meeting.

The Rambler. This individual talks about everything except the subject, uses far-fetched analogies, or gets lost. Sometimes rambling is referred to as "shooting from the lip." It steals meeting time and bores everyone. Thank the person, and then refocus attention by asking him how his point(s) relate to the topic at hand. This allows for self-discovery and reduces the chance of a repeat performance.

Restate the urgency of the objectives and the time constraints. Smile and say, "Your point is interesting, but (while pointing to a flip chart, transparency, whiteboard, or the screen) we do seem to be a bit off the subject. We'd better get back to item three on the agenda, which has a desired outcome of . . ." Or deflect the discussion until the break by saying, "That's an interesting idea. Can you hold it until the break? We'll have more time to discuss it then. Right now, we have to cover these two remaining points."

The Chronic Objector. This person may be an argumentative, combative personality, a self-appointed devil's advocate, or someone who is normally good-natured but is upset by something external to the session.

Keep your own temper firmly in check, be patient, and listen. If the individual thinks that you're not taking her comments into consideration, she will be encouraged to continue the argument—often with greater intensity. So, honestly try to find merit in one of the person's points, express your agreement, then move on to something else.

Sometimes you can make light of the person's remarks; don't be sarcastic, but say something like, "Well, Joel, I can see you aren't taking any hostages today!"

If the combatant continues to push an argument, toss it to the group: ask the other members if they think the topic is worth pursuing, and let them turn it down. Say something like: "How many others share Nick's view and want to pursue it?" Unless everyone is moved by the subject, the lack of interest should stop the argumentative disruption.

Ask the person to make a positive recommendation. "Erin, you've given us a number of reasons for not recruiting at junior colleges. I'd also like to hear you present a couple of advantages."

As a last resort, talk to the offender during a break; see if you can win the person's cooperation or uncover the real issue. Use the firm but friendly confrontation model presented earlier.

The Dominator. This person may be naturally garrulous or a show-off. He also may be exceptionally well informed and anxious to let others know it or may be the most senior person in attendance. If members value what the talkative one is saying and recognize that the person's monopoly of the discussion is temporary, there's no need to intervene.

However, dominators tend to be vocal, full of the "right" answers, and quick to jump to conclusions. Don't let them get a solid foothold in the session. If they do, they will steal "air time," intimidate some group members, stimulate a confrontation with others, or wage personal attacks that distract the team from its goals.

Supportively acknowledge the dominator, then immediately include another individual. Say something like, "I can understand how you feel," or "That's one view of it." Then, after making the supportive statement, actively bring in another group member: "Anna, what are your thoughts on this issue?"

Thank the person for her contribution to the issue and state that you would like to hear what others in the session have to say. Say something like: "It's important to the success of this discussion that we hear from everyone in the group. Please give others a chance to share their ideas."

The Gate Closer. This person may be excited, full of ideas, or a poor listener. Most people are unaware of their gate-closing tendencies and do not do it intentionally or cruelly.

Say to the person who was gate-closed, "Pam, I feel you were just shut out. Would you please continue?" Or say to the person who did the gate closing, "Gordon, please hold it a second; Greg was making his point. When he finishes, I'll get back to you." Then go back to Greg and ask him to continue.

Side Conversations. These spring up when people in close proximity to each other feel a need to talk because they are bored, suddenly have an idea, have been repeatedly gate-closed, or are excited about a point but can't get "air time."

Pause. Look at the offenders. If one of the offenders is seated nearby, place a gentle hand on the person's arm or shoulder.

Directly involve one of the talkers in the whole-group discussion. Say something like, " Polly, what are some other benefits to staying open until 9:30 on Wednesday nights?"

Confront the situation directly. Say something like: "Al, Diane, could we please have one meeting? Judith has the floor."

The Quiet Member. A quiet individual could be bored, indifferent, aloof, timid, or insecure. One person's silence can cause unrest within the group when it becomes noticeable, especially if the other group members are actively participating. Silence also is counterproductive because potentially good ideas are being withheld from the group.

If the person is bored or indifferent, arouse his interest by asking for his opinion. Or draw out the individual next to the quiet person, then ask the quiet person to summarize the points and add his views on the topic.

If you're dealing with someone who feels above it all, ask for her input after indicating the respect you have for the individual's experience. "Nikki, I know you did an awful lot of strategic planning when you worked for Putnam. How can we improve the key economic assumptions we've formulated for next year's operating plan?" However, don't overuse this technique, or the rest of the group will resent it. You also can tweak this superior type by tossing a provocative query his way to see what reaction you get.

If a group member is timid or insecure and is sitting nearby, ask the person a question that can be answered easily. This safely includes the quiet person and makes her more comfortable because the interaction is with the facilitator, not with the group as a whole. Watch for the first time a particularly sensitive person speaks *up*, and then compliment her on joining the discussion. Be sincere!

Finally, institute a round-robin technique a couple of times during the session, where everyone is asked to give his views in rotation around the table. This doesn't look as if you are singling out the quiet ones, but they will be expected to have a say when it's their turn.

The Inarticulate Speaker. This individual finds it difficult to put her thoughts into proper words. She has an idea, but she can't convey it. Assistance is required.

Don't say, "What you mean is this: . . ." Say, "Let me repeat that." Then, put it in better language. Bend the person's ideas only enough to have them make sense, and then test comprehension by asking the person, "Did I get it right?"

Off-the-Wall Comments. These occur when a member, for shock value, adamantly makes a statement that is obviously incorrect. Don't challenge the statement directly; this will only rev up the person and take the meeting on an unwanted tangent. Say, "I can see how you feel," or "That's one way of looking at it." Move the meeting along by stating, "Your point is an interesting one. Who else has thoughts on our cost-benefit analysis?"

Managing Differences

Anyone who facilitates a group session will most likely be dealing with a diversity of facts and opinions. This is a normal and essential dynamic of group sessions. If all members' approaches, perspectives, and values were the same, there would be little need for group decisions at all; certainly there would be virtually no need for facilitation. The very idea of facilitation, in fact, assumes that there will be divergent ideas, opinions, and proposals for solving a common problem, reaching a goal, or making a decision.

Effectively getting the most that a group has to offer requires that the manager never lose sight of a fundamental point: conflict, in and of itself, is neither good nor bad. Whether conflict enhances critical thinking and productivity or undercuts it will depend on how you facilitate the differences at hand. In essence, your challenge is to encourage diversity of thought without encouraging personal conflict—to harness the constructive power of differences without igniting their destructive power.

Differences as a Constructive Force

There are four good reasons for encouraging "fruitful friction" among members of a group as they process information during a group session.

1. *Critical thinking is stimulated.* When an individual or a contingent challenges the direction of a group or takes exception to a proposal that has been offered, the group is forced to reexamine its own beliefs in some detail and to reconsider previously ignored or skimmed-over aspects of the issue.
2. *Innovation and creativity are sparked.* When people are in conflict over acceptable alternatives, this diversity can motivate the group members to work out new and creative alternatives that can be supported by everyone.
3. *Group stagnation is minimized.* Contrary opinions and ideas increase the breadth and depth of each member's understanding of the subject.
4. *Healthy debate and discussion are energizing.* The excitement and energy that spring from interpersonal differences can increase the

motivation and involvement of group members in tackling the task at hand.

Differences as a Destructive Force

Disagreements and differences are destructive when they paralyze the group's ability to realize its desired outcomes. There are four reasons why this cannot be tolerated.

1. *"Winners" are produced at the expense of "losers."* A win-lose situation is individual selfishness manifesting itself in a group. People's energies are directed toward each other in an adversarial atmosphere of total victory versus total defeat. Execution of "the winning decision" is a constant struggle or even impossible because of the active or passive resistance that the "losers" creatively employ.

2. *Polarization is fostered.* In a destructive mode, conflict does not produce "fruitful friction." Instead, opposing opinions cause members to defend their ideas rather than modify them. "Getting my own way" becomes more important than discovering the ramifications of, and the solution for, the group's current dilemma.

3. *Energy is consumed unproductively.* Preparing for battle takes time and effort. In addition, alternately defending one's own position and attacking the opponent's stance in the heat of controversy drains energy from the combatants. This energy is being siphoned off in an internal "we-they" fight rather than being harnessed in a cooperative undertaking of "us against the problem."

4. *A short-term orientation takes hold.* At the destructive level, group members become conflict-oriented (stressing the here-and-now differences) rather than being relationship-oriented (accentuating the long-term consequences of their differences and the methods of resolving them).

Telltale Signs of Constructive Differences versus Destructive Differences

Both you, as primary facilitator, and all team members, as secondary facilitators, need to be aware of the telltale signs of constructive versus destructive differences highlighted in Table 9-1. When differences are constructive, they need to be encouraged because they are the source of alternatives to a decision. Differences are needed to stimulate the imagination, to develop the creative solution, and to get away from the foolish idea that there is only one right decision.

Signals or Cues Indicating Constructive Differences	Signals or Cues Indicating Destructive Differences
High team spirit and a mutual commitment to the desired outcomes remain at center stage.	Members start resorting to personal attacks instead of focusing on the facts and issues.
The task behavior of disagreement zeros in on issues, not people.	These initial personal attacks produce a whole series of attack/ defend spirals that rob the session of its productivity.
The task behaviors of testing comprehension and summarizing are used by everyone to ensure that everyone's viewpoints are understood—even though they may not be supported.	Emotionally charged one-upmanship or the same negative statements presented again and again by the same people is a sure sign of unmanaged and ruinous conflict.
Participants respond to what others are actually saying, not what they think others are saying.	Members do not listen to what others are saying, but rather react to what they think others are saying.
The discussion stays on topic and focuses on achieving the desired outcomes.	Members dig in with unyielding attachment to their own ideas and refuse to seriously explore the merits of other proposals.
Time and energy are willingly spent on modifying ideas and alternatives because members know that this produces better results than any one person could produce alone.	When ideas that go against the majority viewpoint are challenged or criticized, the presenter quickly withdraws under pressure.

Table 9-1 Comparison Chart

Regarding the value of dissenting voices, Heifetz, Grashow, and Linsley argue that these voices must be listened to and understood:

> The voices of dissent . . . are valuable for implementing adaptive change because they are canaries in the coal mine, early warning systems. . . . [T]hey have the uncanny capacity for asking the really tough questions that you have been unwilling to face up to yourself or that others have been unwilling to raise. In many organizations, dissenters get marginalized, silenced, or even fired, which deprives the organization of their valuable,

if unpopular service. . . . [You] protect dissenters by taking
them seriously and listening to them, trying to find the useful
insights in what they're saying without necessarily endorsing
their perspective.[2]

On the other hand, when dissent and disagreement head down the
destructive path, this needs to be recognized and facilitated against immediately to prevent a toxic environment from erupting that destroys the collaborative spirit and interpersonal relationships of the team and shatters
its ability to operate as a dynamic body achieving its desired outcomes.

Managing Differences Effectively

So, when strong differences do crop up that threaten to tear the group
apart or wreck an important decision that needs to be made, how can the
constructive power of dissent be maximized and its destructive effects be
minimized?

The key to managing differences effectively is first to understand where
people are coming from and then to work to resolve areas of diversity.
Differences frequently seem bigger than they really are because in collaborative group sessions, a lot of time is spent discussing different viewpoints and disagreements. Often the group loses sight of both the common
goals and areas where there is agreement. The following process can help
correct the situation by fostering consensus.

Clarify Interests. Start by asking the participants to think about what
they are interested in achieving with respect to the issue in question. Stay
away from positions; emphasize the need to think about interests. Next,
hold a period of silence so that people can collect their thoughts and make
a few notes.

Then, go around the room round-robin fashion and ask each person in
turn to share his interests concerning the issue that is being examined; have
the scribe record all of the perspectives on a flip chart. As the scribe notes
each one, check back with the originator to be sure that the statement is
accurate.

It's possible to have as many different viewpoints as there are members
of the group; however, it is more common to have conflict among several
subgroups of people who share common interests. Remember, stay away
from positions. Get people to talk about their interests—what are they
interested in achieving and why. Interests lie behind positions. It is the
interests that are clashing. If you clarify and understand the interests,
you'll take a huge step toward working through the differences.

Define Areas of Agreement. Ask members to read all of the "interest statements" and help itemize the areas of agreement or synergy among interests. The scribe compiles a list of the areas of agreement on flip-chart pages as the group develops them. Give verbal recognition to any person who demonstrates clear thinking and/or leadership during the agreement definition activity.

As an aid to carrying out this exercise effectively, first sort out common areas for agreement around these six dimensions. Experience shows that if you start with the following checklist, you will uncover several dimensions where agreement substantially exists:

- *Goals.* What end result is the group trying to accomplish?
- *Roles.* Who can, or should, do what?
- *Procedures.* What tools, techniques, methods, or systems should be used for doing things (accomplishing goals, managing changes, solving problems, making decisions, and so on)?
- *Relationships.* How will people relate to, and communicate with, one another?
- *Limits.* What is or is not possible?
- *Timing.* When should things be accomplished or decided?

This is not an exhaustive list; therefore, the group should add other areas that it feels are important. The main task, however, is to search for agreements or synergy among several common areas of interest, no matter how simple.

Define Areas of Disagreement. Next, ask the group to sort out the major points of disagreement among the stated interests. These are noted on a flip chart by the scribe.

Specifying the points of contention will advance all team members' understanding of the situation because then they can see the "essence of the difference." It makes the disagreement more objective by moving it out of the context of feelings, subjectivity, and emotionalism. Also, defining the areas of disagreement moves the problem from the realm of something that is nebulous and unmanageable to the realm of something of substance that is manageable.

Use the same checklist of common areas (goals, roles, procedures, and so on) given earlier as a focal point for defining areas of disagreement. For example, it may become evident that while the group members are in agreement about what end result they are interested in accomplishing (goal), who is to do what (roles), and what is and is not possible (limits), the group has very diverse interests regarding the specific methods for carrying out the task (procedures), and they are split on when key decisions need to be made (timing). This organized process makes it much easier to understand and resolve a difference because the issue has been stripped to the bone.

Uncover the Sources of the Differences, then Resolve the Differences. With the differences plainly articulated, you can engage the group in the task of finding the sources of these differences. For example, have they arisen because of disparate facts, conflicting priorities, contrary values, divergent assumptions, misunderstandings, uncertainty about some aspect of the issue, or something else?

Once the sources have been identified, the group should figure out what steps need to be taken to put an end to the differences. Resolve the least important differences first, in order to gain momentum and confidence that the differences can be dealt with. Don't waste in-session meeting time trying to resolve differences that are extraneous to the group discussion. Set those aside and handle them outside the session. Above all, do not waste any time, inside or outside the session, dealing with differences over aspects of the situation that are mandated or otherwise beyond the group's control.

Reducing Confusion

Groups can get lost in the problems that they are trying to solve. At any time during the processing of information, a group can become confused about what the real issues are, where the group is headed, what it is trying to decide, and the like. A course of action that is clear and simple to six members may be fuzzy and complex to four others. On occasion, the entire group may have difficulty locating its position after it has decided where it wants to go and has begun the journey to get there. In these instances, the facilitator will have to intervene and deal with the group's impending disarray.

Confusion is a serious problem in groups because of the relationship between people's self-orientation and their feelings. Some people feel uncertain and anxious if they don't know where they are. Others may feel that they are making no progress when, in fact, they are. Still others may feel that they are adrift on a sea of muddled thinking.

Confusion has a debilitating effect on group productivity. You should step in to restore focus and direction whenever you sense that the discussion is going around in circles or is splintered in several directions. Verbal cues such as, "Why are we here?" "What are we discussing?"

"What are we trying to decide?" or "What is the objective of this discussion?" are clear signals that it's time to reorient the group. To reduce confusion, stop the group activity and use the maintenance behavior of performance checking. This allows the group members to pause and concentrate their attention on affirming what they are attempting to do and clarifying what they are *not* trying to do.

There are two types of confusion that can clutch a group. *Type A confusion* arises when the group, after determining its desired outcomes and starting on the journey to get there, loses sight of what it originally set out to accomplish. *Type B confusion* materializes when the group gets entangled in the various processes and procedures that it is trying to use.

Type A Confusion: "Where Are We Going?"

The cornerstone for managing this type of confusion is for you to have clearly defined desired outcomes contained in the PDORA document or written on flip-chart pages and posted for all to see.

By putting in place an agreed-upon reference point that describes where the group wants to be after it has worked through a particular topic, you have a focal point to refer to at any time when it is necessary to remind participants of the desired outcomes and get a drifting discussion back on course. If outcomes are clearly stated and posted, Type A confusion can be eliminated in almost every case.

Occasionally, because of the nature of the information that is being shared and processed, the group may decide to alter its course partway through the discussion. Then you should call for a performance check to get the group to redefine the desired outcomes and post them for future reference.

Type B: "What Should We Be Doing?"

Once a group has decided on its destination, it can become so involved in getting there that it gets lost on the way. When the group becomes entangled in the processes that it is using to solve a problem, you need to halt the activity temporarily with a performance check.

After calling for a time-out, ask each person to state what he thinks the group should or should not be doing. As thoughts are volunteered, the information is written on a flip chart by the scribe (see Figure 9-1).

Once all the statements have been captured on flip-chart pages and posted for everyone to review, specific questions (especially those of

Our Group SHOULD Be Working on . . .	Our Group SHOULD NOT Be Working on . . .
Which category of solutions looks best right now	[How the selected criteria will be weighted]
Which criteria we will use to select a final solution	How to implement the solution
How the selected criteria will be weighted	Making a final decision on which solution to implement
etc. etc.	etc. etc.

Figure 9-1 Keeping Your Group Process on Track

clarification) regarding any of the items are taken up. This clarifying step is needed to ensure group understanding of the information on both lists.

When the statements are clear, the whole group examines both lists and identifies any items that appear in both lists. Those that are included on both sides need to be discussed by the entire group. By mutual consent, the group decides on which side of the chart each item belongs. Put brackets around the duplicate item that is eliminated.

Finally, the points on the "should be working on" list are summarized to refocus the group.

For many facilitators, facing up to wheel spinning and working with the group to remedy it can appear to be an impossible task. Attempting to reduce confusion without a road map will demonstrate that a great deal of time can be consumed with nothing to show for the effort. Recognizing which type of confusion the group is dealing with and taking the actions recommended here will greatly diminish the burden of reducing group confusion.

Closing Comments

The techniques presented in this and the other chapters are intended as guides; they are not rigid prescriptions. Some techniques may come naturally to you, while others may require more practice and work. There is nothing magical about them; it's simply a matter of trying them, assessing how things went, making modifications wherever appropriate, and then practicing the behaviors again.

To help you in this endeavor—to move you from book learning to actual practice and use of these behaviors in your job environment—a set of ground rules for conducting your group sessions following the Mining Group Gold system and principles is shown in Table 9-2. These ground rules provide behavioral norms for everyone to follow in order to have more successful meetings.

To put the ground rules into practice, review this list and talk it over with your team. It will be most helpful if all your team members have read *Mining Group Gold* so that they understand the rationale and methodology behind the ground rules that are being discussed. You may decide to use this whole list as your set of ground rules, or you may decide initially to create a smaller set of ground rules by picking and choosing from these items, then expanding your list to encompass more behaviors over time. Either way is fine. The important thing is to have some set of agreed-upon ground rules that all team members will honor as a means of maximizing team meeting effectiveness.

OUR TEAM'S GROUND RULES TO MINE GROUP GOLD		
Start-Up	**Move-Out**	**Wrap-Up**
We will:	*We will:*	*We will:*
Arrive on time.	Show respect for the agenda, but remain flexible.	Conduct a meeting assessment at the close of every session.
Turn off all cell phones, laptops, PDAs, and pagers.	Call for a process check and ask, "What is the best use of our team's time right now?" whenever we see that time on an IP item is running out and we haven't achieved the desired outcome.	Review all decisions that were made, all action items that were assigned, the "parking lot," and any postponed agenda items at the end of every meeting.
Live by PDORA: have a stated purpose, desired outcome(s), four mandatory roles, and an agenda with clock times.	Use a "parking lot"—a separate flip-chart page for collecting information that is important but is not germane to the topic that is currently being processed.	Get our meeting minutes out to all team members within one working day of the meeting's conclusion.
Note each agenda item as either Information sharing (IS) Information discussion (ID) Information processing (IP)	Stimulate contributions by actively seeking information or opinions from others in a sincere manner, using open-ended questions.	Exchange relevant information with any nonattendees who have a need to know.
Use a scribe to record information on flip charts when needed.	Test our comprehension when we are unsure about what was being said.	
Emphasize secondary facilitation because everyone is responsible for creating a successful meeting.	"Open the gate" to bring in quiet or nonparticipating individuals.	
Do an agenda review and provide clarification before heading into the Move-Out phase.		

constructive participation of others to
maintain an open, collaborative climate and
keep people involved.

Summarize and note all decisions and action
items along the way.

Do our best not to be a disruptive meeting
member, but when a person is disruptive, we
all share responsibility for dealing with it.

Welcome and foster constructive differences
as the key to our critical thinking, while
always being alert to facilitate against the
destructive side.

Be flexible in our thinking and our search for
options because we believe that our collective
wisdom produces better ideas than solo or
dictated thinking—we always want the best
solution to win.

Utilize the "feelings, facts, solutions" process
model to help us deal with emotion that
threatens to derail our session.

Table 9-2 Mining Group Gold Ground Rules for Maximizing Meeting Effectiveness

---

WORKSHEET

Develop written responses to the two items listed below.

1. What do you feel are the main learning points from Chapter 9?

~ Grand rule for a motor

~ Commitment to objective

_____

_____

_____

2. Elaborate on why you feel these points are key for you.

~ Notes summary for late person

~ Keep motion moving / And decision

_____

_____

_____

Notes

1. M. Doyle and D. Straus, *How to Make Meetings Work* (New York: Berkley Publishing Group, 1976), p. 105.
2. R. Heifetz, A. Grashow, and M. Linsley, *Adaptive Leadership: The Practice of Mobilizing People to Tackle Tough Challenges and Thrive* (Boston: HBR Press, 2009), pp. 145–146.

Chapter 10

FACILITATING FEELINGS: KEEPING THE GOLD MINE PRODUCTIVE IN THE FACE OF EMOTIONS

CHAPTER OBJECTIVES

- To present a process model and a set of basic how-to tips and techniques for facilitating the feelings portion of the "feelings, facts, solutions" sequence.
- To underscore the disruptive role that feelings can play during a group session.
- To stress the need to deal with feelings when they arise and not to ignore them.

Introduction

Few things in a facilitator's tool kit are more important than an understanding of this simple sequence of group behavior: *feelings, facts, solutions.* This progression originally was set forth years ago by George Strauss and Leonard Sayles[1] to describe the three major stages of the nondirective interview. This sequence also has direct application to groups because it provides the correct succession for the facilitation of feelings. Once again, a look back at Figure 4-1 shows "feelings" as the fourth behavior issue requiring attention.

Figure 10-1 gives you the full process model that will be examined throughout this chapter. While all aspects of the model will be talked about, the focus of Chapter 10 will be on the model's "Processing Feelings" element, which emphasizes tips and techniques for facilitating through a "feelings" bout. The main thing to remember, the facilitation gold nugget for you in handling emotions, is to shift into neutral and be an unbiased processor.

A Quick Overview of the Facilitation Sequence

Feelings

When a group is in the "feelings" or "emotions" phase, it is pointless to say, "Let's keep feelings out of this," because the group is already expressing them. To handle strong feelings properly whenever they crop up in your session, stay neutral, accept the feelings, acknowledge them as real, and manage them in an organized manner.

Should you attempt to press on with the agenda or move forward with problem identification and analysis without adequately processing group members' feelings first, your efforts will be resisted. The group will continue to focus on war stories, anecdotes, monologues, debates, and discussions that release feelings without regard for the planned purpose, desired outcomes, or agenda.

When feelings are getting in the way, the group's ability to move along to the more rational and disciplined process of presenting, understanding, and analyzing the facts; collaborating to create a number of potential solutions to problems; and making team decisions about which of those solutions to implement is severely restricted.

Any time a group goes into the "feelings" phase, where the emotion begins to consume the meeting, you need to encourage individuals to express their strong sentiments, process them in an organized way, and move into phase 2, facts. If this is not done, the session will get bogged down in a directionless emotional confrontation.

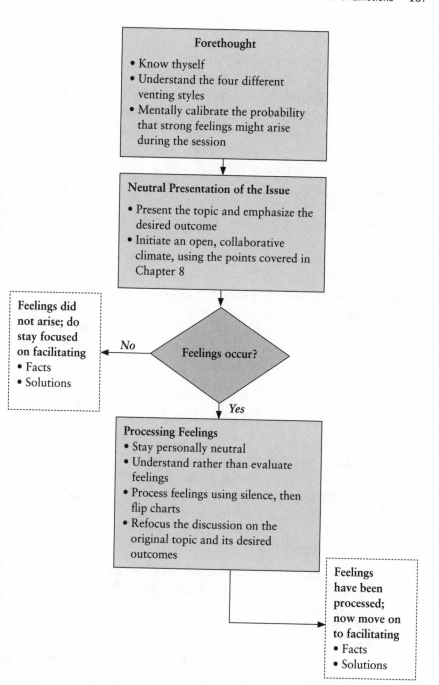

Figure 10-1 Feelings Facilitation: A Process Model

Facts*

Having had a chance to ventilate their feelings in a structured way, the group members are now ready to develop and analyze the facts in a less emotional, more objective manner. You are in a position to help the group generate and use facts and identify and then analyze the problem.

As Sayles and Strauss point out, "Facts may be hard to obtain but at least they are subject to objective inquiry, and it is usually easier to get agreement on facts than it is to get agreement on opinions. Actually, one may lead to the other."[2]

Robert Bales reinforces the importance of facts by stating, "A rich background of common facts lays the groundwork for the development of common inferences and sentiments, and out of these common decisions can grow. No decision rests on 'facts' alone, but there is no better starting point."[3]

In any situation, whether it be conferring, debating, planning, problem solving, or decision making, facts can be handled more smoothly and effectively once feelings have been addressed. Moreover, after they have been addressed, the group is much less likely to fall back into the "feelings" phase and thus require further catharsis.

Solutions

Once the facts have been assembled and the issue in question has been identified, debated, and analyzed, the final stage is reached. The group is ready to generate potential solutions, select one of them, make decisions about implementing it, and develop an action plan to which everyone can commit. In facilitating through this phase, you can take advantage of any of the tools and techniques presented here or in previous chapters.

Movement between Phases

Feelings, facts, solutions is the three-phase sequence for group productivity. The group may, of course, switch back and forth between phases as different agenda items, problems, or issues are taken up, or as new aspects of the same issue are considered.

Most important, don't waste time trying to isolate the facts, opinions, and beliefs before the group has had a chance to express feelings and go

---

*Author's note: As used in the context of this sequence, the term *facts* is broadly defined to incorporate information other than just pure facts. Facts are at the root, but less fact-based statements—opinions, estimations, ideas, values, beliefs—are also included.

through catharsis if this is required. Feelings color information, and as long as the group is emotionally excited, its ability to approach the subject rationally is diminished.

Similarly, you need to avoid the common tendency to facilitate jumping to a solution before getting all the facts. Remember too, as Figure 10-1 shows, that the group many not have strong feelings at any time throughout the meeting—actually, this is more the rule than the exception. In those instances, movement right into the logical facts phase of data and information processing is appropriate.

Finally, there may be times when the outcome for a particular agenda item is merely to discuss the topic as thoroughly as possible; a solution is not required. In those cases, you will only have to help the group complete the feelings and facts phases. In most situations, however, whenever strong feelings do arise, you will facilitate the group through the traditional sequence: feelings, facts, solutions.

Forethought

Know Thyself

Before moving ahead to present the specific processes for facilitating group feelings, a word about you, the leader, as a person is in order. To be an effective facilitator of the group's feelings, you must comprehend your own biases and the triggers for them. In other words, being able to help a group work through its feelings so that it can progress to the facts and solutions phases begins with "knowing thyself."

The manager or chairperson who is facilitating the session is human, and, as such, is subject to the same human frailties as the other group members. However, by understanding your own defense mechanisms and biases, you can make an effort to control them and steer clear of the numerous opportunities to get sucked into the emotional fray as a full-blown "feelings" participant. When this happens, facilitation invariably is nil.

For the most part, getting trapped in the emotion of the situation is unintentional. Still, whether it is unintentional or not, the results are the same. The manager and the group participants wind up engaged in a heated, and often prolonged, discussion without anyone paying attention to facilitation. Your primary defense against being unwittingly drawn into the thick of the emotional exchange is to know thyself.

Edgar Schein, speaking about himself as a consultant, makes some poignant comments on the need to identify one's own emotional response biases and be well aware of how these personal biases operate in group settings.

> As a consultant I have to observe myself in action over a period of time and get corrective feedback from others in order to identify the systematic biases in how I perceived things. Once I know what those biases are I can take greater care in checking things out before reacting to them.
>
> . . . If I have a systematic bias to respond to certain kinds of data with certain kinds of emotions, I need to know what that bias is in order to judge its appropriateness to any given situation. For example, if I tend to respond defensively and get angry whenever a client challenges me or tells me I am wrong, I need to recognize this as a bias and learn to control or compensate for that feeling if my judgment tells me that it would not be helpful to the consultation [or facilitation] process to get into an argument with the client.
>
> . . . In order to make choices and decide what will be most facilitative in a given situation, one needs to know one's biases.[4]

Schein does not imply that learning about, accepting, and controlling one's biases is an easy thing to do. It isn't. However, it is crucial for every manager or group leader to make an honest, ongoing effort to do so in order to elevate her ability to facilitate the "feelings, facts, solutions" sequence for group productivity.

Understand the Four Venting Styles

As well as knowing your personal biases, you need to be aware of typical venting styles. People do bring forth their catharses differently. Over the years, I've built a mental map that has helped me recognize and accept the broad divergence in venting styles. In no way is it a scientific profile based on controlled psychological or personality research. It is just a simple tool I've evolved that has proven useful on more than one occasion when feelings flared and I needed a way to focus quickly on what was happening. Tying back to the necessity of forethought, understanding the venting styles portrayed in the model and giving them consideration ahead of time will help you become more alert to your own venting tendencies and those of others. With this insight, you can be more tolerant, accepting, and encouraging of people whose styles are different from yours.

Figure 10-2 shows a four-cell matrix that breaks venting into four styles. When in a feelings state, a person or group vents, to varying degrees, on two different levels: the *words expressed* level (open or guarded) and the *emotions expressed* level (open or guarded). The words and emotions dimensions, when taken in all combinations, lead to four primary styles.

Expressers (Open Words; Open Emotions). As their name implies, expressers vent freely when they are in a feelings state. Their words and emotions are both congruent and open. You will get good insight into where they stand (words) and why they believe so strongly in their convictions (emotions). I've found that because they have no problem opening up and getting it out, their venting is usually short-lived. They just want to get things off their chests, and then they are ready to move ahead. With expressers, pay attention to the words behind their emotions; many good ideas for problem solving and decision making are often brought forward.

Directors (Open Words; Guarded Emotions). Directors don't really vent with a lot of emotion; outwardly they appear relatively calm. Instead, they vent using strong, powerful words like *exploit, combat ready, take charge, arrogant, challenge, eradicate,* and so on. They speak quickly,

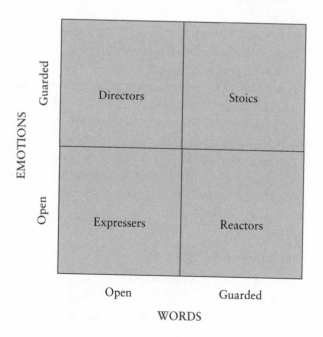

Figure 10-2 Four Venting Styles

confidently, and forcefully. They are good at using nonverbals to emphasize their words—for example, ticking off each point by reciting "point a," "point b," "point c," while simultaneously flicking out their fingers or tapping their pen on the table for each point. Directors have no patience for incompetence, time wasting, confusion, or bureaucracy. They readily vent over these topics. Also, they tend to vent early.

Reactors (Guarded Words; Open Emotions). Reactors can blow off steam at any time if something doesn't set well with them. Their emotions will be clear. Body language, facial expressions, and tone of voice will all reinforce the emotion that is being displayed. However, as opposed to expressers, the words of reactors will often be indirect and obscure. While their feelings are clearly expressed, the reasons or meaning behind them is far more difficult to clarify. It is often a facilitation challenge not to become frustrated with reactors, but if they get any sense that others are not concerned with their emotion, they may express even stronger feelings.

Stoics (Guarded Words; Guarded Emotions). Stoics may have strong feelings, but they are unlikely to let you know about them early. Outwardly they appear calm, and they aren't saying anything that indicates strong feelings. Inwardly, however, stoics may be churning with emotion, brewing an emotional outburst that can take you by surprise with its suddenness and intensity.

Stoics are the opposite of expressers. Be sensitive to their body language and tone of voice when they do speak. Their fidgeting, facial expressions, posture, aura of preoccupation, agitated tone of voice, and the like are your best clues that all is not well regarding their inner feelings.

If you sense that something is amiss, it is wise to test your impression by saying something like: "Claudia, I sense that you are bothered by the direction this discussion is going; you seem very uneasy. What's bothering you?" While Claudia may decline the invitation to respond, chances are that she will probably begin to open up. It's better to short-circuit the stoic's internal churn as soon as you sense it, rather than letting it fester and explode.

Neutral Presentation of the Issue

Getting specific, let us assume that you have just finished outlining the history and dimensions of a complex, controversial subject with which your group must concern itself, and you have followed the guidelines for "initiating an open, collaborative climate" from Chapter 8. At this point, you are at a facilitation crossroads. Depending on the specifics woven into the subject that you just presented, the group will either move into the feelings phase or bypass the feelings, at least for now, and get down to the business of working the facts.

If you know most, if not all, of the people who will be in attendance and you know the subject matter, you will have an excellent understanding of the potential group dynamics. This knowledge is useful in helping you assess whether the group will need to pass through the feelings phase before being able to process facts objectively.

In spite of the neutral stage setting, far-reaching, negative issues (such as product recalls, major reorganizations, facilities closings, sell-offs and acquisitions, account losses, product failures, and the like) are guaranteed to generate strong feelings among those members who are heavily affected by the original crisis and those who will be fully engaged in resolving it. Any upheaval will thrust you into a situation where feelings facilitation is critical. Under circumstances like these, you must plan for this venting/catharsis activity as part of your PDORA by setting aside an appropriate amount of time to handle the emotions that you can be certain will emerge.

Processing Feelings Effectively

For you, acting as primary facilitator, being able to deal with feelings properly is a critical facilitation skill to be honed. As will be shown, the actual techniques and process for handling feelings, regardless of the venting style, are not difficult to carry out. They tend to seem more formidable than they really are because the atmosphere of the feelings phase is potentially explosive. Knowing in advance what to do will notably reduce your sense of intimidation during the emotional portion of a group session.

But what happens if, after the subject is presented, strong feelings unexpectedly surface? In other words, feelings weren't planned for because they weren't expected. Don't panic; don't discount the feelings and attempt to "bulldoze ahead" with the planned agenda; and above all, as Figure 10-1 shows, slide into using the guiding principles presented here.

No discussion is going to be productive as long as strong feelings persist. The way to alleviate this situation is to recognize what is taking place and deal with it by providing the group members with acceptable outlets for venting their emotions. Ask people what they feel and why. Get them to talk, to express their feelings.

In their classic, *Getting to Yes*, Roger Fisher and William Ury underscore the importance of catharsis as a major activity for moving a person or group beyond feelings and back to a more objective, clear-headed phase of processing information and opinions.

> People obtain psychological release through the simple process of recounting their grievances. If you come home wanting to tell your husband about everything that went wrong at the office, you will become even more frustrated if he says, "Don't bother telling me; I'm sure you had a hard day. Let's skip it." . . . Letting off steam may make it easier to talk rationally later. . . . Perhaps the best strategy to adopt while the other side lets off steam is to listen quietly without responding to their attacks, and occasionally to ask the speaker to continue until he has spoken his last word.[5]

So, the bottom line is twofold: open the gate and make individual "feelings" expression easy; and, know that logic is incapable of resolving an emotional situation. Also, keep in mind that logic is in the "ears of the beholder." What is logical and intuitively obvious to one individual may not be logical at all to an emotional listener. Milo Frank's comments bolster the notion that logic loses in emotional situations.

> Emotions are the dark or bright clouds that obscure your thinking process. Recognize that logic loses to emotion. No matter how long the meeting, you cannot convince a person with logic if his mind is blocked by emotion. And further recognize that your logic may not be logical at all to your emotional listener, because the problem you feel is causing his reaction and which you are addressing may not be the problem at all—and usually isn't.[6]

There are four guiding principles that leaders can use to help group members express, and then process, their feelings in a constructive manner, regardless of the venting style being used.

Stay Personally Neutral

First and foremost, you must never get personally involved while you are in the role of facilitator; however, using the process of hat switching, you can provide personal inputs into the content of the discussion. If there is ever a time to keep the role of manager or team leader separate from that of primary facilitator, a feelings discussion is the time. Therefore, whenever feelings do burst forth, the hat you should immediately reach for is the one labeled *facilitator*. This should be almost reflexive—*feelings in the group trigger the facilitator role in you*. A manager or team leader who is drawn into the thick of an emotional battle will find it next to impossible to be a neutral processor of feeling information at the very time when the performance of this activity is needed most. But how can the manager as facilitator behave in a neutral manner? What needs to be done?

Respect People's Right to Have Their Feelings. The group members have as much right to their feelings as you have to yours. Keeping this in mind, you must accept the feelings expressed by group members as being legitimate and convey an attitude that both the group members as individuals and their ideas are worthy of attention.

You are not required to agree with others' feelings, but simply to accept that they exist. At appropriate points, you can communicate your own thoughts and feelings in response to what has been said. Practicing the art of excellent facilitation, you must demonstrate that the feelings that are being shared by others deserve to be heard.

Effective techniques for conveying both acceptance and personal neutrality include letting the person have his say (instead of gate-closing), thanking the person for the comments he made, and practicing the task-oriented behaviors of testing comprehension (to ensure proper understanding) and summarizing (to capture nonjudgmentally what was said).

Encourage and Acknowledge the Expression of Feelings. When group members are in the feelings phase, their expressed fears, doubts, anger, inadequacy, frustrations, and viewpoints are exceedingly valuable communications. Therefore, feelings need to be heard and understood. While the thought of encouraging people to express their feelings may be intimidating to many of you, remember that neutrality makes this process easier.

Performing the maintenance behavior of encouraging the expression of feelings while maintaining neutrality takes discipline, but is not difficult. Feelings need to be brought out so that they can be understood and processed, and using *brief verbal assertions* is the easiest technique for doing this. Acknowledge what is being presented with positive head nods and simple verbal feedback that indicates, "I'm tracking what you are saying." Declarations such as "I understand," "I see," "True," "Okay," "That certainly could be," "Sure," "I hear you," or other similar ones will do the trick for you.

Neutrality through the practice of this communication routine pays significant facilitation dividends. By remaining neutral, you maintain the role of primary facilitator, stay detached from any inflammatory content, stimulate the speaker to open up, and leave little or no residue of unexpressed feelings to fester.

Understand Rather than Evaluate Feelings

For most people, regardless of their organizational role, this is a difficult principle to apply. It is especially troublesome for the manager who is practicing the art of facilitation.

Efficient managers and executives are supposed to absorb a mass of information, sort through it quickly, evaluate what has been said or written, pass judgment, and announce a decision. These characteristics have put them on the "fast track" to promotions. Certainly, many believe skillful use of these behaviors to be the mark of a tough, no-nonsense manager.

On the surface at least, the role of the manager as tough decision maker seems to conflict with the role of the manager as facilitator, where a premium is placed on listening and understanding. Not only are these roles not in conflict, but effectiveness in executing the facilitator role actually strengthens the individual's ability to carry out the manager or team leader role. Skilled facilitation in getting feelings out, understood, and processed provides a much stronger foundation for making a high-quality decision than does running roughshod over team members' feelings, misunderstanding their intent, and making value judgments about them on the way to another "tough call."

Problems involving communication failures and misunderstandings are less likely to occur if the initial tendencies to evaluate and judge are suspended. No matter which of the four venting styles is used, any person who is expressing emotion is calling out the same thing: "Hear me!" "Understand me!" What can a manager specifically do to increase her ability to understand feelings rather than evaluate them?

Probe with the Nonevaluative Task-Oriented Interpersonal Behaviors. The task behaviors of seeking information, seeking opinions, building, testing comprehension, and summarizing are excellent techniques for increasing understanding while staying out of an evaluation mode. When a group member expresses thoughts with obvious emotional overtones, try to gain a fuller understanding of the statement's content and underlying causes by seeking more information and further clarification.

In addition, you can test for comprehension by nonjudgmentally reflecting the words and feelings of the message back to its originator to make sure that it has been truly understood. Statements of this type reflect the feeling and emotion being expressed without implying agreement or disagreement. Opening with phrases like: "I hear your anger over this . . . ," "It sounds like you are frustrated because . . . ," "I get the sense that you are really worried about . . . ," "You seem ambivalent over the . . . ," "I get the impression you're intimidated by . . . ," or "You sound disappointed that . . ." all mirror back the speaker's emotions as he makes his statements. A complete statement might go like this: "Robyn, what I'm hearing from you is a great deal of frustration with our consensus process because it seems like we're getting nowhere. Am I right in my understanding?"

Finally, using the summarizing technique to capture the status of the situation after a 10- to 15-minute exchange of thoughts and feelings is critical to keep confusion and misunderstandings in check.

Be Sensitive to Verbal and Nonverbal Cues. Quite often during a feelings discussion, you will fail to connect the verbal and/or nonverbal reactions of group members to the statements being made. Being a miner of group gold requires that you have a sharp "third ear." Recognizing and listening for subtle and indirect reactions—especially with directors and stoics—is essential for gaining a full understanding of what is being said. If these emotional reactions (a sharp tone of voice, a scowl, a raising and lowering of the speaker's eyebrows, a crossing of arms while debating a point, or a tapping of a pen on the table to emphasize certain words) go unheeded, the emotional climate is being managed inefficiently.

As long as the manager ignores the feelings behind the words, the group members will keep pulling the group back to the feelings phase and never allow the session to move fully into the facts phase. Or, if this does not occur, another equally negative response is for those whose feelings have been ignored to withdraw from all discussions and become uninterested, passive members for the remainder of the session. The result is that valuable meeting talent is lost.

On the other hand, the manager who recognizes and encourages the expression of feelings not only acknowledges the seriousness of the problem, but also helps make the session's dialogue less reactive and more proactive. Freed from the burden of unexpressed or ignored emotions, the group members become more willing to work on the problem from a facts and solutions standpoint.

Process Feelings Using Silence, then Flip Charts

Silence. When feelings arise and reach the point where formal processing is required, the processing should always begin with silence. Before you move ahead to facilitate the group's feelings, a short period of silence is essential. This period of silence allows people to calm down, to reflect on their feelings, and to think before they blurt out something that they might regret later. The need for this period of transition between the arousal of feelings and processing them is elaborated on by Avery, Auvine, Streibel, and Weiss.

> A session spent working with anger, frustration, fear or other unpleasant feelings can start with a few minutes of silence. Each person can use this time to identify and clarify his or her own feelings, and to become composed enough to prevent a destructive interchange later on. Silence is an opportunity for members to think for a moment without distraction, but it has benefits that go beyond the rational thought that occurs during this period. Silence is often soothing, allows members to become "centered," and breaks the flow of a competitive, overexcited interchange. Often during silence, a member will realize that a point he or she was arguing for so urgently is not really that important after all.[7]

Flip Charts. Once the period of silence has been completed, the processing phase begins. To make it clear that feelings are not being ignored, and to capture what may be invaluable data for later use, you should employ the aid of an indispensable tool—the flip chart. Here are three simple, nonthreatening approaches for sorting out and understanding feelings in an organized way.

- *Bring in the whole group.* This method is useful if there is a subset of people within the whole group that is holding common feelings. You should obtain a statement of the subset's feelings by using the interpersonal behaviors of seeking opinions and information, testing comprehension, and summarizing. Have the scribe write the results on a flip chart. Once that statement is noted, ask this contingent to elaborate on what circumstances or factors are driving their feelings, that is "what is causing your feelings?" Have the scribe write these on a flip chart. Finally, ask the rest of the group what it thinks about the contingent's expressed feelings and the causes behind them—"What do you support? What do you take issue with and why?" Have these responses written on a flip chart.

Taking all of the data provided by both the contingent and the rest of the group, write a summary statement for each side that acknowledges its current feelings and viewpoints on the matter at hand, thank all the group members for their participation, and post the summaries. Where appropriate, this information can be used in the later stages of the session as input to the debate and discussion.

• *Round-robin.* This approach is good to use when the whole group seems to be in a feelings mode, and it's difficult to get a reading on the general themes of these feelings. As facilitator, go around the room and have group members summarize their feelings on the issue and why they feel that way. Then engage the whole group in categorizing the feelings based on common themes. Once this is done, thank the group for its participation and post the information for all to see (as well as for possible use later in the session).

• *Buzz groups.* This technique is expedient when the whole group seems to be into feelings, but it could be threatening to some individuals to expose their feelings on a round-robin basis. To use this approach, break the whole group into buzz groups and let the members of each buzz group express their feelings to one another. Each buzz group is charged with taking notes on the common themes and choosing a spokesperson to provide a summary of these themes to the whole group. Write down these summary comments, thank the group members for their participation, and post the information for possible future use in the session.

All three methods are analogous to the steam valve on a pressure cooker. They are utilized to provide a structured means for you to encourage the necessary expression of group feelings without losing control of the session.

More often than not, the feelings that come forth are doubts, concerns, or fears about an action or plan. These feelings arise because one or more of the group members are, in some way, affected by the action or plan. Therefore, if you believe that immediate processing of the posted information is required, work with the group to

• Combine, condense, and refine the list of concerns so that all items are discrete.

• Use weighted voting to shorten the list to the three biggest concerns of the group. The mechanics of weighted voting are simple. Participants are given nine votes each and are told to distribute them in the following manner: five votes to their number one concern, three votes to their number two concern, and one vote to their number three concern. There is to be no deviation from these voting ground rules. When the voting is finished, add up the total number of votes for each item. Circle the three items receiving the highest vote totals to isolate them as the three biggest concerns.

- Hold a positive discussion in which the group, working collaboratively, focuses its energies on reducing, eliminating, or avoiding its three biggest concerns.

Many times this information-processing exercise is not necessary. Merely giving group members the opportunity to voice their feelings, to clarify them, to know they are understood, and to discover how others feel is enough to satisfy the participants.

Remember, your task is to process the group's feelings, not to debate, deny, defend, attack, object to, or question them. When wearing your manager's hat, you can share your personal views.

Refocus the Discussion on the Original Topic and Its Desired Outcomes

After people have vented their feelings in a structured way, it's time to refocus. The major tool here is the interpersonal behavior of summarizing. Summarize the main points of the feelings discussion. If a flip chart was used, these sheets can be reviewed. Then recount the desired outcomes of the original topic.

For example, you can refocus the discussion by saying something like, "That was a stimulating discussion on going outside the company to get the video made. It's clear that everyone now feels strongly that we should get the job done inside, and two people still feel ambivalent about using our own employees to play the parts instead of hiring professional actors. Let's keep these feelings in mind as we continue to look at specific things that our department can do to help improve return on assets (ROA) this year."

Sometimes you may have to be assertive in getting the group to refocus on the original topic because of a phenomenon known as the "feelings merry-go-round." Nothing robs a group's energy more than members who constantly repeat their feelings after these feelings have been heard, understood, accepted, written down on a flip chart, and posted.

Bringing a feelings merry-go-round to a halt requires that you remind the person that she has said something several times, show her that it has been recorded in her own words, ask if she has any new information to add, and if not, move forward by refocusing on the original topic and its desired outcomes.

Pointing to the words on the flip-chart page, you could say, "Roy, I know your point is important to you. You've already said that three times, and I've got it written down just the way you wanted it recorded. I accept your feelings. Is there anything new you'd like to add? If not, we must move on and explore other things our group can do to improve ROA this year."

Cutting off a feelings merry-go-round is an essential facilitation activity that you will have to carry out from time to time. It requires that you be assertive in taking charge of the situation and stop it before it multiplies into a beast that consumes the whole meeting.

But What if the Group Manager Has Strong Thoughts or Feelings on the Subject?

Acting as primary facilitator does not, in any way, prevent the manager from participating in the content aspects of the topic that is being debated. During the processing of the group's feelings, you may find it essential to share your thoughts or feelings on the issue that is being discussed. You have every right to add your input. However—and this is of the *utmost* importance—*you must verbally indicate that you are momentarily stepping out of the facilitator role and into the role of formal manager of the group.*

Verbal hat switching is necessary in order to avoid any confusion about the source of the message: it is from you, the manager, speaking in your role as group manager. For example, while pointing to a flip chart listing the feelings of others, and with much force, you could say:

> After listening to the views of Daneale, Scott, Sean, and Pat, and understanding why they feel the way they do, let me switch hats from facilitator to team manager and respond this way. I'm quite disturbed by the idea of using consultants. It will suck $15,000 out of our budget to pay for outsiders to teach our Power of Recognition Workshop. Consultants have no conception of how our business operates; most of them probably haven't worked for a single day as a manager in a high-tech company. I can't see the necessity to pay outsiders to do a job that we can do better ourselves. I firmly believe that we will get

acceptable delivery of content, and a heck of a lot deeper discussion about practical applications, if we train a group of our own managers to teach the workshop. That's the approach we used at EnerCo when I worked there, and it was terrific!

There can be further dialogue between the manager and the other group members. However, the manager cannot lose sight of his substantial obligation to the group—to return to the role of primary facilitator and be attentive to the group process. At no time after shifting to the role of manager should you get so heavily drawn into the discussion that you forget your facilitation role. Therefore, after an appropriate amount of dialogue, you need to signify a return to the role of primary facilitator and concentrate on assisting the group process, as opposed to directly contributing to the content.

In situations where you find yourself becoming personally embroiled in an emotional discussion, but where the group includes an individual who is skilled enough to handle the primary facilitation role and who is not caught up in the heat of the moment, you have the luxury of being able to switch to your manager's role and assign the primary facilitator's role to this other person. This gives you the opportunity to become fully immersed in the content and emotion of the subject without having to worry about primary facilitation responsibilities. However, after the emotional issue (for instance, staff reductions) is concluded, you should reclaim the role of primary facilitator.

If you are fortunate enough to have facilitation flexibility, you should take advantage of it when necessary. Still, in the innumerable instances where the role of the primary facilitator cannot be temporarily assigned to another person during a particular discussion, the most effective way for you to facilitate a feelings discussion is the one recommended in this chapter. That is, practice a process of controlled entry and exit into and out of the feelings discussion, while never losing sight of the critical role of primary facilitator.

Feelings, facts, solutions is a sequence that does lead to group productivity. When a group hits the feelings stage, it is pointless for you to urge movement into the facts and solutions stages without helping the group deal with its feelings. By providing a practical means for letting the group members vent their feelings and by recording those feelings on a flip chart, you can prevent the session from breaking down into an aimless emotional confrontation.

For most managers, dealing with group feelings is an unpleasant, tension-ridden, and often intimidating chore. Many times, a cardinal mistake is made: ignoring the feelings and "getting on with resolving the blasted issues." Managers do this to avoid dealing with emotional issues, as well as in a misguided attempt to keep the meeting on track. However, by facing the situation and following the techniques presented in this chapter, you can significantly increase your chances of successfully handling group feelings.

Caravan Freight, Inc.: A Case Study

Lloyd Price is business operations manager for Caravan Freight, Inc., a national trucking company with profits of $34 million on revenues of $850 million. Caravan, like so many firms in the highly competitive trucking industry, is faced with unrelenting pressures to keep costs down.

In early January, J. P. Richardson, the president of Caravan, sent a memo to his direct reports urging them to "do everything possible—short of downsizing—to trim costs and increase productivity." The goal given to the senior staff was an 11 percent productivity increase, companywide, by year end.

In response to the memo, Lloyd Price decided to set up a strategic planning meeting with his six managers to determine how to deal with Richardson's difficult request. So Lloyd sent out an e-mail memo to his team announcing Richardson's productivity initiative and the key particulars for the four-hour strategic planning meeting. He also included information on the session's purpose, desired outcomes, role assignments, and agenda. The meeting was scheduled for the day after tomorrow.

Price's e-mail elicited an angry reply from his billing manager, Cathy Carr (a reactor). The gist of her message was: "You've got to be kidding. If J. P. would just come down from his ivory tower and see the way my team is configured, he'd find out that we can't even begin to think about his ridiculous task. It's always take and no give! How can you be productive when you're just a payroll number?" Several other reactors shot other angry e-mails to all team members—including Lloyd. The lid had blown off.

Driving home that night, Lloyd admitted to himself that he was feeling frustrated and stressed. While productivity certainly had to be increased, when would the stream of crisis projects end? Caravan was also in the midst of a major restructuring, its quality improvement teams were dying on the vine because management was spread so thin that it couldn't provide proper support, and Caravan's parent company had kept all budgets and head-count numbers flat while increasing sales revenue targets by 8 percent for the year.

On the morning of the session, right after Lloyd welcomed the team—but before he could review the purpose, desired outcomes, and agenda—Peter Best, the repair shop manager (a director), spoke up first. Forcefully, point by point, and pounding the table with his fist for each one, he articulated six reasons why he had neither the time, the resources, nor the desire to commit to this task. Asking only a few simple clarifying questions, Lloyd wrote all of Peter's points on a flip chart.

Ruth Brown (an expressive) chimed in, attacking the 11 percent productivity goal as stupid and unrealistic. She cited a recent benchmarking study by industry leader Morrison Van Lines in the trucking industry that hailed 4 to 6 percent year-over-year productivity gains as being outstanding. She also reminded everyone about November's thoroughly abysmal attitude survey results. Handing out a copy to everyone, she highlighted the "employee motivation and commitment section," where the rating was only 55 percent positive. Then, standing up and waving her arms, she said: "Anger is not a strong enough word to describe how I feel. Totally pissed is better, but it still falls short!" With only positive head nods and reinforcing comments like "Good point," "Okay," "I've got it noted," and so on, Lloyd duly noted all of Ruth's thoughts and feelings on the flip chart.

Jim Lowe (a reactor) said that he was going to paint his office door green as a visible protest against Richardson's greed for his big bonus at the expense of the "little guys." Richie Valenzuela (a reactor) told everyone: "I've had it. I'm giving my two weeks' notice right now." Cathy Carr (a reactor) said: "This company has to have a monopoly on stupidity. I just know it does. No company in the world could possibly make dumber decisions, faster, than Caravan!"

Although he felt like he was being indirectly attacked, Lloyd wrote their comments on the flip chart, always checking back to be sure he was writing down exactly what they were feeling, and when finished, he tore the sheet off the pad and taped it to the wall. Then, Lloyd said, "Look, I know how upset you all are. I feel the same way. We need to continue to process our feelings, but in a little more structured way. Let's all take a moment of silence, reflect on our feelings, and write them down. After that, I'll go around the room, round-robin style, and capture everyone's feelings by adding them to our chart. If you already have something on the chart from before and want to add to it, that's fine. I'll be fully participating in this exercise myself."

The team did as instructed. When the silence process was finished, but before beginning the group processing, Lloyd asked Ritchie Valenzuela if he would be the scribe. Ritchie immediately responded, "I'd rather call in Donna my administrative assistant to be the scribe. She has better handwriting and can spell better than I can." Lloyd said, "This is an important discussion that we need to have as a team. I'll keep things going at a pace that allows you to capture everyone's points without being overwhelmed. Pristine handwriting and perfect spelling are not a requirement for scribing. Just write what people say and keep moving along. Also, I'll make sure you get a chance to get your own points recorded. You are an important team member not just our scribe. "Ritchie, with a hint of sarcasm, replied, "Okay, boss, but I'm still quitting." Lloyd, without comment, handed Ritchie the marker.

First Lloyd called upon Clarence Henry, who had been silent throughout the previous discussion. "Clarence, it looked to me like you were getting quite irritated during our team's little outburst a few minutes ago, but you weren't saying anything. I'd really like to hear how you feel about our productivity task." Clarence replied: "Yes, I was upset. Still am. What really fries me is that neither Richardson, you, nor anyone else on the senior staff really appreciates the hoops we have to jump through to carry out a major request. We get no budget or head-count relief to help us, and nothing comes off the plate in terms of current tasks. When will Richardson realize that you can't put ten pounds of garbage in a five-pound bag? Furthermore . . ." (The stoic was getting it out sooner rather than later.)

Lloyd went completely around the room at a comfortable pace, with Ritchie writing down everything from everyone. At one point, Lloyd shared a his own thoughts from his drive home the other night. He added that he was angry because Richardson had made the productivity decision unilaterally. There had been no discussion. It caught the entire senior staff by surprise. At another point, Lloyd gate-opened for Ritchie to write down his feelings which he willingly did.

Throughout the structured venting process, Lloyd, as primary facilitator, and several others from time to time, as secondary facilitators, made sure that everyone's feelings were heard, understood, acknowledged as real, and accepted.

When the process was finished, the team had 38 items on four full sheets of paper. The atmosphere in the room had lightened considerably. While people weren't overjoyed, they all admitted that they felt better for having had the opportunity to say what they felt and get it off their chests.

Clarence asked Lloyd what he intended to do with his sheets. Lloyd replied: "I personally don't plan to do anything with them. These are our data. We need to process this information further. Even though they came out as feelings, there is a wealth of ideas on those sheets. I'd like to propose that Clarence, Cathy, Ruth, and Peter take these sheets and consolidate them. Categorize the feelings into buckets according to issues like aspects of the assignment itself, workload and pressure, J. P. Richardson, Lloyd Price, employee motivation and morale, and any other categories that seem reasonable. Don't change any words; just bucket the statements."

The team of four agreed. Lloyd asked the team how it would like to deal with the new list at the next meeting. After some discussion triggered by a proposal from Jim Lowe, the team decided that it would discuss each category and further clarify any of the feelings statements within them. Then, using the distributive voting process (described in this chapter), it would select the top two categories and develop some meaningful actions that would help alleviate the emotion attached to the project. For example, Richie volunteered: "Lloyd, I've talked with plenty of people the last few days in other sections, and they are at least as upset as we are. If you could just get together with the rest of J. P.'s direct reports and, as a united staff, communicate to him the intensity of all our feelings, it would make me feel a whole lot better knowing that he knows. I'd feel so good, I wouldn't even quit!"

Everyone had a hearty laugh. Lloyd said: "Those are exactly the things I hope we can accomplish next time to ease us through this feelings phase. But I want to caution every one of you, I know J. P. well. We *are* going to have a productivity initiative for this year. He may back off a bit on his requirements if the senior staff plays its cards right in our meeting with him. But the assignment will *not* go away, and whatever it turns out to be, it will be on top of everything else we have to do. Our team's challenge will be to 'mine our own group gold' so that we can figure out how best to minimize the workload, pressure, and disruption that this necessary task assignment brings to our operation."

The session evaluation at the end revealed a great deal of satisfaction with the meeting. A breakthrough had been made when all seemed hopeless. Just as the team was preparing to leave, Lloyd asked: "Could you hold it a second? I want to show you something. You know Peter never gave me a chance to present today's agenda. He was on me like a wildcat. But, just as an FYI, notice that, based on your e-mail and feedback, the only agenda item I had was 'controlled venting' with a desired outcome of 'team feelings processed.'" Ruth commented as she left with Lloyd: "I know, I know. Feelings, facts, solutions."

WORKSHEET

Develop written responses to the two items listed below.

1. What do you feel are the main learning points from Chapter 10?

_____

_____

_____

_____

_____

_____

2. Elaborate on why you feel these points are key for you.

_____

_____

_____

_____

_____

_____

_____

Notes

1. G. Strauss and L. Sayles, *Personnel: The Human Problems of Management* (Englewood Cliffs, N.J.: Prentice-Hall, 1972), pp. 231–232.
2. L. Sayles and G. Strauss, *Human Behavior in Organizations* (Englewood Cliffs, N.J.: Prentice-Hall, 1966), p. 293.
3. R. Bales, "In Conference," *Harvard Business Review* 32, no. 2 (1954), p. 47.
4. E. Schein, *Process Consultation, Vol. II: Lessons for Managers and Consultants* (Reading, Mass.: Addison-Wesley, 1987), pp. 71–72.
5. R. Fisher and W. Ury, *Getting to Yes* (New York: Penguin Books, 1983), pp. 31–32.
6. M. O. Frank, *How to Run a Successful Meeting in Half the Time* (New York: Simon and Schuster, 1989), p. 132.
7. M. Avery, B. Auvine, B. Streibel, and L. Weiss, *Building United Judgment* (Madison, Wis.: Center for Conflict Resolution, 1981), p. 73.

Chapter *11*

FACILITATING VIRTUAL TEAMS: CASHING IN ON COLLABORATIVE BRAINPOWER WHEN APART

CHAPTER OBJECTIVES

- To understand how technology is beginning to affect group sessions.
- To describe the benefits and drawbacks of four categories of virtual interaction.
- To furnish facilitation guidelines for conducting real-time distributed sessions.

Introduction

Every day each of us gets a little splashed, if not fully soaked, as wave after wave of new technology washes across our daily lives. From the cell phone to the iPhone, from ATM banking to online banking, from paper maps to navigation systems in our cars, we all experience the effects of technological change. Some of us exult in the progress that it brings; others doggedly resist each and every intrusion on our usual way of doing things.

Technological developments introduce seemingly radical changes, yet at the same time, certain proven principles of fact and experience hold steady and continue to operate as the bedrock for the new technology. The ability to synthesize the new opportunities of today with sound principles from the past helps reduce our fear of the unknown so that we can learn to use a new technology to its maximum advantage. For instance, access to online banking in no way suspends our responsibility to manage our personal budget prudently, but it can make our banking task more convenient and provide greater flexibility and freedom to our lives.

Collaborative work sessions are no different. The face-to-face meeting is never going to go away because in many instances, as a result of the purpose and the desired outcomes, there is no substitute for them. While the vast bulk of meetings throughout the world will continue to be conducted in the traditional face-to-face manner for decades to come, there is no denying that technology will have an increasing effect on group processes in the future. But even as hardware and software gain greater acceptance in group settings, the underlying principles for maximizing their impact on teamwork and collaboration will not radically change. *The methodology for facilitating virtual meetings will be essentially the same system that I've stressed so far in this book. The process for mining group gold is the one compelling constant that is capable of bridging the old and the new.*

Categories of Group Interaction

New technology is constantly revolutionizing the way executives, managers, and nonmanagers alike perform their work, both internally and externally, whether across the street or around the world. Robert Johansen has classified work group interactions into four categories across the dimensions of place and time.[1] Using Johansen's dimensions, a matrix that labels and links the four categories can be set up, as shown in Figure 11-1.

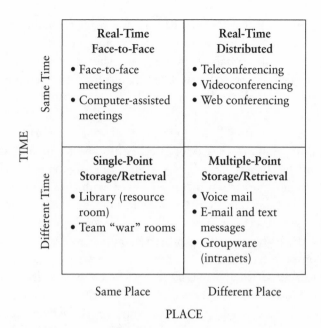

	Real-Time Face-to-Face	Real-Time Distributed
Same Time	• Face-to-face meetings • Computer-assisted meetings	• Teleconferencing • Videoconferencing • Web conferencing
Different Time	Single-Point Storage/Retrieval • Library (resource room) • Team "war" rooms	Multiple-Point Storage/Retrieval • Voice mail • E-mail and text messages • Groupware (intranets)

Same Place   Different Place

PLACE

Figure 11-1 Group Interaction Categories

Technology is currently being developed and applied across all four categories of group work. While all four are interesting and will be cited briefly, the dynamics between the technology and people who are utilizing "real-time distributed" meetings are crying out for the systematic application of Mining Group Gold collaborative practices. Therefore, the spotlight in Chapter 11 will be on how to get the most out of work sessions when people are distributed in different locations but are trying to collaborate during the same period of time.

Real-Time Face-to-Face: Same Time, Same Place

The real-time face-to-face meeting has been the focal point of this entire book. However, one wrinkle to this type of meeting—which changes nothing in relation to what you have learned in the previous 10 chapters—is to use one or two computers attached to LCD projectors to project computer images on a screen or screens. The computer, with its projector, and its operator act as an electronic flip chart and scribe.

Projected on-screen electronic meeting technology creates a focal point for the meeting. In addition to speaking and hearing, meeting participants can now see key ideas, agreements, and actions composed online. Visual reinforcement of critical thoughts, combined with the ability to modify and expand them quickly and neatly, keeps things moving.

Creativity can be enhanced by the use of automated brainstorming, grouping of ideas, weighted voting, and charting software applications. Action items are simpler to ferret out and discuss to ensure feasibility and commitment.

There are several drawbacks to this type of session versus a traditional "flip chart" meeting. Increased logistical issues and technology costs are obvious, but the biggest drawback—a huge one—is that only one page can be seen and worked on at a time. Even with two computers, projectors, screens, and operators working in tandem, the participants are able to see and process only two full pages of work or, at most, several smaller, harder-to-read windows projected on the screens.

The constant back-and-forth movement between pages to modify, update, review, or discuss them is irritating to many people. It destroys processing continuity; it is the source of a lot of fumbling, scrolling, zooming in and out, and closing and opening of windows as the operator searches for the right page(s); and it breeds a lot of confusion, as people's requests to recall points on previous pages often require an ad hoc search. Also, it takes a good-sized room and special arrangement to accommodate the hardware and the operator (especially with two setups) so that everyone can see the screen(s).

With computer-assisted meetings, you lose the panoramic view of many flip-chart pages hung on a wall that can be seen by all and can stimulate the thinking of anyone at any time. Processing and integrating information is a simple task of saying, "Let's look at flip chart number ten, point four, and try to mesh that idea with item six on flip chart one."

Real-Time Distributed: Same Time, Different Place

Relative to virtual team facilitation, "working together while apart" in real time is the sweet spot for mining group gold tools and processes. Same-time, different-place meetings come in three formats: audio, video, and computer (Web-based) conferencing.

Videoconferencing. A great deal of effort has gone into making remote collaboration a commonplace business reality. Invented in the 1960s, videoconferencing took hold only in the 1980s, when digital telephone networks became feasible. Only recently has it begun to show signs of becoming an effective medium of remote collaboration. Videoconferencing is coming of age as the technology matures, and as it spreads, the demand for skilled facilitation of videoconferences will grow to avoid myriad meeting problems.

Until the 2000s, videoconferencing was not something that executives could really depend on. Corporate networks, for example, lacked the bandwidth to handle video. Connecting far-flung participants across different time zones required endless fiddling by the company's IT department. We all have been frustrated by no picture or poor, slow-motion picture quality, coupled with a one- or two-second delay between the words being spoken at one site and finally coming through to the other locations. Seeing lips saying one thing but hearing the words spoken seconds later was both amusing and frustrating. Stepping on one another's lines as a result of the audio delays also retarded effectiveness.

The new systems, in particular Halo by HP and Cisco's TelePresence, are so state-of-the-art and reliable that companies have no hesitation about using them to conduct sensitive contract talks and other high-level meetings. These top-end systems are not inexpensive. But given the sophisticated technology, in concert with proven techniques to mine group gold, results-oriented meetings can be conducted far more easily. Also, the time and money saved by doing so can have a positive impact on both a company's travel expenses and the wear and tear on its managers and executives.

Teleconferencing. While a bit more old-fashioned, audio teleconferencing can still be a very economical way to hold excellent virtual meetings. Much gold can be mined using this method without having people schlepping across the country or around the world to meet face to face. One caution: try to avoid any audio connections that are half duplex, meaning that voice can go only one way at a time. With such phone lines, it is impossible to interrupt a speaker to ask clarification questions, to amend critical information, to remedy incorrect data, or to gate-close a dominator, a rambler, or an angry tirade. Any feedback is impossible until the person stops talking, and then when an individual does speak up, that person now controls the airwaves.

Computer Conferencing. Web-based computer conferencing is used to conduct live meetings, training, or presentations via the Internet. In a Web conference, each participant sits at her own computer and is connected to other participants via the Internet, using either a downloaded application on each of the attendees' computers or a Web-based application distributed by e-mail (a meeting invitation) to enter the conference.

A *Webinar* is a specific type of Web conference. It can be one-way, from the speaker to the audience with limited audience interaction, such as in a Webcast. Typically Webinars are two-way using voice over Internet

Protocol (VoIP) and include polling and question-and-answer sessions to allow full participation by both the audience and the presenter.

How to be a miner of group gold when acting as primary facilitator for a videoconference, teleconference, or computer conference to enhance the power of those kinds of sessions will be treated shortly in more detail.

Single-Point Storage/Retrieval: Same Place, Different Time

This configuration does not really involve meetings per se. Here a team builds a base of information—think of a library, resource center, display room, or war room—where people must physically go to obtain information or view objects. As a "same-place, different-time" operation, team members go to the designated place at their convenience and obtain whatever information they need in order to solve problems, make decisions, or manage some other aspect of their jobs. Team members obviously can go in small groups and discuss the information together in the designated place as it is acquired.

Multiple-Point Storage/Retrieval: Different Place, Different Time

This is truly the electronic "at your convenience" or "when you need it" category. Sending and responding to e-mails and voice mails are good examples that fall into this classification. Like the "single-point" model just discussed, the "multiple-point interaction" is not really a meeting as such, but rather a means of having an electronically stored database that can be accessed, read, and, if authorized, manipulated at a time and place of the user's choosing. The goal here is to allow individuals to access and read company blogs and Web pages, to perform group writing and editing tasks, to create and manage group calendars and address books, to provide direct input into group projects, and so on. However, Tim Brown has summarized some problems with this use of technology.

> [The problem is] e-mail has done little to support collective teamwork. The Internet helps move information around but has done little to bring people together. Creative teams need to be able to share their thoughts not only verbally but also visually and physically as well. . . . Too much has been focused on mechanical tasks such as storing and sharing data or running a structured process and not enough on the far messier tasks of generating ideas and building consensus around them.[2]

Mining Group Gold: "Real-Time Distributed" Virtual Meeting Fundamentals

Premeeting Planning

Who Should Attend? Once you have your purpose and desired outcomes figured out, and the upshot is that you need to call a real-time distributed virtual meeting, be exceedingly judicious in whom you invite. You must adhere to the rule: *invite the smallest number of people necessary to achieve the desired outcome(s)*. Even more so than with face-to-face sessions, because of the technological logistics, the additional interpersonal burdens brought on by being apart, the intervening hardware and software, and the difficulty of getting consensus over a distance, meeting size is your first decision, and it requires razor-sharp thinking on your part. Small beats large when holding a virtual meeting.

The one exception to the "less is best" rule is if you are planning on holding a one-way information-sharing event involving several remote sites, with a fixed amount of time set aside for Q & As over phone lines. In that case, numbers really are irrelevant.

Ensure Vested Interests. Engage special needs or interests of those you intend to invite. Correspond personally with all invitees in advance to confirm their meeting participation and to make certain any special issues or concerns are understood and mapped to the desired outcomes to increase commitment to the session. Also, don't invite anyone you know will not fully embrace the content of your planned agenda.

Mittleman, Briggs, and Nunnamaker citing their research on virtual meetings note: We found that when a potential participant was unable to articulate a vested interest in the outcome of a meeting, that participant never showed up for the virtual meeting. Over the almost 100 sessions we have completed, we had a zero attendance rate when vested interest was absent.[3]

Develop the PDORA Document. Regardless of whether the interaction format of the meeting is video, audio, or Web-based computer conferencing, the meeting caller must complete a PDORA document and send it out to all the attendees *before* the virtual meeting occurs. This is the most significant action that the virtual facilitator can take because the key particulars contained in the PDORA—date, building and room numbers for all the remote sites, start time, end time, call-in number, and access code—along with the meeting's purpose, desired outcomes, roles, and agenda with clock times (including necessary breaks), with each item coded as IS, ID, or IP, will be the load-bearing structure for the entire session.

When people are separated by place, your PDORA will be every attendee's "lighthouse beacon," the constant reference point, helping all of the virtual team members stay on time and on track. You cannot expect to have a successful virtual meeting without a PDORA document in the hands of everyone before you go on-air or online!

Set Roles. The roles of primary facilitator (the caller of the virtual meeting), secondary facilitators (all), timekeeper, and minute taker are as essential here as they are in a face-to-face meeting. Those who will hold the timekeeper and minute taker roles can be determined in advance and included in the PDORA or can be solicited during your PDORA review. When you are videoconferencing, a scribe may be needed. Therefore, the flip charts or whiteboard need to be placed in a position where the camera can easily be turned to focus on them.

Get Out the Prework. Any prework should go out with the PDORA, along with clear instructions and enough lead time for all attendees to do it justice. Check to see that the prework is completed—don't assume that everyone will believe it is important or will follow your instructions. Send out a follow-up e-mail to double-check that it is being completed. Require an electronic confirmation. In a virtual meeting, prework that was completed by only a few is disastrous from a processing standpoint and a huge time waster.

Start-Up

Who Is Present? The first order of business for any virtual meeting is to hold a process check immediately to see who is online. With videoconferencing, teleconferencing, or Web-based conferencing using VoIP, hold a round of introductions to establish the audience and to give attendees a sense of one another's voices. For computer conferencing without voice, use an electronic sign-in sheet. Also check to see how long each attendee will be present at your meeting.

Review the PDORA. Once you know whom you have online and for how long, review the PDORA from top to bottom and answer any questions about the purpose, desired outcomes, roles, or agenda for the meeting. When covering the principal roles, explain expectations if people are not sure what their duties entail.

For videoconferencing and Web-based computer meetings, show the PDORA in a separate window to add focus and to give you the opportunity to make check marks as agenda items are completed and edit the agenda along the way in real time.

Move-Out

Make Your Opening Remarks. Make any general stage-setting or background remarks, then start working your way through the agenda, item by item. Keep your opening remarks short and sweet. You want to utilize the brainpower of the group, not dominate it with your thinking.

Stay Flexible. Be flexible with the agenda; adjust your schedule if things move more quickly or more slowly than you expected. Time is harder to plan for and to manage when you are facilitating a virtual session than with a face-to-face session because of the extra unknowns. First-rate timekeeping is an invaluable service, so choose a conscientious person for that role every time.

Make Your Transitions Crystal Clear. The action of moving from one process stage to another should be complete and explicit. If virtual participants do not follow a transition, then they will be lost during the subsequent activities. At the conclusion of each topic, declare an end to it, summarize decisions and action items, and double-check to make sure that the minute taker has them noted. Then be unequivocal in announcing the next agenda item or process step to be used.

Reflect Users' Names When Facilitating. When you are verbally interacting with a virtual participant, use her name to address her at every opportunity. This not only pulls that participant more into the meeting, but identifies that participant to others and serves as a direct reminder to everyone that the named participant is actively engaged.

Keep the Desired Outcomes at the Forefront. If you start to go into the weeds, forcefully restate the desired outcomes to get back on track. You as primary facilitator, and all others as secondary facilitators, need to keep checking the desired outcomes against the output that is emerging and monitoring whether that output has the breadth and depth expected. If not, keep referring to the desired outcomes and throw in provocative ideas to stimulate new avenues of exploration.

Stay on Point. Relevant and well-facilitated virtual sessions that stay on point are a necessity if you want to keep your participants engaged because their distractions will be endless. With virtual meetings, any time the process breaks down—people making long-winded, self-serving comments; the group repeatedly straying from the agenda topic; presenters who are unprepared and bungling; and so on—will cause others to tune out far more quickly than in a face-to-face session. The reason is simple: it's because they can. The remoteness of the parties and the ease with which they can become involved in outside tasks without others knowing it makes it convenient for them to read their e-mail, catch up on unrelated work, or engage in a social activity while keeping just one eye on the meeting.

Ask Questions and Give Feedback. For all topics, keep using open-ended questions, whether they are direct, general address, return, or relay. Encourage others to do the same throughout the session. Just because you are meeting virtually doesn't mean that strong debate and probing have to fall by the wayside.

Feedback and responding are vital for virtual meeting excellence. Without them, attendees become observers rather than participants. They start thinking, "Am I the only one here?" They experience a low sense of presence, and little or no feedback from others on their comments and contributions enables this feeling. This lack of feedback also leads to less interest in the meeting and inhibits debate and convergence to a decision.

Use Frequent Process Checks. The leader or facilitator should engage the team in process checks more frequently than would be appropriate in a face-to-face meeting. Multiple process checks with all participants, round-robin style, throughout the Move-Out phase to make sure that everyone is on the same page at the same time is a key facilitation activity.

Proactively gate-open for the less-involved virtual participants every 10 to 15 minutes by asking, "Beth, are you with us? What comments do you have regarding the direction we're headed with this issue?" These process checks provide opportunities for individuals to offer feedback and keep virtual participants more engaged in the overall process. For Web-based computer meetings, enabling groupware features (such as comment numbering) that encourage online conversational feedback is a good idea.

Research shows that meeting members are more prone to get lost as to "where we are" or "what are we trying to accomplish" when they are distributed in different locations. They also may lose track of who is virtually present at the meeting and who is not. Furthermore, they may feel less a part of the team, contributing to lower buy-in to the meeting results.

Encourage Verbal Expression of Feelings. Even with videoconferencing, body language is tougher to read than in face-to-face meetings, and with the other formats, it is impossible.

So, depend on secondary facilitation in the following way. Have a ground rule that members are encouraged to speak up and verbalize what they are feeling so that it doesn't fester. If they are frustrated, they should say so; if they are angry, they should say so; if they are bored, they should say so. It's the only way to have a transparent meeting when body language and verbal cues are missing. As primary facilitator, you will need to take the lead in sharing your feelings and pause now and then to check on the others: "How do you feel about things at this point? How do you feel the meeting is progressing?" Use the round-robin approach, and solicit feedback.

Manage Multiple Conversations. If two or more people are speaking at once, either you or someone else in the role of secondary facilitator must step in quickly, gate-close all the offending parties, and then sort out a speaking order. Nothing is worse in a virtual meeting than people talking over each other. It occurs far too often, and it is both annoying and nonproductive.

Have a Solid Plan if Decision Making Is to Be Part of Your Meeting. Idea generation (divergence), along with the follow-on tasks of idea discussion and idea narrowing, can be done quite nicely in virtual distributed sessions. However, idea evaluation and selection, resulting in a final decision (convergence), is exceedingly difficult in a real-time distributed meeting than in a face-to-face session. The increased difficulty might be due in part to limitations in bandwidth, making give-and-take negotiations more structured and rigid. Or it might be due to a decreased focus on the group and an increased focus on self, making compromise more difficult.

So to get a decision rendered, it may be better to use the entire virtual team to generate and discuss many ideas, then narrow them down to, say, the top three alternatives. Once that is accomplished, as primary facilitator, set up an ad hoc team to negotiate an integrated solution. The facilitator can assign representatives of differing camps to the team to sort through the final going-in set; negotiate differences, either online or offline using side process channels; and report a resolution back to the full team.

Facilitate the Entire Virtual Team. An important issue that you, as primary facilitator, will have to deal with is not getting caught up in facilitating only your own local audience, to the exclusion of audiences in the other remote locations. If you do, participants in those locations will quickly cease to focus on the meeting and engage in other unrelated online work. You are the primary facilitator for the entire virtually networked meeting, and you must stay attuned to participation from all locales. One thing that can help you do this, especially if there are a number of remote sites, is to appoint a person at each site to be a "site-specific" secondary facilitator and make sure that this location is fully involved in all information processing by gate-opening for that site if it is being overlooked.

Set Ground Rules. For any virtual group that is going to meet over time, putting a set of ground rules in place and gaining commitment to them will be critical. There are three starting points to assist you in this matter: (1) draw from the ground rules document at the end of Chapter 9, (2) draw from the 21 main points presented here in the "Mining Group Gold: 'Real-Time Distributed' Virtual Meeting Fundamentals" section, or (3) draw from the sample ground rules shown here.

The smoothest way to set ground rules is for you to think hard about the ones that you believe are most important and make up a formal document. Send it out with the PDORA for your first meeting, and set aside 30 minutes early in your first agenda. Then review, clarify, and modify the items with the virtual team. Be sure to test for consensus from each person when a final list is developed. The final set must be owned by the whole virtual team, so all its members need to "work it over." However, a well-thought-out list, initially proposed by you as a solid base from which to operate, will make this job pretty routine.

Developing ground rules is not a silly exercise to be taken lightly; they will be your virtual team's code of conduct and provide the template for all secondary facilitation. Here are a few virtual team ground rules as starter examples. *We will:*

- Schedule times on our calendar to attend our real-time distributed meetings.
- Have a PDORA sent out to all members in time to be read before the meeting starts.
- Complete all online premeeting input ahead of the call.
- Show up on time, on the phone or online.
- Verbalize our feelings.
- Stay focused and avoid distractions during the meeting.
- Communicate early and often, ask questions, and give feedback.
- Be mindful of background noise.

Wrap-Up

Finish with Snap. The wrap-up process for a virtual meeting is the same as that for a face-to-face session.

- Ask the minute taker to review the core outcomes: all decisions and action items.
- Dispense with any "leftovers" (agenda items that were not completed, were postponed, or were dropped), handle all parking lot items, and seek agenda items for the next session.

- Hold a session critique: go round-robin, asking participants to give specific views on what was done well and what could be improved. Use your ground rules as the benchmark against which the session is critiqued.

Burying Virtual Gold

These comments, by a person who was locked into a series of poorly conceived and facilitated real-time distributed sessions, while humorous, should cause every virtual meeting planner or facilitator to stop in his tracks and think long and hard about the real devastation created by every slipshod effort. Don't bury your group gold, mine it!

> Understand—this is coming from a man who often was compelled to spend the better part of one day a week on a bi-coastal video conference call with two dozen people. Staring. Wishing death. Listening to the CTO opine at length about how exciting it would be to build and sell a national yellow pages app from scratch. If there had been cyanide capsules on the table instead of M&Ms, I don't think I would have hesitated to indulge. "Boil the ocean" business models and long meetings are the cocktail for making Merlin Mann wish harm upon himself.[4]

Mining Virtual Gold

The following account will end this chapter on a high note. After completing a Mining Group Gold workshop for a client who runs a national chain of automotive service centers, R. A., an assistant district manager, sought me out. Our discussion revolved around how he could maximize the effectiveness of a series of teleconferences that he was responsible for planning and facilitating on the critical subject of loss prevention with managers dispersed throughout the Midwest. We spent a couple of hours together, and I coached R. A. through a strategic process that incorporated much of what has been covered in this chapter. At the conclusion of our discussion, he was confident and energized.

I asked him to let me know how things were going after he got a few sessions under his belt. What follows is R. A.'s summary of his teleconferencing process and the results of those actions. His account is both insightful and instructive.

Subject: My General Process for Teleconference Meetings

Tom, since our meeting, I've organized a series of conference calls with our Zone loss prevention managers; each one has used the Mining Group Gold (MGG) process. The calls have been regarded as successful and well organized, and for the first time in years we stayed on track and ended with actual outcomes.

Today we held another call using MGG, and this time my manager also attended. He warned me that he was concerned that we could not accomplish our desired outcomes and address all the issues, but he agreed to the agenda. Well, the call took place, and we stayed on track and on time. Here is the general process I've been using.

Once a date is established for the call, I ask each call member to commit to take the call from a landline (no cell phones) and to use the handset, not a speakerphone (to limit call drops, break-ups, and background noises). Then I limit the call duration to no more than three topics because I know the level of passion will be high, and I want to ensure that we limit the duration of the call to 90 minutes max.

To determine the topics, I ask each call participate to provide his or her top two or three topics for the call and ask that he or she provide these topics only to me (not the others). This is done to limit any crosstalk between the members before the call occurs, and gives the members a chance to offer topics anonymously. Once I receive the topics, I compile a master list and then ask each participant to vote on the three that we should discuss (all by e-mail). Again, I ask for private votes from each person. This process naturally prioritizes the topics and identifies which topics we will process.

Because I can't manage the environments and distractions of each call participant, I know that keeping everyone engaged is a constant challenge. So the first thing I do is consult a couple of the call participants individually who I know have a passion about the topics, seek their precall thoughts, and ask for their full participation. This ensures that I will not be the lone voice throughout the call.

Next, I devote time to planning the PDORA. Regarding roles, I consider the personalities of each call participant and assign persons that I feel might be prone to "drifting" to roles that require their attention (timekeeper or minute taker). Then, as I develop the call agenda, I consider the group's personality. Knowing that the group tends to attempt to solve every issue 100 percent in a single discussion (which I find is rarely possible), I specifically write the desired outcomes for a particular subject so that the goals break the problem solving into doable segments—this also gives a sense of accomplishment as we move along.

Within 24 hours before the call, I send everyone the premeeting materials (agenda, list of topics, and other items) and ask that each have them available for the call. During the call, I make sure that all attendees have the documents in front of them (it gives them something to focus on, too).

Once we get started, I follow your techniques of asking quiet members for their thoughts and suggestions and retarding dominant personalities (myself included). My Zone counterparts, as well as our technical advisor, all have strong "type A" personalities, which made past meetings frustrating and often unproductive. I am conscious of participation balance and practice gate-opening and gate-closing quite often.

At the conclusion of the calls, we hold a critique and commit to a follow-up call date. We've now had three calls, and all have followed this process, with very positive results.

I work best when I can organize and manage things. So this process comes naturally to me; however, I absolutely believe that any engaged and motivated person can use MGG to increase teleconferencing productivity and results.

WORKSHEET

Develop written responses to the two items listed below.

1. What do you feel are the main learning points from Chapter 11?

_____

_____

_____

_____

2. Elaborate on why you feel these points are key for you.

_____

_____

_____

_____

_____

_____

Notes

1. See R. Johansen, D. Sibbet, S. Benson, A. Martin, R. Mittman, and P. Saffo, *Leading Business Teams: How Teams Can Use Technology and Group Process Tools to Enhance Performance* (Reading, Mass.: Addison-Wesley, 1991), pp. 15–22.
2. T. Brown, *Change by Design: How Design Thinking Transforms Organizations and Inspires Innovation* (New York: Harper Business, 2009), p. 30.
3. D. Mittleman, R. O. Briggs, and J. F. Nunnamaker, Jr., "Best Practices in Facilitating Virtual Meetings: Some Notes from Initial Experience," *Group Facilitation*, Winter 2000.
4. M. Mann, "Running More Productive Meetings," *43 Folders*, February 21, 2006, online blog.

Part IV

ANALYZING THE DYNAMICS OF A GROUP SESSION

"Let's Have a Team-Building Session": A Mining Group Gold Integrative Case Study to Wrap Up Your Learning

- To use an actual work example as the means for demonstrating the manager's use of a variety of facilitation tools, techniques, and processes presented throughout this book.
- To highlight the power of secondary facilitation in action.

Introduction

The case you are about to read is the actual transcript of a meeting involving Al, the manager, and his seven direct reports. This particular meeting is a follow-up to one that had been held the previous week, in which the same group had *more or less* decided to hold a team-building session for itself. The consequences of that nebulous decision will be felt in this meeting.

As you read this case, notice that Al demonstrates a process that allows him to function both in the role of primary facilitator and, when needed, in the role of active group participant. At no time does Al abdicate the role prescribed by the formal organization—the role of manager of the group.

The case also shows facilitation as a shared responsibility. Thus, people other than Al demonstrate good facilitation skills as the group members share responsibility for successful facilitation. However, they are not perfect; mistakes are made.

Finally, I have included my comments next to the group dialogue as a way to bridge back to key learning points from the previous chapters. My intent is to hit the highlights and to note briefly some of the more subtle interactions. You are urged to dig deeper and look for understanding and learning beyond my points. Have fun with this case. Pretend that you are sitting in a corner watching this group operate. What do you see? What feedback would you give the group members regarding things that they did well? In order to improve, what would you challenge them to do differently next time?

"To Team-Build or Not to Team-Build? That Is the Question"

Al: Okay. Well, I'm glad we were all able to get together today, given our hectic travel schedules and workload. [Flipping back a blank top page to reveal a prewritten flip-chart page, Al points to the different items as he continues to speak.] The purpose of today's session is to share and process information relative to holding an off-site team-building session. Our desired outcome is "team building: go/no-go decision

A model beginning. The purpose, desired outcome, role assignments, and agenda with clock times were all prewritten, posted, and reviewed before any other business was transacted.

made." I'll be the primary facilitator for this meeting; the rest
of you, of course, have the role
of secondary facilitators. Kathy,
would you take the minutes and
note all decisions plus any action
items that arise? [She nods in
agreement.] Also, Andrea, would
you be the timekeeper? We would
like to be finished 30 minutes
from now, at 2:00.

Andrea: Fine, no problem.

Al: Good. You'll see on the
agenda that the first 20 minutes is
allotted to examining the logistics
and the pros and cons of holding
a team-building session. The last
10 minutes will be used to make
our decision. Any issues with the
purpose, desired outcome, roles,
or agenda for this session?

*Checking back with the group
to make sure that everyone is
on board and committed to the
meeting's direction. Anyone with
a differing perspective has an
opportunity to speak up.*

Everyone: Looks good, fine, let's
go, and so on.

Al: Okay. I think it's going to be
easy to tie down the loose ends
from the team-building discussion we had at last Monday's
staff meeting. I think we're pretty
well in agreement on most of the
particulars. One new point to
add is that Ike Delock, the vice
president of human resources,
has sort of invited himself to sit
in on this, and I said okay.

*Uh-oh. This substantially changes
the situation. Al has made an
autocratic, unilateral decision on
an issue that has ramifications
for the whole group. This was
not his decision to make alone.
Al would have been better off*

telling Ike that he would have to run it by the team members first to see if they approved of having Ike at the team-building session. Well, it's too late now. Let's see how the group responds to Al's pronouncement.

Diane: Oh, good!

Supporting.

Tom: [With anger] You've got to be kidding me! I don't want Ike to be there!

Feelings, disagreement. How will this be handled?

Bob: Why not? What's the problem with him?

Good secondary facilitation. Direct question, seeking information, trying to understand.

Tom: [In a sharp tone of voice] Because he's not part of our group. He's an outsider.

Still in feelings. Notice that at this point, Al has not said anything. He has not gotten defensive or argumentative, even though he precipitated the discussion and was directly challenged by Tom.

Diane: Well, Tom, I might look at that a little differently. Maybe it's an opportunity to develop a little openness and trust vertically rather than just among ourselves.

Disagreeing. Opinion giving. Trying to counteract feelings with logic. Even though Diane might have a good point, this argument is not going to convince Tom to change his mind, since he is in the "feelings" stage.

Andrea: I agree with Tom. This workshop could be important to us as a family group.

Encouraging by supporting.

Tom: Thank you.

He shows appreciation for Andrea's encouragement through her support.

Andrea: Having an outsider there could completely destroy it.

Opinion giving.

Kathy: But Andrea and Tom, there are pluses and minuses to this. It could go either way. I think we should talk about it a little. Let's explore it. What do you think, Jeanne?

Good secondary facilitation. Harmonizing by proposing that communications be kept open and that the group take a balanced view. Good use of a direct question to gate-open for Jeanne.

Jeanne: Well . . . do you know Ike?

Direct question. Seeking information.

Tom: [With exasperation] No, I don't know him.

Giving information.

Jeanne: Super person. Really, I think he might . . . He's got a lot of skills, and I think he really just wants to observe our process.

Jeanne is selling. She's trying to convince Tom that Ike is "a good guy." This is not doing what is most needed right now—clarifying and better understanding what Tom feels and why.

Tom: [With a burst of anger] Fine. I don't have anything against the man personally, but I just don't want to have a corporate spy in our midst!

Tom is an "expresser"; strong feelings of anger are backed by a highly negative label: "corporate spy."

Kathy: Spying! That's pretty harsh, Tom. I don't know if I'd really want to put it that way.

Opinion giving. Kathy is not helping the situation at this moment. She is evaluating Tom's feelings ("pretty harsh" and "I wouldn't put it that way"). Kathy has a right to her feelings. However, she needs to make it clear to Tom that she understands what he feels, and why, before stating her contrary views. This is a common problem when feelings arise. People jump in and basically tell the person, "You shouldn't feel the way you do" (which is wrong), "you should feel the way I do" (which is right). Al or someone else must step in soon and do what needs to be done: try understanding what Tom feels and why, rather than evaluating his feelings.

Tom: [Heatedly, with emphasis on the word "I"] Well, I would put it that way. Who put you in charge of what I think?

Defensive. An attack on Kathy. The group is on the verge of destructive conflict.

Ron: Do you really feel that he is going to be spying or . . .

Excellent secondary facilitation. Ron does exactly what is needed at exactly the right time. He tests comprehension by trying to understand Tom's feelings. He gets gate-closed before he can finish.

Tom: [In a much calmer voice] Well, spying . . . Maybe I'm saying more that he would just inhibit our freedom to speak up among ourselves.

Information giving, very useful insight into Tom's feelings. Ron's probe has helped settle him down.

Ron: Well, I can certainly understand how Ike's presence could hinder our communications, but I'd like to follow up on Diane's point about the vertical slice. . . .

Ron supports Tom, then shifts to harmonizing to look at Diane's side of the coin. Some things to note: Al has not said anything. However, throughout this skirmish, his nonverbal cues indicated rapt attention to what was going on. He was fully in charge. He was mentally monitoring everything. Had Ron not clarified Tom's feelings when he did, Al would have had to intervene and do so. The point is, Al was waiting. He was staying out of the content and monitoring the process. Remember, just because you are the primary facilitator doesn't mean that you have to facilitate if you are getting good secondary facilitation. Al was receiving excellent facilitation support, so he waited, he watched, he listened, and he monitored.

Diane: Yes, and even take the word spy. You can turn that over and look at the other side. He has an ear to the top. In watching our processes, he can relay back that we are doing pretty well. Also, he can see firsthand what problems are caused by some of the mandates that come down from "on high." Why, you remember last year when they changed that hiring procedure? It took us six months to get things rolling again. Why, the first few days I had 50 phone calls. . . .

Diane grabs the little opening that Ron provides by gate-closing him to explain the merits of her position. However, notice that she begins to ramble and starts getting "revved up" on an unrelated tangent, the hiring procedure.

Al: Help me understand how that's going to help us move ahead with this issue.

Firm but friendly confrontation. Al steps in to gate-close Diane's unproductive rambling.

Diane: Well, if Ike had been there, perhaps some action could have been taken in six weeks, not six months. I see that as a positive aspect of his presence.

Diane stops rambling and crisply explains her position.

Ron: So you think Ike should be at the workshop? [Diane nods in agreement.] Tom?

Direct question, testing comprehension, gate-opening for Tom.

Tom: [In a conciliatory tone] I don't think that if we are going to try to pull together as a team, we need any outsiders looking at our team process at this stage of the game. While I appreciate Diane's position, I can't agree that this should be a vertical workshop. I don't see it that way.

Tom now states the issue in situational rather than behavioral terms. He is starting the transition from feelings to facts.

Ron: Would you participate in the workshop or . . .

Seeking information; still trying to understand Tom's perspective.

Tom: [Forcefully, but without anger] I guess, [answering the question]: if Ike's going to be there, I don't think that I would show up.

Giving information. Strong message indicating how deeply Tom feels about this being only a team building for just Al and this team, with no outsiders.

Bob: [Irritated] Wait a minute. Wait a minute. At our last staff meeting we had decided exactly what we were going to do. We knew we were going to do this thing. We had reached consensus. Everybody agreed. And here we are rehashing the same thing over again. We simply won't take yes for an answer. Diane, you were given the action item for pulling this thing off. What is it that we decided?

Mini-feelings. Giving information, summarizing points from previous staff meeting. Direct question to gate-open for Diane. Actually a good piece of secondary facilitation.

Even though there are divergent views, the group is now working at processing information. Communications are open; there are no personal attacks; there is no destructive conflict at this time. The group is starting to problem-solve. It has moved into the "facts" phase.

Diane: Well, if we're getting back to asking the question of what were our goals, maybe we weren't exactly clear enough about that. I think maybe we all assumed that we knew what our top priority was and what the possibilities were. Maybe we just didn't take that far enough.

Opinion giving. But more important, Diane has uncovered the root of the conflict: lack of good clarity about the intent of the team-building workshop (its goals) at the close of the previous meeting. A major breakthrough.

Andrea: As timekeeper, I'd like to interject a quick performance check and remind everyone that we are halfway through our session, with 15 more minutes to go.

Performance checking; giving information to assist the group process.

Ron: Thanks, Andrea. That Rolex keeps good time.

A tension-relieving exchange. Nothing boisterous, well-timed, a brief interlude to inject a bit of levity.

Andrea: At $29.95, it had better. [The group laughs.]

Ron: Getting back to our team-building issue, I think both Tom and Diane raised good points. I also think that Bob's got a good point on the process itself that we used last week. Al, you've been silent on this one so far. You've talked to Ike personally about coming down. What's your position on having him participate?

Encouraging. Another piece of good secondary facilitation by Ron. He also uses a direct question to gate-open and draw Al into the content side of the discussion. It's perfectly proper for a subordinate to draw the manager into the discussion if there is a felt need to do so.

Al: Well, first let me take off my facilitator's hat and look at it from the role of team manager.

Now we see the substantial benefits of a manager who stayed out of the content but was totally

I . . . obviously, he [Ike] pointed out to me that he would like to invite himself, and I said, "Sure, come on in." I was pretty comfortable with it. I don't feel threatened by it. I may be the farthest in the spectrum away from Tom's position in terms of comfort in seeing him join us. I don't have any issue with that. On the other hand, when I put my facilitator's hat back on, and I listen to the issue from Tom's perspective, I hear the "other voices." It may be that where we really got off was that when we were discussing this and planning it, we weren't very clear about our goals. We said, "I've got a great idea. Let's have a group meeting, a team-building session." But we may not have identified what it was that we wanted to accomplish with that. I think that, on the one hand, if it's to improve our internal relationships and facilitation skills as a team, then Ike's an outsider and an interloper, and he probably wouldn't be a contributor. He's certainly not a key person. On the other hand, if the purpose of the team-building session is to improve our relationship with corporate human resources, then Ike becomes a key player. And so we've got a lack of clarity in our goals, or, at least, we haven't set them in place. Maybe we ought to test and see what kind

tuned in to the group process through listening and mentally monitoring the dynamics. Al does a nice job of signifying his shift in roles by "hat switching." He also does a superb job of summarizing the main issues and clarifying his personal position. Notice that everything that Al says is stated in situational, not behavioral terms. He defines Ike's role under two different goal conditions. Al gets to the heart of the problem and clarifies its essence: by first determining the goal of the team-building session, the staff will have defined Ike's role as being either involved or not involved. Addressing the goal issue, Al now performs the consensus-testing activity by asking each person, in turn, if he or she can support the goal of the team building as being a team-only session. Al has moved the team into the "solutions" phase.

of consensus we've got on the goal of team building. Maybe that's where we ought to begin. Let's test the alternative that this should be a team-building session just for our team. Kathy, how do you feel about this?

Kathy: I would agree that it should be a session for our team only.

Al: Okay. Bob?

Bob: I agree. Our team only.

Tom: Our team.

Andrea: Just our team.

Ron: I think our team is best for now. I think it's important that we do it ourselves first, before we start bringing in other people. I think Tom's got a good point.

Jeanne: That's our goal. I agree.

Al: Okay. Diane?

Diane: Well, I still think that optimally we could get both during the same session. But, Tom, if what you're saying to me is that you don't think we can, and you're forcing me into a choice, well, the choice is an easy one because I would much rather have your input into our team-building session than Ike's.

Opinion giving. Diane reiterates her original position and then supports the consensus of the group. The word "forcing" does leave some doubt that she is truly committed to a family group session.

Jeanne: Diane, you said Tom was forcing you into your choice. So you feel pressured?

Summarizing followed by an excellent example of testing comprehension. Jeanne picked up on the word "forcing" and checked to see if that is what Diane really meant. A critical piece of secondary facilitation.

Diane: Oh, no, no, that's not what I meant. It was a poor choice of words. I fully support having this be a family group session. My arm's not being twisted.

Information giving to clarify her position. We know now that Diane really is fully behind having the team-building session include just the current team.

Al: Okay, I also agree that we make this a family group session. So what we're really saying, then, is that we've got a two-step plan. Our goal, first of all, is to improve our own team relationships and facilitation skills. And if that's our goal, that makes Ike an outsider, and we probably ought to note that this is where we are headed, and we probably ought to un-invite Ike. And then we have a secondary issue, which is that at some point we want to address the goal of upward facilitation and interface with human resources. And if that's the case, then Ike moves from being a peripheral player to being a key person. We will want to address that down the road.

Al gives his consent last. He waited so as not to unduly influence the group. Al summarizes what was agreed to and also takes steps to make this a win-win outcome by offering the option of holding a team-building session with Ike after this one. Diane can still meet her original goal with Al's proposal. This will cement her commitment even more. The group has reached a true consensus. Everyone has verbally acknowledged that he or she either "agrees with" or "agrees to support" the idea of a team-only session as the first team-building activity.

Tom: Good.

Diane: Let's do it.

Ron: Fine. That leaves just one last thing regarding the action item that Kathy is putting in the minutes. Who is going to call Ike?

General address question. A nice piece of secondary facilitation to make sure that all action items are "buttoned up."

Al: Tom, do you want to do it? Do you want me to do it?

Direct question. A curious statement. Why would Al ask Tom if he wanted to call Ike? Tom wasn't the one who invited Ike.

Tom: I think you can do that.

What would you expect him to say?

Al: No problem. I think that's fine. Well, that's an interesting one. Somewhere along the line last week we made a classic assumption in terms of what the goal was and slid right by it. I think we all learned something from that. Bob, as a first step in planning for our team-building session, would you check out the prices for room rentals and food at several local hotels and report back with options at our next staff meeting on the twenty-second?

Solid wrap-up and close.

Bob: Will do.

Al: Kathy, please note Bob's action item in the minutes. [Kathy nods.] Finally, here is a copy of the "Group Session Effectiveness Evaluation" that we have been using to critique our meetings. Please fill it out and give it to Kathy so that she can put the results in our minutes. We'll discuss any issues on the twenty-second.

The road to managing conflict and strong feelings is rarely smooth or straight. As this case illustrates, it requires a team effort to work through diversity. Al, acting as primary facilitator, in combination with other group members performing as secondary facilitators, practiced a number of tools, techniques, and processes for mining group gold. Doing so enabled them to turn a potentially explosive situation into one that reached a productive conclusion. The team was able to discover that the true source of conflict and feelings was its collective failure to define the team-building goals at the end of the previous week's staff meeting. Once the real problem was identified, the group took action to resolve it. In doing so, the team proceeded along the "feelings, facts, solutions" sequence to group productivity.

A Concluding Thought

Will Rogers once said of Congress: "When all is said and done, a lot more is said than done." That is often the case with planning and facilitating group sessions—people say a lot about what needs to be done, but they do little in the way of changing and improving the facilitation and productivity of their meetings. I hope this book will give you the confidence and ability to become a true "miner of group gold" so that, "When all is said and done, a lot less will be said and a lot more collaboration will be done."

As I wrote in the preface, "Without your desire to use them, the ideas presented here are useless. You are completely in charge of what Mining Group Gold will ultimately mean to you and your organization."

WORKSHEET

Develop written responses to the two items listed below.

1. What do you feel are the main learning points from Chapter 12?

_____

_____

_____

_____

_____

_____

_____

2. Elaborate on why you feel these points are key for you.

_____

_____

_____

_____

_____

_____

_____

_____

INDEX

Note: Boldface numbers indicate illustrations; *t* indicates a table.

ABOUT THE AUTHOR

Tom Kayser is the President of Kayser Associates, Inc., a human resources consulting firm. He is an expert in organizational behavior and change, group facilitation, team-building design and facilitation, and executive coaching, and he speaks at many universities and professional organizations. He lives in Akron, Ohio.

If you are interested in contacting Tom Kayser to discuss Mining Group Gold workshops, team building initiatives, or other consulting activities, you should e-mail Tom at:

KAYSER1@ROADRUNNER.COM